The Last Emperor of China
My Husband Puyi

我的丈夫溥仪——中国的末代皇帝

Told by Li Shuxian
Written down by Wang Qingxiang
Translated by Ni Na

CHINA TRAVEL & TOURISM PRESS

Contents

- Preface .... Li Shuxian 001

- Chapter One 005
  My Childhood

- Chapter Two 012
  Seeing Puyi for the First Time

- Chapter Three 018
  My Courtship with the Last Emperor of China

- Chapter Four 025
  The Setting of Our Love

- Chapter Five 038
  The Last Emperor's Grand Nuptials

- Chapter Six 049
  The First Week of Our Honeymoon

- Chapter Seven 057
  Hopes of Having Children Vanish into Thin Air

- Chapter Eight 063
  Teaching Puyi Domestic Chores and How to Live a Normal Life

- Chapter Nine 073
  Hangovers from the Previous Lifestyle of the Royal Family

- Chapter Ten 077
  Mortals and Secularity

- Chapter Eleven 081
  Puyi——A Great Fan of Peking Opera

- Chapter Twelve 089
  Accompanying My Husband Back to the Place Where He Ascended the Throne as Emperor

- Chapter Thirteen 096
  Visiting Historical and Cultural Sites Together with Puyi

- Chapter Fourteen 105
  Our Sincere Love

- Chapter Fifteen 114
  The Refusing of the Feudal Protocols

- Chapter Sixteen 121
  Reunion with the Former Servants

- Chapter Seventeen 127
  Puyi's Contacts with People from All Circles of Society

- Chapter Eighteen 139
  Receiving Foreign Guests with Puyi

- Chapter Nineteen 143
  The Publishing of the "Earth Shattering" Book

- Chapter Twenty 153
  The Tour to Southeast China

- Chapter Twenty One 171
  Tour to Northwest China

- Chapter Twenty Two 179
  Being Attacked by Cancer

- Chapter Twenty Three 183
  "Tricky" Situation that Happened in Puyi's Ward

- Chapter Twenty Four 186
  Friendship with Our Neighbour

- Chapter Twenty Five 191
  Performing the Rights of a Citizen

- Chapter Twenty Six 195
  "Hurricane" Blew Suddenly

- Chapter Twenty Seven 202
  The Puyi Who Dared to Speak Out the Truth

- Chapter Twenty Eight 212
  Our Venture in "Red August"

- Chapter Twenty Nine 219
  Bitter Taste of Revenge

- Chapter Thirty 225
  Being in Bondage to an Incurable Disease

- Chapter Thirty One 230
  Puyi's Last Summer

- Chapter Thirty Two 235
  I Watched Puyi Passing Away

- Chapter Thirty Three 243
  Puyi's Memorial Ceremony Was Held Thirteen Years Later

- Chapter Thirty Four 251
  Publishing of My Memoir and the "Puyi Craze"

- Chapter Thirty Five 257
  The Publishing of *The Second Half of Puyi's Life*

- Chapter Thirty Six 261
  Apologies from Edward Behr

- Chapter Thirty Seven 266
  Drawing a Satisfactory Conclusion to the History

- Epilogue 279

Preface

I am overjoyed that *My Husband Puyi* is to be published. Aisin-Gioro Puyi was the last Emperor of the Chinese feudal society era. He was placed on the throne as Emperor Xuantong at the young age of three, but less than three years later his forced abdication was announced. Afterwards, according to The Articles Provided for the Favourable Treatment of the Great Qing Emperor after his Abdication, decided upon by the Provisional Government of the Republic of China, he was still allowed to live in the inner court of the Forbidden City, acting as an Emperor "behind closed doors*". For the following 13 years he lived this role, until in 1924, when he was expelled from the Forbidden City by the celebrated Christian General, Feng Yuxiang. Following this, it was arranged that he would stay at the Japanese Concession in Tianjin.

At home

In 1932, the Japanese secretly sent him to northeast China to be the Puppet Emperor of the Manchukuo** set up by Japanese Imperialists. With the final surrender of the Japanese Imperialists in August 1945, Puyi then fell captive to the Russian Red Army, being escorted first to Chits, then to Khabarivsk (two Russian cities in the far

---

* Following the success, of the Wuchang Uprising on the October 10th 1911, to ensure the abdication of Emperor Xuantong (Puyi), the Provisional Government of the Republic of China, after negotiations with a representative of the Qing Dynasty Government, "The Articles" were formulated. They also stipulated that, following his abdication, Puyi's title of dignity would be retained, that he should receive an annual allowance of four million *taels* of silver, and that he could also live in the inner court of the Forbidden City.

** Manchukuo: A puppet regime created in China's northeastern provinces by Japanese Imperialists, 1931-1945

east, close to northeast China), where he was placed under house-arrest for a period of five years.

After the establishment of the People's Republic of China, the Chinese and the Soviet Russian governments, following the bilateral talks, finally decided to extradite Puyi back to China. Puyi was then detained for ten years at Fushun War Criminals Prison*, located in northeast China. He was reeducated and remoulded there, through physical labour and being imbued with communistic ideas. Finally, Puyi realized his wrongdoing, so repented for his role in aiding the Japanese Imperialists in enslaving the people in northeast China. He started a new life with a completely different outlook, which resulted in him becoming an honorable, respected citizen of the New China, and my good husband.

His autobiography *The First Half of My Life—From Emperor to Citizen* has been popular at home and abroad, as a book which has continued to rivet the world's attention, since it was published in 1964. Now, to the reading public who are interested in Puyi, I'd like to present this book, *My Husband Puyi* which is about his new life after 1960, when he was granted special amnesty. He enjoyed this new life for only eight years, as he died of kidney cancer in 1967. Eight years is a much shorter period com-

Mr. Wang Qingxiang and I at my home, Xizhimen, Beijing

* This was a special prison for politically important high-ranking Chinese and Japanese war criminals.

Li Shuxian (1924-1997), a native of Hangzhou

pared with the first half of his life which lasted for more than fifty years, but much more valuable, if viewed in the light of his life's significance. Puyi and I were married for five and half years, but if taking into account from the day we were introduced to each other, we were together for almost six years. We were fortunate to have experienced a sweet courtship, a happy home life and our attendances to each other when we were both ill.

In 1984, the first edition of my memoirs, *Puyi and I* was published, creating a major sensation in China. In its preface, I explained how I came to write the book, as follows: I remember that it was in September of 1979, when Mr. Wang Qingxiang, a historian from the Historical Research Institute of the Jilin Provincial Academy of Social Sciences, paid a visit to my home. He urged me to write the memoirs of my husband, for he believed that it would prove to be a great contribution to our Chinese nation. The principle we agreed on was that I should write down every event and sentence as they came to my mind, and that he would help me to draw out my memories to the greatest extent possible. He said to me: "Your memoirs must be first-hand data as precise as possible. They will be an invaluable document for historical research. So every single word of it must conform to historical facts." I also held this view.

My memoirs were written intermittently during a period of six months. Whenever I thought of the past, I relived the memories of the life that we had spent together more than ten years earlier. It had been as though my husband was standing lifelike in front of me, when the reminiscences flooded back to me. I have no idea of how many times I laughed whilst savouring the happiness and sweetness of that time or how often the tears suddenly welled up in my eyes, due to the sadness of losing him. My memoirs may not be perfect but I'm confident that they are realistic. While helping me with the compilation of my memoirs, Mr. Wang Qingxiang reiterated that his desire was to make an accurate historical record and that he preferred to omit any unclear details where my memory failed me. My original memoir, *Puyi and I* is the result of our mutual cooperation. First, he collated my oral accounts by cross-referencing them with the manuscript left by Puyi. Then, he came to Beijing to go over every single word and sentence together with me. I'm glad that the final text successfully conveys the essence of my spoken accounts. Of course, my memoirs mostly show Puyi's home life. They obviously couldn't cover every aspect of the second half of his life. In order to get a well-rounded view of citizen Puyi, my memoir should be read alongside Puyi's own diary and articles, which were written during this period, to supplement your understanding.

Twelve years later, Mr. Wang Qingxiang and I again worked happily together to thoroughly revise *Puyi and I* by adding to it with many more details of our common life. My difficult experiences during the Cultural Revolution as Puyi's widow significantly contrasted with my improved life and situation in the new era. By 1978, China had begun to implement the progressive policy of reform and was opening up its doors to the outside world. During the previous ten years, more and more Chinese and foreign reporters, historians, readers of my book, tourists and personalities of various circles had come to visit me. These visits greatly helped me with my book revision and they also aroused again affection and love for my dear husband. These foreign reporters had often laden me with various questions about our courtship, marriage, our daily life and work, our tours, our times in hospital, as well as the relationships between Puyi, the Aisin-Gioro Clan and also between him and the State Leaders. To answer their questions adequately, I used to write down the key points as I remembered them. Later on these recollections naturally became useful material for the revision of my former memoirs.

I named the revised book *My Husband Puyi*, hoping that it might convey my affection for my dear husband. I'm greatly indebted to Mr. Qiao Huantian, the Executive Director of the People's Publishing House and the editor of this book. It is their support and kindness which have given me this opportunity to bring my story to the reading public. Finally, I'd like to express my gratitude to all the friends who have helped me, as well as the readers who will enjoy the reading of this book.

Li Shuxian
September 23rd, 1996

Chapter One

My Childhood

I was born in Hangzhou, on 4th September, 1924. With its picturesque West Lake, Hangzhou is famous, at home and abroad, as a "Paradise on Earth", but while it was a paradise for the rich, it was not so for the lower classes, such as my family. I had a miserable childhood there.

My mother, Li Changsi, was a housewife. She took my elder brother, thirteen years my senior, and I to live in Hangzhou, whilst my father, Li Jinshen, a junior bank clerk, continued to work in Shanghai. We relied on the monthly remittance, which my father sent us for our needs. As my parents were not on good terms, my father seldom came

My photo taken at the age of 33, 1957

back home, so my elder brother and I would see him only at festival times. When my father did come back home, my parents often quarrelled. Eventually, my father found another woman in Shanghai and sent us ever smaller sums of money, making our life increasingly difficult.

Fortunately my mother, though uneducated, had a clever mind and deft hands, and was excellent at sewing fur coats and *Qipao* (a close-fitting woman's dress with high neck and slit skirt). With accurate cutting, delicate needlework, superb workmanship with lifelike designs of embroidered flowers, insects, birds, fish, flying dragons, dancing phoenixes, etc., the dresses made by her were prized more highly than those produced at a professional tailor's shop. As a result, a lot of potential customers preferred to send their materials to my home rather than dress-maker's. Even so my mother's income was not enough to cover our daily needs. Sometimes in order to make ends meet, mother had to take my elder brother and myself to the suburbs, with a bamboo basket slung over her shoulder, to gather edible wild plants. I still to this day miss a kind of wild plant, called *Malantou*, it tastes very delicious. During summer time, our astute mother regularly dried the surplus edible wild plants and bamboo shoots growing in our courtyard and preserved them for winter use.

Although we were poor, our mother valued us and we loved our mother, so we had a warm family life. In the Chinese feudal society, most of the parents favoured their sons. My mother was no exception and she laid her hopes on my elder brother, Amao, often encouraging him to keep on working hard at his lessons so as to pass the university entrance examination. She was sure that after my elder brother graduated from university, he could obtain a good job and support her in her old age. To raise the tuition fees for my elder brother, mother always cooked simple meals, rarely bought meat for our meals. Unexpectedly one day, I believe it was during the summer vacation of that year when he was about to graduate from senior high school, my elder brother suddenly fell ill following a visit to the West Lake. My terrified mother couldn't afford the hospital expenses, nor did she have an elementary knowledge of nursing. All she could do was to watch his condition deteriorate rapidly. A few days later, my elder brother died. He was only 19 years old. My poor mother sank into extreme depression. She missed her son and his death crushed her completely. With tear-stained cheeks, she would often take leave of her senses, though my strong mother always clearly remembered to escort me to and fro from school and she continued doing the sewing work for others. However, in 1932, when I was only eight years old, she finally grew world-weary and with a heavy heart, she lay down and died. My poor mother was not then yet forty years old.

After my mother's passing away, as an eight year old girl, I was incapable of taking care of myself. My father returned to take me to Shanghai, to his home in the British Concession. A woman was living with him. Evidently, they had been living together for a long time. Dad wanted me to call her mum, but I was reluctant to do so. From the very beginning my harsh-natured stepmother didn't like me. When I got home from school, she would order me to do chores. Her dislike of me grew; I was like a thorn in her flesh. She kicked me, beat me and swore at me whenever she was unhappy with me or in a bad mood. I was frequently beaten black and blue by her, especially when I quarrelled or fought with my stepbrother. She would always beat me first, never wanting to hear my side of the story. After being beaten or reviled by my stepmother, I never dared to complain to my father, because stepmother had already threatened me that she would beat me to death, if I did. When noticing that my eyes were swollen, my father would question me closely:

"Has she beaten you?"

"No," I replied.

"Has somebody been bullying you?"

"No," I reiterated.

"Then, why are you crying?" he asked.

"I fell over and hurt myself," I said.

Anyway, my father still cared about me, and finally he realized the truth. He was indignant with my stepmother and argued with her. Father pitied me, trying his best to console me with his love. I remembered once before a festival that he kindly bought me a beautiful coat and a pair of leather shoes. He proudly showed them to me when he came back home, saying: "Xiaomei, come and put them on and let me have a look at you!" Knowing that I liked fruit, my father often brought some home for me. He always put the fruit into my hand personally, because he worried that my stepmother wouldn't let me eat it when he was away. Being jealous of this, stepmother would get very angry so that an argument would break out between them.

When I was 12 years old, I caught typhoid fever. It had happened after my father took me to see a celebration at a popular Buddhist Temple, where people had come from many different places. That evening I started to run a fever and vomit. Without hesitation, my anxious father sent me to hospital, where I was diagnosed as having typhoid fever. After a few weeks I recovered, but I had a relapse and ran a fever again. During the following few days, all of my hair fell out. The doctor suggested that I had better be hospitalized so as not to infect others, but father insisted on taking me back home so that he could look after me himself. He made me a comfortable bed downstairs in the spacious sitting room which was airy and sunny. But, stepmother wanted me to move upstairs, to a smaller bedroom. She said that she wanted to hold a party downstairs to celebrate her birthday. Father didn't agree with her, shouting at her: "My daughter's life is more important!" My father asked a well-known Chinese doctor to treat me. According to the doctor's prescription, to aid my nutrition, he ground sesame into powder and made up a hot soup for me to drink. In the mornings, my father would get up very early, first going to buy live tortoises and phytin, then he would come back to stew a bowl of phytin and crystallised sugar for me. Before leaving for work, he made sure that I ate it all. Almost every evening, he steamed tortoise meat to make clear soup for me. He took care of me meticulously until I regained my health.

But, the unexpected always happened; hating the fact that my stepmother was

The Last Emperor of China My Husband Puyi

mistreating me, my father was often depressed and slowly his health deteriorated. When I was 14 years old, another tragedy befell me. My dear father, the only person in this world who really loved me, took a turn for the worse and lay incapacitated in bed for several months. Finally, he grasped my hand in his and while still filled with concern for me, drew his last breath.

With my father passing away, I had nobody left to defend me. Stepmother didn't allow me to go to school any more, but made me stay at home to do all the housework. Everyday I had to get up very early to cook breakfast and in the evening I couldn't go to bed until I had finished all the chores. Besides cooking, washing and tidying up rooms, I had to heat the opium and make it bubble for my stepmother, while she smoked it. At times, when she was smoking opium, due to fatigue and lack of sleep, I couldn't help dozing off, while attending to

Mr. Wang Qingxiang and I, 1992

her needs. Seeing this happening, and while not saying a word, she would suddenly poke my hand with a scalding, sharp opium pin. It would sear my hand terribly. I screamed with the intense pain, but noticed that she would just stare at me angrily. I felt like I was Cinderella in the fairy tale, with nobody to pour out my grievances to. Later on, my vicious stepmother planned three items of domestic punishment for me. Firstly, I was only allowed to eat one small bowl of food each meal time. Secondly, I only received the leftovers from the last meal to eat. Thirdly, I had to eat in the kitchen and never with her and my stepbrother. I never had enough to eat and was often hungry, so I had to sneak scraps whenever I could. Once, my stepmother stewed a pot of pork with soy sauce. When she left the kitchen, using my chopsticks, I would quickly pick up a piece of pork from the pot and put it into my mouth. Unexpectedly on one occasion, my stepmother came back and caught me. She glared at me fiendishly and hit me with a walking stick. Blood dripped from the top of my head, staining my coat. She didn't send me to hospital, but instead she grabbed several handfuls of incense ash and rubbed them into the cut to help stop the bleeding.

One of my classmates, named Ruifang, lived close to my home. We were best friends and we still saw a lot of each other after I stopped schooling. She had a rich and powerful father whom often entertained friends at home. One of these friends, a fat old man, was a millionaire. He was always glad to meet me there, tapping my shoulder and warmly calling me "little sister" and praising me by calling me beautiful. When he heard that my father had already died and that I was mistreated by my stepmother, he told Ruifang's mother that he wanted to marry me, although he already had a wife and a concubine.

Hearing the conversation between her mother and the fat old man, Ruifang hurried down to my home to tell me the news. Soon after, her mother, as the matchmaker, came to deliver the fat old man's proposal. My stepmother was excited. Since my father had died, our family had lived on the limited remainder of his money and the quality of our life was getting worse each day, while the fat old man owned a big company, with seemingly limitless funds. He promised that he would present my stepmother with a considerable sum of money as a bride price and that he would buy her a modern western-style house. He also told my stepmother that he would allow her to live together with us, supporting her for the rest of her life. I was frightened. This fat old man was even older than my father, so how could I ever marry him? My stepmother took this as a rare opportunity to make a fortune——by devious means. From then on, she began to "care" about me. She affably advised me:

"Since your father's passing away, our life has been getting more and more difficult. Mum has no money, so we suffer, but the 'uncle' you met at Ruifang's home likes you and he wants to marry you. If you agree to marry him, you will enjoy wealth and rank all your life. He has promised to buy you a luxurious house, car, clothes, and everything you want."

"Okay," I said sarcastically, "You may marry him."

She cunningly replied "Yes, I really want to marry him, but unfortunately, he doesn't like me."

Knowing her deceit hadn't worked, she switched tactics by trying to terrify me. She shut me in a room without food for several days. Not long after that, the fat old man gave a dinner in a popular restaurant, inviting Ruifang's family, my stepmother and myself. My stepmother didn't tell me who had invited us beforehand, but made me dress up. I had a slim figure, fair complexion, bright and big eyes, and a shiny and thick plait of hair reaching down to my waist. She looked me up and down, and smiled craftily. As I followed her into the splendid dining hall, I spotted the fat old man seated at the head of the table. Understanding everything in a flash, I turned tail and ran, ruining their plan. Upon returning home, my stepmother became exasperated and gave me a sound thrashing. She swore to me angrily: "I will starve you to death!" I was shut up in my room again and had very little to eat. It was almost unbearable, but I would never agree to marry that fat old man, no matter how cruelly she tortured me.

I was in misery. Contemplating my suffering over and over again and tired of being so ill-treated, I decided to follow my father by ending my life. One day, whilst my stepmother was taking a nap, I quietly swallowed several of her opium "hits". I was soon struggling in agony on the floor, startling two of our neighbours. They ran down and forced the door open, finding me already unconscious. The two good souls quickly sent me to a nearby hospital. The contents of my stomach were pumped out and my life was saved. On my return I was confined to the house where my stepmother still exerted pressure on me to marry the fat old man. I was clearly aware that I was still in danger and I thought of my aunt. She was actually my father's step-sister, and had liked me from my earliest days. I managed to escape from my home, close to the field on Jing'ansi Road, to find my aunt who lived on Mabel Park Road. She was a landlady, relying on rent for a living. Very soon, my stepmother angrily came to fetch me home. My aunt tried to put her off the trail, saying that she hadn't seen me and that I hadn't been there. My stepmother didn't believe her, so she paid some dubious characters to wander

My colleagues and I at Guanxiang Hospital, 1960

around my aunt's house to spy on us. My aunt was anxious that she would snatch me back, so she decided to send me to Beijing, where her older married daughter lived (her younger daughter had married a dentist and lived in Shanghai). So, for my own safety, I went to Beijing. My elder cousin's husband, a native of Canton, had been a businessman who had long since died. Widowed at the age of 27, my cousin, with her two little children, made ends meet by doing laundry for others. My coming had added to her burden, making me feeling guilty. After two years, she couldn't carry on and had to return to her husband's home town, to get help from his relatives. I was left alone in Beijing.

As a girl of 19, without any knowledge of the ways of the world and in the midst of the chaos of war, I couldn't live independently and so had to marry a Chief Police Officer. But I never expected that I was entering into such a deplorable marriage. He was a playboy, and later on, even kept a mistress outside. I found this out when I was three months pregnant and the shock of learning this caused me to lose the baby. Later, my husband simply left me, to live with his mistress, leaving me at home by myself.

In August 1948, I eventually freed myself from my disgusting husband, by moving out of his home. To improve my education, I became a student at the Beijing Yuwen School. Six months later, Beijing was peacefully liberated and on October 1st of the same year, a new country, the People's Republic of China was officially established. I saw hope in my life and I glowed with joy. I was young and determined to learn a skill to support myself. One day, while glancing through the newspapers, I was delighted to discover the general regulations for the enrolment of nurses for the Huiyin Nurses Training School. They were recruiting Nursing students at Lishi Lane in Dongsinandajie Street. With a few of my girl friends, I took the entrance exam and fortunately, was accepted at once. I enrolled for two years of intensive study in Basic Nursing Theory, after which I followed our teacher, Madam Shu Yueping, to practice nursing in a clinic. I was scared the first time I watched a baby being delivered, but after two years of practicing, I had mastered this and other skills of clinical nursing. In 1955, I began to work as a Nurse at the Jingshan Clinic in the Chaoyang District in Beijing. The clinic was opened by Doctor Ni, from Taiwan, who had a Japanese Medical Degree, specializing in paediatrics. He was a very distinguished Paediatrician attracting a lot of patients. Although busy with his own work, Dr. Ni kindly squeezed in time to give me extra tuition everyday. In my two years there my clinical nursing abilities were improved, and my medical and clinical knowledge grew. In 1958, the Public Health Bureau of Chaoyang District Government amalgamated several private clinics and turned them into the Guanxiang Hospital which covered a variety of Western and Chinese medical practices. I was always busy and happy to have become a nurse in this new hospital.

Chapter Two

Seeing Puyi for the First Time

I finally divorced my first husband in 1955, after I had started to work at the Jingshan Clinic. For the first time ever, I had become financially independent, earning my own salary.

Having already suffered one unhappy marriage, I was hesitant whenever my friends and colleagues introduced an eligible man to me. Our hospital's management quite often expressed their concern about finding a good match for me. I was introduced to high-ranking government officials, rich and handsome engineers, doctors, teachers, etc. I gave each of them a lot of consideration, but would always politely decline their advances. Time passed very quickly and I was by now already used to being on my own.

Three-year-old Puyi on his throne, with his father, Regent Zaifeng, in the background

On 10th February 1962, I returned to work after a break of five days for the Chinese New Year holiday. That day, Mr. Sha Zengxi, an editor at the People's Publishing House and one of my old friends, came to the clinic to see me. Because I had been snowed under with invitations from friends and colleagues during the New Year, and having dined at some of their homes, he hadn't been able to catch me at home. So finally he had decided to visit me at the clinic following the New Year celebrations.

"I'd like to introduce an eligible gentleman to you. Would you be interested in meeting him?" he asked me, when nobody else was in the room.

"Where's he from? What kind of job does he have?" I enquired.

"Trust me! I would only introduce a decent man to you, wouldn't I?" he responded.

"How about telling me about his background first," I asked.

"Please come to my home when you have some time, then I'll tell you all the

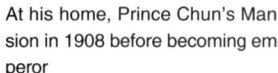

At his home, Prince Chun's Mansion in 1908 before becoming emperor

details," he revealed.

Of course, I couldn't refuse his kind offer. Two days later, I found time to go to his home. Only then, did he tell me the full story.

"He works for the Research Committee of the Historical Accounts of Past Events (HAPE), which is affiliated with the Chinese People's Political Consultative Conference (CPPCC)," he explained.

"What is his name?" I asked.

"Emperor Xuantong," Mr. Sha blurted out, watching my reaction. This was a name known to everybody in China! "You've got to be kidding!" I said, knowing that he had been the Emperor. I was frightened.

"Why are you scared of him? Do you know him?" he questioned.

"I hate the notorious Emperors in the films and traditional operas. I don't want to see him," I stressed.

The emperors on the stage had left a very deep impression on me from childhood. They were majestic-looking but extremely pompous and exceptionally cruel. How on earth could I make friends with an emperor?!

"He has been fully reeducated and as far as I know he has very high standards when choosing a lady friend," he added.

"Then, I won't go at all," I responded, feeling somewhat inferior.

"I have already arranged your meeting with him, come and have a look first," he suggested. Then, jesting he added, "I myself have never seen the 'Last Emperor'. I'd like to take this opportunity to see him too, to broaden my own horizons."

I thought it over. Mr. Sha had fixed the appointment on my behalf, because as a loyal friend, he cared about me. I had no reason to refuse his help and considered that it might be nice to see what the "Last Emperor" was like. This was the way it turned out. Mr. Sha had a fellow-townsman*, named Zhou Zhenqiang. Mr. Zhou had been a former National Party General and had once held the position of Captain of Chiang Kai-shek's bodyguards. But later on, he was taken captive by the Chinese People's Liberation Army (the PLA), and was reeducated in prison for ten years and finally getting Special Amnesty, together with Emperor Xuantong (Puyi). They had both been assigned jobs at the Research Committee of the Historical Accounts of Past Events (HAPE) of the CPPCC, sharing the same office. Knowing that the "Last Emperor" was living alone and couldn't take care of himself at all, Mr. Zhou had felt sorry for him. Once, when he mentioned the matter to Mr. Sha, Mr. Zhou had immediately thought of me. They had discussed this matter together, concluding that Emperor Xuantong and I might be suitable for each other. Then Mr. Zhou had taken my photo from Mr. Sha to show it to "the Last Emperor", after which Puyi had gladly agreed to see me. In fact, Mr. Sha hadn't told me anything about that beforehand. The photo that he gave to Mr. Zhou was an old one that I had sent him some time before.

Several days later, on a Sunday, Mr. Sha accompanied me to the Cultural Club at Nanheyan Road to meet the "Last Emperor", Puyi, as arranged. When we entered the grounds of the club, we immediately saw two men standing in the bitter northern wind. Mr. Sha greeted one of them, Mr. Zhou, and then he introduced me to the other tall

---

✶ In China, the fellow-townsman means coming from the same county or province. In Chinese society, being a fellow-townsman, requires you to help each other as much as possible, even if you have never met before.

Puyi in his prime, in Tianjin

gentleman, Puyi, who shook hands with me warmly. I don't know why I was so nervous but I couldn't look him in the eye.

I had opportunity to observe the graceful manner of "The Emperor" after he had invited us to sit down in a private area of the club and had asked an attendant to serve us coffee. He had sleek hair and was wearing a dark blue Mao jacket and a pair of shiny black leather shoes. His genteel talk and actions immediately created a favorable impression in my mind.

In our conversation, Puyi inquired politely about our clinic, my age, my hometown, what ward I worked in and did we have a lot of patients each day? At that time I was still studying nursing at a part-time Medical School, so I had come with a medical textbook in my hand. Seeing it, Puyi changed the topic of our conversation:

"I have an interest in Chinese medicine. During the period of my reeducation, I had even dreamt about working as a doctor later in life, so I made the best use of the time to study traditional Chinese medicine. I read a lot of books about it and sometimes volunteered to assist in our prison clinic, measuring blood pressures, giving injections and learning how to treat different kinds of illness."

I asked him about his personal life. "Now, I'm living on my 100 yuan monthly salary. It's not really enough, but sometimes I get a state subsidy," he replied.

Again, he questioned me about my life. I told him that both of my parents had passed away when I was a child, which aroused his sympathy. He sighed: "You have had a sad life!" He wanted to know what my father's profession had been. I told him that my father had been a junior bank clerk.

Before this meeting, I had found out some information about him also, knowing that he had once ruled the whole of China as Emperor Xuantong. Later he had become Emperor Kangde of the Manchukuo, which was in northeast China. At the time, his portrait was hung on the wall of each family in the country. The people had to "kowtow" to his portrait every day, but now here sat a different Puyi in front of me: one with a broad, warm smile on his thick lips. I had to wonder, "Was he really that Emperor?" His manner wasn't the slightest bit haughty. He was no different from ordinary people! He was honest, amiable and wore plain clothes, not at all like the emperors in the traditional operas.

It was our first meeting, but we talked congenially, not being aware that our meeting had lasted almost four hours. Outside the gate of the Cultural Club, Puyi made sure to ask Mr. Sha for his address and the telephone number of his work unit, taking a small notebook from his pocket to write it down. Evidently he had been too shy to ask me.

While watching Puyi get on the bus to return back to the CPPCC Headquarters, Mr. Zhou Zhenqiang was very excited, "Wonderful, this time I think we have done it!" he beamed to Mr. Sha and I. "How do you know that?" Mr. Sha said with a smile.

"Going by past experience, if he didn't like her, Puyi would always leave after exchanging a few words with the lady and matchmakers. Whereas this time, he was very relaxed and talked with Comrade Li for several hours. He definitely likes Comrade Li," explained Mr. Zhou, who had a sanguine disposition, thus speaking with a positive attitude. With a cryptic look and a twinkle in his eye, he continued:

"We have introduced more than ten eligible ladies to him, but he didn't like any of them."

"Really!" Mr. Sha responded, wanting to know more.

"He wanted to find a relatively young and pretty one, as the CPPCC often arranges for him to receive foreign guests. Protocol requires him to be accompanied by his wife sometimes, so he considers that he must marry a woman who is presentable," Mr. Zhou further explained.

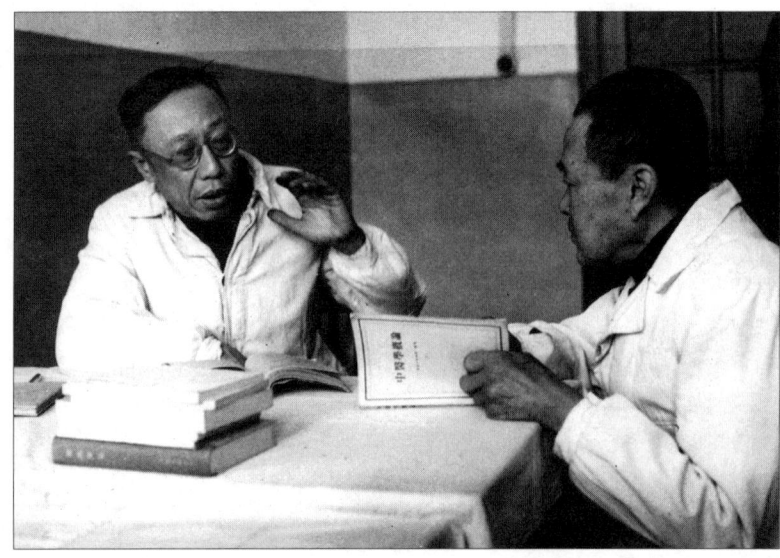

"I have an interest in Chinese Medicine."

"Emperor Kangde" Puyi, reigning from 1933 to 1945

Seeing Puyi for the First Time

Chapter Three

My Courtship with the Last Emperor of China

Our second meeting took placed on the weekend, only five days after the first one. Puyi had phoned Mr. Sha Zengxi, inviting us to attend a ball that was to be held at the auditorium of the CPPCC Headquarters. We accepted the invitation, leaving for the ball in plenty of time. Surprisingly, after getting off the bus and walking for only a few steps, we saw Puyi coming to welcome us, beaming with delight. I felt very content to sense his warm sincerity again. Inside the auditorium of the CPPCC HQ, the band was repeatedly playing "The Friendship Waltz", with the couples dancing happily. At first, Puyi remained seated by Mr. Sha and me, accompanying us while we sipped tea. Later on, Mr. Sha politely asked a lady to dance, intentionally leaving an opportunity for Puyi and me to talk freely, but it seemed that he couldn't find a suitable subject to talk about.

When, after an intermission, the music started up again, Puyi stood up and, following the example of the other male dancers, invited me politely, saying: "Comrade Li, let's have a dance," but he added: "I can't dance, so I'd like to learn from you. Maybe I'll make your shoes dirty."

I said: "I can't dance either!"

Very soon, I realized that he really couldn't dance! He had no idea about rhythm and he couldn't follow the beat. Sometimes his shining leather shoes trod on mine, which was followed by a gentle voice: "I'm sorry," or an apologetic smile. However, he could follow "the slow step" by meeting my steps, albeit unskillfully. When the music changed to "the quick step", he immediately got muddled up, so that finally he just simply dragged me around in circles.

"You were Emperor for so long, why didn't you learn to dance?" I asked, when we returned to our seats by the small round table. I was perspiring profusely!

"Back then, I was the 'Son of Heaven', when even my parents had to kowtow to me, when they saw me. Ordinary people were accused of discourtesy if they even dared raise their heads to look at me. No lady was willing to risk her life by dancing with me, or even placing her hand on my shoulder, so it was impossible for me to learn how to dance. Now that I'm an ordinary citizen I hope that you'll be able to teach me, and make up for lost time," he stated. Afterwards, he said to me in a whisper: "May I phone you directly, to avoid having to bother Mr. Sha?"

He asked for the telephone number of our hospital and I gave it to him. But at the same time I softly explained my concern to him: "You enjoy such a great reputation, it might make it difficult for me to get along with my colleagues in the hospital, if they know who you are." Puyi smiled: "I won't say that I'm Puyi. If your colleagues want to know my surname, I'll just tell them that I'm Mr. Zhou." From then on, our hospital received more and more telephone calls, asking for me. Many of my colleagues therefore became aware that I was dating a man called Mr. Zhou.

Puyi (second from left) with his collegues

The ball came to an end just after 10 pm. It was extremely cold outside that evening, and a thick layer of ice had formed on the ground. With great care Puyi escorted Mr. Sha and I to the bus stop. When the bus drew up, Puyi again reminded us to be careful when getting on the bus as the footboard was very slippery. I thought to myself that "The Emperor" was really good at caring about others.

On our way back, Mr. Sha asked me what I thought of Puyi. I told him that I would like to spend more time getting to know him. I added that as he and Mr. Zhou had graciously introduced us to each other, that it was important to spend this time with Puyi. Actually, I was very keen to continue a friendship with him.

"As an old friend of yours, I was able to introduce him to you and arrange meetings with him, but I can't decide whether to marry him for you!" Mr. Sha remarked.

"I notice that he is kind and ready to care about other people," I uttered.

"I have already told you that he had been 'remoulded' completely. Now he is neither 'Emperor Xuantong' nor 'Emperor Kangde' (called this name during the time of Manchukuo). Why are you still judging him by his previous role and lifestyle?" he questioned. While voicing these comments, he sounded to me as though he was very pleased with himself. However, I didn't expect that the Last Chinese Emperor would be so easy to approach.

Our third meeting was arranged by a direct phone call to me from Puyi himself. He invited me to watch the well-known film, *The Yangtze River flows to the East*, which was to be shown in the auditorium of the CPPCC HQ. He informed me that he had already reserved some seats for us.

The film's plot captured his attention from the beginning. When seeing the scene of the male protagonist forsaking his original wife, even though she had cared for him unerringly and had also shown filial respect for her parents-in-law, and had cared for their son, Puyi condemned him indignantly: "The man is despicable! He was lucky to have such a virtuous wife at home, but still sought pleasure from outside and then finally drove his wife to commit suicide by jumping into the Yangtze River. He was so heartless!" Upon hearing this, I knew that he was a kindhearted man.

After the film was over, Puyi saw me off at the Baitasi bus stop. On the way there Puyi asked me whether I felt cold or not. He expressed that he would prefer to accompany me back to the Guanxiang Hospital. I was grateful for his kindness, but wouldn't let him do that. He returned home after watching me get on the bus.

Not long after that, on another Saturday and for the second time, Puyi invited me by phone to meet him in front of the auditorium of the CPPCC HQ. Unfortunately, on that day, all the buses were jam-packed with passengers. After being unable to board several full buses, I finally managed to force my way onto one. Because I had missed several buses, and the bus I journeyed on was overloaded and slow-moving, I didn't

The auditorium of the CPPCC Headquaters

arrive on time.

Seeing that I was too late to meet him in front of the auditorium as planned, I made a detour along the office building to his apartment, a single-storey house in the compound of the CPPCC HQ, but there was no light on inside. I decided to go back to the front of the auditorium to see if I could find him there. A few steps from the auditorium, I ran into Puyi, who was anxiously returning from the bus stop. Because he was so delighted to find me, he hugged me spontaneously. Lots of people were hurrying past the front of the auditorium and they all laughed when they saw him hug me, making me feel embarrassed. Puyi suddenly realized what he was doing and roared with hearty laughter too.

Puyi and Ma Lianliang, one of the most distinguished Peking Opera master

A few of his acquaintances came up to banter with him: "Why is the old man so delighted?" He hastened to explain to me, "As I didn't find you at the bus stop, I was anxiously looking for you everywhere and didn't expect to bump into you here. Why shouldn't I be happy?" I commented to him in a whisper, "How forgetful you are! You should know where we are." He replied to me jokingly: "You were not punctual for our meeting, so this is the punishment I have given you!" I was lost for words.

That evening, we enjoyed the very popular Peking Opera *The Concubine Gets Tipsy*. He was very fond of Peking Opera, the leading school of the traditional Chinese operas and one of the "Four Chinese National Treasures" (The four national treasures are Chinese painting, cuisine, medicine and Peking Opera). He was able to distinguish the different singing tones of its various schools. While watching it, he excitedly explained to me its plot and special creative art forms, airing his appreciation of them. From that evening on, as he took me more and more to watch the Peking Opera, I gradually began to appreciate and thoroughly enjoy it.

When the opera finished, Puyi suggested that I have a look at his apartment. He had informed me concerning the location of his apartment, but this was the first time I entered it. I found that it consisted of a sitting-room and a bedroom. The bedroom was about 20 square meters in area, with a desk, a pair of single sofas, a small round table, several chairs, a double bed and a door leading to a tiny washroom. The sitting-room was larger, having a writing table, a bookcase, a crescent-shaped sofa and a teapot. The furniture, his clothes and utensils were scattered around the room, in no apparent order.

He invited me to sit on the sofa in the sitting room and offered me a variety of cakes, fruit, melon seeds and sweets. Seeing that I was reluctant to reach out and get them for myself, he picked up an orange and some sweets, stuffing them into my hands.

Puyi remarked that our several meetings had already left him with a good impression of me and that he was not able to tear himself away from me. He wanted to know whether I was also glad to have the pleasure of his friendship. I expressed that I hoped to keep seeing him regularly, to give our friendship a chance to blossom. Then, with the appropriate words of that time, he asked me whether or not I was satisfied with him. I replied that we should continue to have mutual positive criticism and help each other in the future. He beamed with pleasure.

At that moment, Mr. Wan Jiaxi, Puyi's fifth younger sister's husband came in. It seemed that they had planned this beforehand. Puyi informed me that on the next day, a Sunday, they would like to go to my home. Considering that our relationship was still in its early days and that Puyi was a very unique figure, I didn't think that it was suitable for him to come to my home. I felt that I must decline him: "Our living quarters are a hodgepodge of small houses and it is far from here, so it is better not to go there!" Puyi asked in reply, "Why don't you want me to go?" I recognized that he was determined to go and that it would be impolite for me to reject them again, so I reluctantly agreed.

Around 9 am the next morning, Puyi and Mr. Wan Jiaxi found my home, in Chaowai Jishikou. Actually, my home consisted of only one tiny room, and was soon filled by the three of us. Later, Puyi later commented about my tiny room, "Both Wan and I liked your small room. It's not big, but clean and neat, with the simple furniture placed in the right positions." It had been a surprise to me that the imposing Emperor Xuantong even wanted to come as a guest, to the tiny room of an ordinary citizen.

After chatting for a few moments, Mr. Wan made his excuses and took his leave, so that there was only Puyi and I left in the room. He kept on smoking, but didn't say anything for a while. Finally, Puyi broke the silence: "Now, in your home, I'd like to have a heart-to-heart talk with you. I have a lot of things that I want to say to you."

"Certainly! I'd like to know what you have to say," I answered.

"As you know, I was the former Puppet Emperor of the Manchukuo. I followed the Japanese Imperialists for thirteen years, as their 'lap-dog' and during that time, I committed a lot of crimes against the people. I owe the Communist Party of China and the Chinese People a large debt."

I responded: "I think that you have been remolded completely and have a very high political consciousness now. Anyhow, Chinese history is quite complicated. Let the past be past, now we should look forward!"

Puyi and members of Aisin-Gioro Royal Clan at Puyi's fifth sister's home. On the far left is Wan Jiaxi, Puyi's fifth brother-in-law.

Puyi continued, "I appreciate your words, but I'm determined to do more for the Chinese people in my remaining years."

"Both of us should do more for our people," I stressed.

It seemed that my words had helped to free his mind from some of his misgivings. Immediately he revealed a very happy expression and then changed the subject of our conversation.

"Because I was touched by the warmth of the Communist Party's Policy and after lengthy consideration, I presented to the government 468 rare national treasures, including platinum, gold, diamonds, pearls and jewelry. Before I left the Forbidden City in 1964, I had selected them all from the vast treasures which had been stored in the Forbidden City. I had taken them with me while in northeast China and Russia. Now, I'm only living on my 100 yuan monthly salary, without any other income. So, I wouldn't be able to provide you with a high standard of living, if we were to marry."

I further remarked, "It was not because you were Emperor before that I'm enjoying and appreciating your company. I think that virtue is most important and that money cannot buy real love."

He continued: "I'm nearly twenty years older than you. I worry that the age gap would affect our love." Evidently, he had been weighing up this matter for some time.

I decided to tease him, to see his reaction, so in a gentle voice I uttered, "I hadn't thought about that." An uneasy look appeared on his face. "But energetic and lively people always look younger," I added. Hearing what I said, he was happy again,

The Last Emperor of China My Husband Puyi

Emperor Qianlong's topaz seals and jadeite bracelets. They are among the 468 pieces of the rare national treasures Puyi presented to the government in 1957.

saying: "Do you think that I'm lively and energetic? .... Since knowing you, I have been very happy."

"Actually, I would prefer to marry a gentleman who is a little bit older. I lost my parents when I was little, so I need love and affection and an older husband who knows how to take care of a younger wife," I spoke out, honestly.

That day, we had enjoyed a long and open-hearted conversation. But I was still not sure that we had firmly established our relationship. We had only had several meetings together and both of us still hoped to gain more mutual understanding. For me, marriage was a major matter. Puyi also thought that his choice of wife needed great care. He had told me in a very secret tone: "This is the concern that Chairman Mao Zedong shared with me!" He excitedly described to me that only half a month before our first meeting, Chairman Mao had held a banquet in his home in Zhongnanhai to entertain Puyi, encouraging him to consider marriage again. "You need to consider your marital situation very carefully, don't enter into anything lightly. You must find a suitable wife. It will have a great impact on your remaining years. You must have a wife."

Aunt Li was one of my neighbors. She had taken me as her own daughter, always doing her best to take care of my daily needs. When she heard that Puyi had come, with an awestruck and curious mood, she came to see him while we were still talking. To her amazement, Puyi was such a likable gentleman. He greeted her kindly, calling her "aunty", as well as inviting her to have lunch with us, at a nearby inn. Afterwards, she complimented Puyi to me: "Who would have thought that the emperor could have become an ordinary person like us!"

Chapter Four

The Setting of Our Love

After the meeting at my house, our courtship entered a new phase. If I had considered previously that our love tree had already budded and grown to be a sapling, now the tree was starting to put down deeper roots. We started to have even more meetings together, with Puyi wanting to see me almost every day. Sometimes, Puyi came straight to my house without prior making a telephone call.

In the first half of 1962, our country was still in a state of great economic difficulty. In order to help take care of Puyi and the other party members, the government issued each commissioner of the Historical Account of Past Events at least ten meal coupons per month. With these coupons, they could enjoy better meals at the dining rooms in the CPPCC HQ, or the Cultural Club. Puyi often came to meet me before dinner on Saturday or before breakfast on Sunday and then we would go together to eat there. Sometimes we would see some of his colleagues, who were eating there as well. They always cheerfully came over to greet and joke with us, asking us when we were going to get married and telling us to remember to offer them some wedding sweets. (Wedding sweets and cigarettes are memorable features of a Chi-

Puyi at the Forbidden City at the age of 14

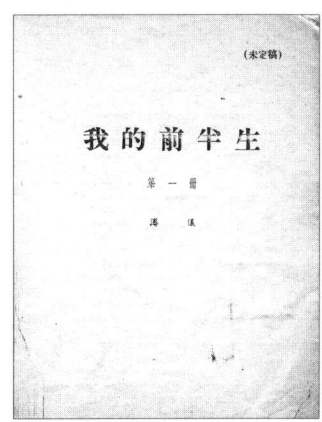

The front cover of *The First Half of My Life* (uncompleted)

Wanrong (1906-1946), Puyi's Empress at the time of "Grand Nuptials" December, 1922

nese wedding, given out to friends and relatives shortly before or after the wedding.)

To give me a different selection of food, every now and then Puyi would also take me to the high class National Minorities Hotel or to the Xinqiao Hotel, to dine there.

During this period, Puyi had been busy making amendments to his book *The First Half of My Life* with the assistance of the Masses Publishing House. Once, while working through his manuscript with the editor, he took me to the publishing house and showed me a lot of the original photographs. Among them were the photos of

Wenxiu (1909-1951), Puyi's "Virtuous Concubine" at the age of 13

The Last Emperor of China My Husband Puyi

Wanrong, his former empress, and Wenxiu, Tan Yuling, and Li Yuqin, all of whom were former concubines. This was the first time I had seen their photos.

Strolling around the streets was one of his hobbies. On Sundays, he was very fond of sauntering along the streets with me, looking at department stores, food stores, bus-stop signs, rubbish bins, as well as shop assistants with white caps and the young girls in blue uniforms who were walking on the streets. These were everyday sights for anyone, but most intriguing for him.

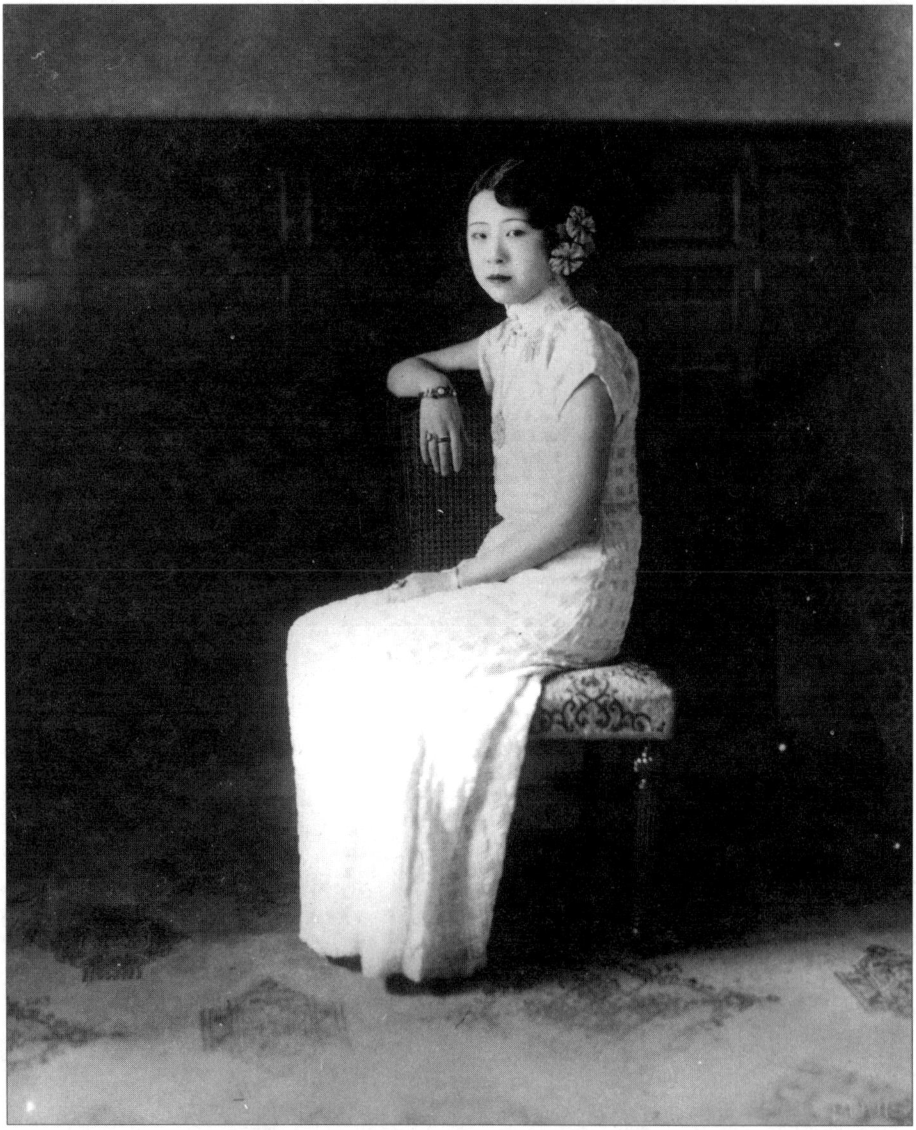

Tan Yuling (1920-1942), Puyi's third wife, who was conferred the title of "Auspicious Concubine" when she married Puyi in 1937

In the spring of 1943, 15-year-old student Li Yuqin was selected to be Puyi's fourth wife, being conferred the title of "Fortunate Concubine".

After he had entered the Forbidden City at the age of three, he had been constantly under the close supervision of several high consorts. There was "strict observance of rules", and he was always being followed by a group of retinue who were always ready to serve him and care for him. He told me that he had hated his "prison life" in the Forbidden City, which had lasted for many years. At long last, he had gained his freedom and he loved the "open space between the blue sky and the vast earth".

I remember once when we ate at a small restaurant on Xisi Street. Sitting at a square table, we bought two bowls of steamed rice, a plate of fried shredded pork and a bowl of soup with meat balls. A man eating near us suddenly recognized Puyi and blurted out: "Isn't that the 'Little Emperor'?" When everyone in the restaurant heard this, they put down their bowls and chopsticks, and then crowded around us, whispering, "Look, it's Emperor Xuantong!" Some gazed at me in wonder: "Is she the Empress?" I was frightened, and didn't dare to raise my head, but was only too aware that my face had turned red, my ears were humming and my head felt numb. For the first time in my life people were staring at me, gossiping about me and treating me like a monster. But Puyi didn't care at all, he was glad to chat with the people, nodding at them, and laughing heartily.

A scholarly-looking old man, with a long white beard, came to shake hands with Puyi and to show his great respect. Puyi invited him to join us and chatted while they were eating.

"What are you doing now?" he asked.

"I'm at the CPPCC," Puyi replied.

The Last Emperor of China My Husband Puyi

"I heard that you work at the Research Institute of Culture and History," the old man commented.

"Actually I worked at the Research Committee of the Historical Acccounts of Past Events connected to the CPPCC," Puyi replied.

"Is your lifestyle busy now?" he continued.

"Most of the time, I check and approve the historical accounts of past events, also correcting them if necessary. Besides that, every week I like to find time to go to the Beijing Botanical Garden to do physical labour," Puyi went on.

"You're looking very healthy, would you mind telling me how old you are?" the old man questioned.

"Uncle (a term of friendly respect used when speaking to the older generation, which doesn't necessarily imply a blood relationship), can you guess?" Puyi asked in reply.

"You look around forty years old, but..." the old man looked Puyi up and down, counting on his fingers, "Xuantong's reign was from..."

"I'm fifty-six years old this year," Puyi butted in, smiling.

"You don't look that age, you really don't look that age," said the old man, shaking his head and sighing with emotion: "You're not at all haughty nowadays!"

On August 25, 1931, Wenxiu left her home in the Quiteness Garden in Tianjin, when appealed to divorce Puyi. The news appeared in major newspapers in China with this picture of Wenxiu.

"I'm an ordinary citizen now. How could I be haughty? I'm proud to be an ordinary worker," Puyi remarked.

Puyi answered all of the old man's questions politely. Finally, the old man asked Puyi who I was. Puyi told him, with a respectful look: "She is my lady friend!" The old man was staggered: "Is that really true! When you were Emperor, would you ever bring your lady friend to eat at such a small restaurant?" Puyi answered him emotionally, "Of course, I couldn't do it then. But the former Puyi is dead, and the one you see now is the new Puyi."

After that meal we said our farewells to the old man. Holding Puyi's hand in his, the old man invited Puyi to go to his home: "My home is at Xisi Street, if you are ever free, then please come to my home as my guest."

Puyi at the time of his "Grand Nuptials"

Puyi then waved goodbye to the waitresses and the diners in the small restaurant.

Leaving the restaurant, I complained to Puyi: "Just now, I really wanted to slip away but we were surrounded by so many people!" Puyi disagreed with me, "the old man and those around us were friendly. They were just showing that they care for us. They are our friends. We shouldn't leave the restaurant without talking with them. That would leave them feeling disappointed."

The Last Emperor of China My Husband Puyi

This little incident at the small restaurant gave me an even greater respect for Puyi. He was so modest, and willing to mix with the working class. I couldn't believe that he was the former "Son of Heaven". I was sure he hadn't been one of the notorious "Sadists". Although Puyi was often ashamed to tell me about his "hideous behaviour" from his early years, I simply couldn't believe that it was true. I was in love with this wonderful man and could only see his good points which set him in such a positive light for me. Maybe I am proof of the saying, "love is blind".

Of course, I didn't mean that Puyi had no faults. During the many years spent at the Forbidden City, and especially the period when he acted as "puppet Emperor", he was constantly under surveillance, which made him suspicious of others. He told me that he hardly ever ate meals outside, except at his younger brothers' and sisters' homes, for fearing that somebody might poison him.

Once at my home at the beginning of the March, 1962, he suddenly asked me: "Comrade Li (this was what he liked to call me before our marriage), you must be good at cooking southern-style Chinese food?" I nodded, "Please come here next week, and I'll cook for you." The following Sunday, he happily came and brought some cans of fish and meat with him. I cooked several Shanghai and Hangzhou-style dishes for him. But strangely, he wouldn't touch them, although I kept inviting him to eat. He just sat there. I was deeply disappointed, having to eat by myself. Later, I realized that at that time he wasn't yet ready to trust me unreservedly.

Sometimes Puyi liked coming to my house before I returned from my work. Actually, he was aware of my work schedule, so why did he do this? I slowly learned that he needed to find an excuse to visit Aunt Li. At her home, Puyi made detailed inquiries about my habits. Did I return home late every evening? What kind of friends came to my home? Were there any male comrades among them? How careful and thorough his investigations were! Puyi thus set up a good relationship with Aunt Li and following our marriage, he still liked going to visit her.

I was not only once an object of his suspicion, but also on one occasion, he had a tiff with me. Whilst around my house, Puyi mentioned his former empress and concubines. He confessed that he had no idea about the normal affection between husband and wife then and that he considered his wives as toys and ornaments, going to enjoy their company; when he was unhappy he would cut them dead. In fact, he said that he didn't love any of them. Upon hearing this, I bantered with him: "You won't treat me like that in the future, will you?" My joke unexpectedly offended him and he became angry, saying: "If we can't really share our lives happily together, then let's just be good friends!" Abruptly, he put on his coat and left.

Why did Puyi get so angry? I understood his way of thinking only some years later.

After being granted special amnesty from the government, what Puyi valued most were the fruits of his ten years of reeducation. What Puyi hated bitterly was being judged by people because of his past position as emperor. They had not made a distinction between the first half of his life from the second half of his life. He would often say that "yesterday's Puyi is the enemy of today's Puyi". Therefore what I said to him had unintentionally touched a "raw nerve".

Following the tiff, Puyi didn't come to my home for three nights. Aunt Li asked me why she hadn't seen Mr. Puyi for several days. I had to put her off, saying that I hadn't phoned him.

Three nights later he eventually appeared again at my house. He excused himself, saying that he had caught a cold.

"I regret making you angry!" I said.

"Forget it!" he replied. I was sure Puyi hadn't forgotten the tiff. He had been ready to apologize to others and examine his own mistakes. Then, he offered his apology to me. "I have experienced reformation and I shall never treat my wife like my former empress or concubines." I looked at him. It seemed as if he was waiting to hear my opinion. Puyi was too frank sometimes, even naive, but at least he was really straightforward and honest.

Before long, the CPPCC Headquarters sent officials to our hospital to examine my personal life. Puyi worried whether or not I would be considered acceptable and if our marriage would be approved. Some days later, a leader of the CPPCC called Puyi to his office, formally notifying him that "Comrade Li Shuxian is a good comrade, with a clear po-

Puyi liked Chairman Mao's poems and calligraphy, hanging them on the wall of his lounge.

The Last Emperor of China My Husband Puyi

litical record and moral integrity and has proved to be honest, understanding a woman's role in society. So the leaders of the CPPCC have ratified your application for marriage. But do you mind that she is a divorcee? This is your decision." Puyi answered, "I have carefully considered the situation. She was right to get out of a miserable marriage forced up on her by the feudal society."

That evening, Puyi came around. Taking my hand in his, he appeared so happy, so I teased him, asking if he had come across a lost purse on his way to my home. He answered me, excitedly, saying, "The CPPCC HQ has sent officials to your hospital, to investigate you at the Personnel department. They have given you a good evaluation. My leader has informed me that they have ratified our marriage, so I needn't worry about it anymore. How could I fail to be happy? Now, you are the person I love the most. If I had lost you, because our leaders wouldn't ratify our marriage, how painful it would have been for me!"

Puyi, after being captured by the Russian Red Army in Shenyang Airport, August 1945, being taken to the Soviet Union

Puyi witnessed at the International Military Tribunal for the Far East, Tokyo, Japan.

From then on, the "Comrade Zhou", who had often phoned our hospital, now referred to himself as Puyi. It created a sensation in our hospital that I was dating "Emperor Xuantong". All of my colleagues were gossiping about it in amazement. Being supported by the authorities of both sides, it became much easier for Puyi to see me. He sometimes went to my house during my working hours, and if this happened, Aunt Li would immediately phone the leaders of our hospital and they would give me permission to return home straight away. Hurrying back home to receive Puyi, I would chat with him for a while, before walking with him to the bus stop to see him off. Afterwards, I

Puyi reading at home

would return to my hospital, to resume my work.

Later on, Puyi changed his practice and would come to my home in the afternoons. Every day, he would first go on the No.1 trolley bus from the Baitasi stop in Xicheng District and get off at the Chaoyangmen stop in Dongcheng District. Then he would walk over to my house. He gradually became familiar with the routine, and so he eventually dared to come to my home in the evenings. In those days, I was quite busy with my daily work, and on top of that we had political study sessions or professional meetings, almost every evening. Thus, I would return home late. Before opening the front door, my neighbours would come to tell me: "Mr. Zhou has arrived, he's waiting for you in your room." They still liked calling Puyi "Mr. Zhou".

China at that time was still suffering from the "Great Famine (1959-1961)". Every month, at a discounted price, Puyi would get a ration card from the CPPCC HQ and would go to buy biscuits, sweets, fruit and canned food from a specially designated shop. He would always bring them to my home and share them with me.

After "going steady" with Puyi for four months, I had made up my mind that I would spend the rest of my life with Puyi. But even so, there were some of my colleagues, who cared deeply for me and advised me to think over the matter carefully. They would say, "How can an emperor share common ground with ordinary people?" From my personal experience of courting Puyi, I was convinced he was no different from the rest of us, the ordinary people, and that he had many fine qualities and virtues which endeared me to him.

However, a lady working in the control lab of our hospital couldn't understand why I was seeing Puyi. She advised me, "You are still young, why are you planning to marry Puyi? How can you live together with a feudal Emperor?" I answered her: "Thank you for caring about me, but he loves me and I love him."

One of my close colleagues was Ms. Wei, whose sister-in-law worked in the hospital's Personnel Section. Upon hearing the news that the CPPCC HQ was sending officials to investigate me, she came to question me about it: "You didn't take a fancy for any of the gentlemen introduced to you previously, but you settled on Puyi. I don't get it. Are you after his money?" "No, he is very poor," I answered, "both of us depend on and live on our own salaries."

"Then, what do you love about him?" she asked.

"I love him for who he is. He is honest and loves me deeply." I tried my best to let her understand our relationship, but failed. She warned me that she would finish our friendship if I married Puyi. (And after our marriage, she did just that!)

The love between Puyi and I was deepening continually. He knew that I was in poor health, so he would always remind me to wear more clothes when it was cold. Once I caught a cold and he came to see me right away. Seeing that I was suffering from a sore throat and that I couldn't speak, he became very anxious. He urged me to go and see a famous Chinese doctor called Mr. Chang, who worked in the Navy Hospital. This was because Puyi favoured Chinese Medicine. I assured him that I would recover in a couple of days, so that I needn't see a doctor. To my surprise, he turned away sadly, with tears running down his face. He stopped crying only after I consoled him for a long time. A week later Puyi phoned and told me that he was ill with a high fever. On my break I hurried to see him with some of his favourite food. I took his temperature and it was 38 ℃. I offered to go to the hospital with him, where he could get an injection to help him recover quickly. He seemed touched greatly: "At long last, I have a true friend! You came a long way to see me and I'm feeling much better now, so I needn't go to hospital." Then, there was a silence. He squeezed my hand tightly and gazed into my eyes: "Tell me, please, when will you marry me?"

"Let's wait a little while!" I said.

"Why wait?" he beseeched me, "Marry me, please. Let's get married soon!"

"Are you worried that I might change my mind?" I queried. I could read his thoughts. "A little bit, I love you, so I'm afraid of losing you and I cannot live without you!" said Puyi speaking from his heart.

Puyi telling a reporter his exciting feeling after being granted Special Amnesty, 1960

"I know a Chinese proverb," I responded. "I'd like to use it to show you my heart: 'Seas may run dry, rocks turn to dust, but I'll always be loyal to you.'"

Hearing what I said, Puyi was so happy that he nearly jumped out of his chair with excitement. Like joining a pair of Chinese couplets, he sung out the following words:

> *A mountain has its summit,*
> *The river flows from its source.*
> *The flower of our love will never wither.*

Our love affair had reached its high tide. Like many young sweethearts we then also "pledged our troth" and planned to marry.

Chapter Five

The Last Emperor's Grand Nuptials

Puyi kept asking me to marry him. He urged me: "Shuxian, what else are you worrying about? We have been going steady for some months. Let's get married soon! Then I won't have to hurry to your home every day." I hated to disappoint him, so we agreed to set our wedding day for April 30th 1962, because the following day would be the May 1st Labour Day. Puyi who had been the Emperor of China, wished to connect this day of "great personal rejoicing" with the workers' festival.

The top leaders of the CPPCC paid special attention to Puyi's marriage plans. They knew that both Puyi and I had lived a single life for a long time and kindly advised us that since we were setting up home together for the first, we needed to plan it well.

Puyi and I at the Golden Water Bridge in front of Tian'anmen Gate, 1962

"Before your wedding day you had better purchase all the domestic articles you will need such as pots, bowls, plates, chopsticks and the like. All of your expenses will be paid by the government," they said.

Not long before our wedding day, the top leaders of the CPPCC dispatched a colleague, named Zhao Huatang, to help us with the shopping and they also offered us two introduction letters to two special department stores, the Wanfujing Department Store and the Friendship Store. As this was a time of great hardship, ordinary stores

Puyi and I, 1964

had very few household goods available.

Actually, I wasn't short of everyday clothes, but I was eager to take this opportunity to buy some beautiful dresses. I heard that leaders from all circles would attend our wedding ceremony, including many celebrities as well as Chinese and foreign reporters. As the bride, I certainly wanted to look my best!

Standing by the counter of the store and pointing to the fabric and the dresses I had chosen, I looked at Puyi, wanting to seek his opinion. But it seemed he didn't understand me. Mr. Zhao Huatang, who was accompanying us, had to interrupt us, saying:

"Getting married is the greatest day of your lives. You shouldn't be tight-fisted with your bride!" Puyi turned to me, gently explaining to me: "The government is so kind to pay for our shopping expenses this time. So we should be conservative and cut down on our expenses, only buying essential household

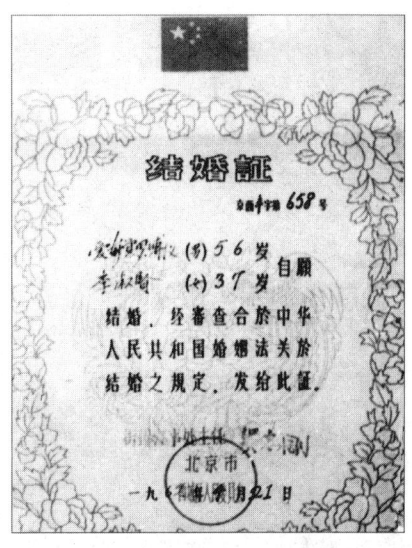

Puyi and Li Shuxian's marriage certificate, 1962

Puyi with his brothers and sisters and Zhao Huatang (far right), his colleague, who often kindly took care of Puyi

items. I think you should buy only one top quality dress this time. Why don't we buy some more dresses for you later, when we have future savings?" What he said was reasonable. Our country was still suffering from great economic hardship, but the government was trying its best to take good care of us, therefore in turn we should do what is right for our country. So, from the two stores, we only bought a bed cover, a quilt, and a western-style skirt for me. Puyi didn't buy anything for himself.

Mr. Zhao became anxious when he saw that Puyi hadn't bought any new clothes for himself. He persuaded him: "You shouldn't leave here without buying anything for yourself!" But Puyi stuck to his guns, saying that his old suits would cover his needs. Later, Mr. Zhao Huatang often complimented Puyi as a "person with political understanding*".

On April 25th, Puyi came to my home to see me. I happened to be suffering from a sore throat and I found it difficult to speak. He became quite uneasy, saying to me: "The reporters of the Xinhua News Agency (China's state news agency) heard that I was going to get married and hoped to issue a photo of me with my "bride to be" before

---

* In 1962, the well-known and tragic "Great Famine" had just ended but China was still in tremendous financial difficulty, so Puyi did his best to cut down the expense for his wedding ceremony for which the government had offered to pay.

our wedding day. They have invited us to tour the Summer Palace tomorrow, to take some photos there. But you are ill now. What can we do about it?" After saying this, he sat down and wept sadly.

"What are you crying for?" I asked him in a hoarse voice.

"I'm afraid your illness will worsen and that our wedding will have to be put off."

"I've only caught a cold. I will recover very soon. I will go to the Summer Palace if I feel a little better tomorrow. It won't hinder the plans of the Xinhua News Agency," I assured him.

I got up to pass Puyi a towel to wipe away his tears. He cheered up again and smiled. On the next morning, Puyi came in a car dispatched by the CPPCC Headquarters. We completed our planned tour to the Summer Palace smoothly.

On April 29th, the CPPCC HQ sent a truck to my home to take my simple furniture, as well as several suitcases packed with my dresses, personal luggage, pots, bowls, basins, and other sundry items to Puyi's apartment.

The following morning, in a car provided by the CPPCC Headquarters and accompanied by Puyi, I went to have my hair set at the noted "Silian Luxury Salon" in Wangfujing Street. Afterwards, he sent me back to my now empty home, outside Chaoyangmen. During the afternoon, Puyi came back in the same car, taking me and several of my colleagues to the CPPCC Headquarters. We enjoyed a meal together there, at their canteen.

At about 6:30 pm, after the dinner, the buses and cars, provided by the CPPCC HQ, drove in convey to the grand wedding ceremony at the Cultural Club on Nanheyan Road. Our bridal car, decorated on the bonnet with a huge silk crimson flower was in front of the convoy. Because the next day would be the "May 1st Labour Day", all of the main streets in Beijing were beautifully-decorated with lanterns and festoons, also adding colour and beauty to our ceremony.

When we reached the Cultural Club, Puyi and I were immediately surrounded by a large group of guests as we got out from the car. Among them were the leaders of the

The Cultural Club of the CPPCC, the place where Puyi and Li Shuxian's Wedding Cremony was held on April 30th, 1962

The Last Emperor of China My Husband Puyi

United Front Work Department of the Central Committee of the Communist Party of China (the CPC) and the CPPCC, the leaders of the United Front Work Department of Peking Municipal Committee of the CPC, cultural and artistic celebrities, the Commissioners of the HAPE, my hospital colleagues and our relatives and friends. They all followed us into the hall, introducing and greeting each other happily.

In the hall, all of the guests were ushered to the long tables covered with snow-white linen tablecloths with teacups, cakes, sweets and fruit on each table. Puyi and I took our seats first and shortly afterwards he took me to each table, introducing me to the guests. We shook hands happily. Puyi and I expressed to them our warm welcome and they all greeted us and gave us their sincere congratulations. Mr. Wang Yaowu, a former Nationalist Party (the Kuomintang) Lieutenant General and the former Chairman of Shandong Province, but now the commissioner of the HAPE, expressed his congratulations to Puyi, "Mr. Pu, tomorrow will be May 1st Labour Day. It's interesting that you're holding your wedding ceremony today. It's wonderful!" Puyi was overwhelmed with delight: "'May 1st Labour Day' is the 'Grand Festival of the Workers'. I'm one of them now, and it touches my heart," said Puyi.

Mr. Li Jue, a former National Party Lieutenant-General and then a member of the CPPCC and the Director of the General Affairs Department of the CPPCC HQ, played the role of the Master of Ceremonies. At 7 pm, he announced the commencement of our ceremony.

First of all, Mr. Zaitao, Puyi's seventh uncle, a former Navy Chancellor of the Qing Dynasty, and the one who was also presiding over our Wedding Ceremony, made his congratulatory speech. At the age of 77, his voice was still sonorous. He declared:

Zaitao (1884-1970), one of Emperor Daoguang's grandsons and Puyi's seventh uncle, in his youth. He was one of the principle organisers of Puyi's "Grand Nuptials".

Today, I'm delighted to join this wedding ceremony. In your new married life, I hope both of you will learn from each other, making your own contribution to our Socialist revolution and construction, and thus repaying the thoughtfulness and care of the government to you both. Finally, I wish you both a harmonious life together, till you are both old and grey.

Mr. Zaitao sat down after making the speech. In 1922, he had been one of the main organizers of Puyi's Grand Nuptial held in the Forbidden City when Puyi married both Wanrong, his "Empress" and Wenxiu, his "Virtuous Concubine", and in 1937, he helped Puyi to confer the title of "Auspicious Concubine" on Miss Tan Yuling. This time, he presided over a completely different wedding ceremony for Puyi. The two former wedding ceremonies had become fresh in his mind and therefore all sorts of feelings were welling up in his heart.

Next Mr. Li Jue, the Master of Ceremonies, announced that it was the groom's turn to make a speech. Puyi strode to the front and with an air of confidence spoke the following:

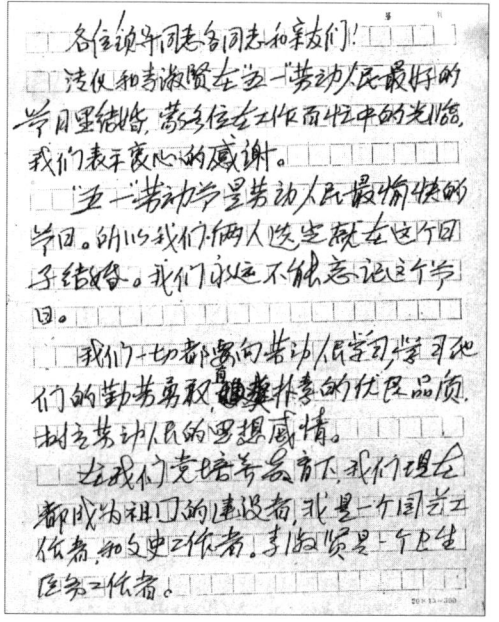

Puyi personally wrote a draft beforehand for his wedding ceremony speech.

Leaders, comrades, relatives and friends, Madam Li Shuxian and I are marrying on the most important festival of the working class. We are cordially grateful for your presence at our wedding ceremony today. We chose this day to hold our wedding ceremony because it is the happiest festival of the working class. We will remember this day and continue to learn from the working class all our future days together, following their excellent virtues of being valiant, industrious, forthright and simple and the noble ideas and affections of the proletariat. I hated the first half of my life, for it was a humiliating experience of an exploiter and parasite. Following the ten years of reeducation, I have turned into a "glorious" worker with the ability to earn my own living. Now, I'm a horticultural worker at the Beijing Botanical Gardens and also a historical records worker at the CPPCC. My wife is a respectable medical worker. We are setting up our home together on the eve of the festival of workers. This is the happiness I've been pursuing. Now, this happiness is at hand. It is given to us by our government and our people. Now, on behalf of my wife and I, I'd like to inform our guests of our desired intentions. We will mutually encourage each other, be ready to overcome our short-

comings and mistakes, do our respective work well, be loyal to the people's cause and devote our strength to our motherland, just as she desires.

Actually, Puyi had made good preparation for the speech. He had discussed the matter with me several times: "Shuxian, I will definitely be asked to make a speech at our wedding. I think that you should say something then too. It would be very significant." I told him that I was afraid to talk on formal occasions. Puyi persisted, "You can make a draft and practice it repeatedly beforehand!"

I didn't agree with him outwardly, but did prepare one secretly, so that I was prepared. When Puyi had finished his speech, all of the guests strongly insisted that I should say something. The Master of the Ceremonies walked to me and politely said to me: "You'd better satisfy the request from the guests!" I became aware that it was impossible for me to refuse it, so I uttered a few words. I took out the draft I had prepared and stood up to read it:

Puyi and I at our wedding

Leaders, comrades, relatives and friends: first of all, I'd like to express our sincere thanks to you for being so kind as to attend our wedding. Through a long period of mutual understanding, we have gradually built up our affection and love for each other and our common interests have also helped to tie our futures together. Our love has matured and led to today's Wedding Ceremony. We are excited to finally realize our dream. On this unforgettable moment, Puyi and I want to present our heartfelt thanks to our Socialist Motherland because she has given us a happy home for our married life together! Finally, I'd like to thank you all again.

As soon as I completed reading the draft, I heard someone say:

"I didn't expect the Bride to make such a brilliant speech!"

Then Mr. Li Jue, the Master of Ceremonies, on behalf of the CPPCC leaders, happily conveyed their warm congratulations to us.

When the ceremony was over, the guests rearranged the seats into a circle and the hall was brimming with cheers and laughter. Madam Feng Lijuan, wife of Mr. Zheng Tingji, a former National Party General and now a Commissioner of the HAPE, was the most vivacious lady, with her voice resounding more than everybody else's. Pointing her finger at Puyi, she said: "Aren't you interested in medicine? Now you are married to a 'fighter in white*'. You dream has finally come true."

Mr. Liao Mosha, a famous writer and the director of the United Front Work (UFW) Department**, affiliated with the Beijing Municipal Committee of the CPC, was sitting near us and kept looking over at us with a broad smile on his face.

According to Chinese civil custom, the bride and groom should entertain guests by pouring tea and lighting cigarettes for them. But Puyi didn't seem to know this. He stayed in his chair, excitedly chatting with the guests. I was afraid that they would be unhappy with this, so had to remind him to follow the custom. Instead of doing that, he stood up and announced to the guests: "Please help yourself to cigarettes and tea!" How angry I was! I had to amuse the guests myself, hurrying around the hall to light cigarettes for former National Party Generals, Mr. Du Yuming, Mr. Shen Zui, Mr. Zhou Zhenqiang and other noted guests. They all arose from their seats and thanked me politely. Several times, Puyi had whispered to me to take care of myself and to have a rest. I was exhausted that day when we returned to our bridal suite. With concern, Puyi said to me: "Luckily, Mr. Wang Yaowu, Mr. Zheng Tingji and Mr. Fan Hanjie didn't smoke; otherwise lighting cigarettes for them would make you very weary!"

The photographers from the China News Agency and some other leading newspapers in China attended our wedding by invitation. They eagerly took a lot of "historic photos" for us. Taking this very rare chance, they shot a special family photo of the Aisin-Gioro Royal Clan. I had been a southerner of Han Nationality extraction, but from this day, I had become a formal member of this "Family of Great Renown", which had declined after the "Xinghai Revolution" (the 1911 Revolution, which overthrew the Qing Dynasty).

We were not driven back to our bridal suite in the CPPCC HQ until after 9 pm that

---

* In China, people like to refer to doctors and nurses as "fighters in white".

** The purpose of the work of the UFW, known as "Tong Zhan Bu" was to attract and unite celebrities outside of the CPC to engage in the work of the socialist revolution and construction, thus accomplishing the great cause of the unification of China.

Puyi's colleagues in CPPCC HQ expressing their congratulations to Puyi and I at our wedding ceremony

evening, when we were accompanied by some of my colleagues from my hospital and Mr. Zhou Zhenqiang, our matchmaker. After being assigned work at the CPPCC HQ, as an unmarried man, Puyi had been given a temporary apartment, which had been converted from offices. These were located next to the Secretary's Section of the CPPCC HQ. Actually, this had been especially suitable for him, for his office and apartment were then in the same courtyard, making his lifestyle easier. This same apartment had been redecorated to become our bridal suite. We received group after group of well wishers there. We lived there for a few months until the government chose another residence for us later.

Madam Fu Xuewen, wife of Mr. Shao Lizi, visited us. She put two bottles of vintage wine on the table, merrily telling us, "Mr. Shao will come, in the next few days, to drink your wedding wine with you. He said that I should ask you if you can cook some delicious dishes for him then!" Puyi smiled and said, "We look forward to his visit!" Mr. Shao Lizi, her husband, once used to be the National Party's Minister of Propaganda, The Chairman of Gansu Provincial Government and Chairman of Shaanxi Provincial Government. He had been quite a popular progressive personage and was referred to as "the old man seeking peace". Later, he had become a member of the Standing Committee of the CPPCC.

The Commissioners of the HAPE who had received the Special Amnesty in the first, second and third groups came forward in twos and threes to offer their congratulations. Some of them were the famous former National Party Generals, such as Mr. Song Xilian, Mr. Liao Yaoxiang, Mr. Du Yuming, Mr. Shen Zui and so on. Most of them wore the "blue Mao jackets" issued to them when they were in the Fushun War Criminal Prison. As gifts, some of them presented us ashtrays and some gave us children's toys—apparently they knew Puyi's hobby!

Mr. Shen Bochun, Mr. Lian Yinong and Mr. Ping Jiesan, three of the leaders of the CPPCC, brought with them a very pretty quilt cover. They offered their congratulations: "Hoping you live together happily until you reach a hundred years!"

Mr. Yu Dejun, a botanist and the director of Beijing Botanical Garden, came too. In the March of 1960, according to the suggestion of Premier Zhou Enlai, the Civil Affairs Bureau of Beijing Municipal Government had assigned Puyi to the Beijing Botanical Garden of the Chinese Academy of Science.

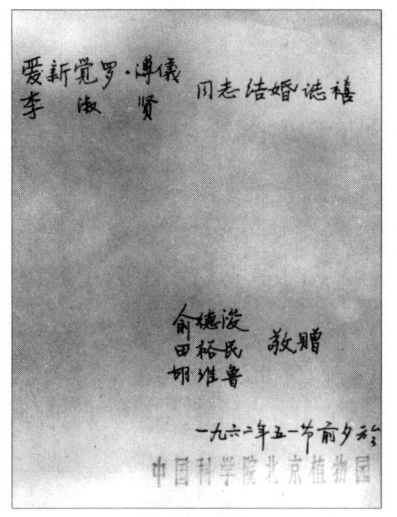

Puyi's wedding present

Puyi had spent one unforgettable year there, working in the morning and writing and studying in the afternoon, developing a profound friendship with his colleagues there, sharing their common work and life. He had taken the Botanical Garden as his native home and still returned there to visit them, once a week, after he had been transferred to work at the CPPCC Headquarters. Director Yu himself brought us a wedding gift, together with two other previous leaders of Puyi, Mr. Tian Yumin and Mr. Hu Weilu. The gift was a set of hard backed books, being the *Selected Works of Mao Zedong*, with a dedication written on the front flyleaf of the first volume:

Congratulations on the Marriage of Comrades Aisin-Gioro Puyi and Li Shuxian.

Respectfully presented by:

Yu Dejun
Tian Yumin
Hu Weilu

On the Eve of May 1st Labour Day 1962

Beijing Botanical Garden
Chinese Academy of Science

The Leaders of the Masses Publishing House came along to our apartment too, giving us an exquisite hanging scroll of a poem written by Chairman Mao Zedong, in his own calligraphy. They knew that Puyi loved Chairman Mao's poems and calligraphy.

The Last Emperor of China My Husband Puyi

Puyi and I and members of Aisin-Gioro Royal Clan at our wedding ceremony

Puyi immediately hung it on the wall of our lounge. He praised it with appreciation, saying: "The Chairman's calligraphy is wonderful, so are his poems!"

Mr. Zaitao, the seventh uncle of Puyi, also came to see us. He gave Puyi a pair of marble ashtrays as a wedding gift.

Mr. Pujie, Puyi's second younger brother and his Japanese wife, Sagahiro, were also there. They presented their elder brother with a snow-white shirt and a pair of socks and explained that they believed the second half of Puyi's life would be "as white as snow". Their gifts to me were a delicate purse and a white cloth dotted with black flowers to use for wrapping things in. I said to him that Mr. Pujie and his wife's gifts had special significance, symbolizing our future industrious and frugal life. Puyi happily nodded, saying that both of us "should be fortunate" and that "we would live together till we were both old and grey".

Mr. Puren, Puyi's fourth younger brother, also came. He brought his gift, a small electronic watch. Later on we hung it on the wall of our home, to serve us, by counting every minute and second for us.

Each of Puyi's younger sisters and brothers-in-law came at different times, bringing various gifts which had special significance.

It wasn't until 11 o'clock that night that all of the guests had left to return home. Then our sweet honeymoon week began.

But one of my hopes was soon to be dashed!

Chapter Six

The First Week of Our Honeymoon

The news of Puyi and Li Shuxian getting married was the top story that night in all the major newspapers in Hong Kong. Up until then, for more than forty years, thousands upon thousands of newspapers and magazines had reported about Puyi's every movement, but the only report Puyi cut out and kept was the one entitled "Newly-married Puyi's house crammed with well-wishers".

[Beijing] April 30th. Puyi got married to a lady named Li Shuxian. The bride, a native of Zhejiang, aged 36, worked at a hospital in Beijing. At their wedding ceremony, Puyi made a speech. He said:

"Now I am an academic on culture and history. We are delighted to be setting up a happy, new-style family home." He expressed his intention that in the future he and his wife would encourage and help each other so that they could make progress together. Li Shuxian also made a speech.

The news of Puyi and I getting married was the top story in all Hong kong newspapers.

Among those who joined the wedding ceremony were Puyi's relatives Zaitao and his wife, Pujie and his wife, his younger sisters and Mr. Zheng Dongguo, Mr. Qin Yizhi, Mr. Huang Wei, Mr. Li Jue, Mr. Lu Chongyi, Mr. Du Yuming, Mr. Liao Yaoxiang, Mr. Fan Hanjie, Mr. Song Xilian, and Mr. Wang Yaowu plus many relatives and friends of the bride and groom. All together there were more than 100 guests. They lined up to wish Puyi and his wife a happy

The Last Emperor of China My Husband Puyi

On May Day, 1962, Guo Moruo (left) and Bao'erhan (right) cordially received the bride and groom at the auditorium of CPPCC HQ.

life together.

The next day, May 1st, was the "International Labour Day". At 9 am, the annual "celebration" meeting and various performances were held in the auditorium of the CPPCC HQ. Shortly after 8 am Mr. Xing, the Secretary General of the CPPCC, came to our home, telling us that Mr. Guo Moruo, Deputy Premier of the State Council and Mr. Bao'erhan, deputy chairman of the CPPCC and Uyghur Nationality leader, were in the lounge of the auditorium. They wanted very much to see us before the start of the celebrations. When Puyi and I followed Mr. Xing into the lounge of the auditorium, Mr. Guo and Mr. Bao'erhan stood up immediately and eagerly came over to shake hands with us. Puyi introduced me to the two highly-esteemed old men. Mr. Guo greeted us with a smile.

"Congratulations! Mr. Puyi, I congratulate you on your marriage and starting a new life together! I hope your love will last forever!" Afterwards he asked: "Where is your bride from?"

"Hangzhou, Zhejiang Province," Puyi answered.

"Oh, she is a southerner, too!" Mr. Guo commented positively.

Mr. Guo Moruo was from Sichuan Province, in the south of China. As his gift for our marriage he gave Puyi two luxurious tins of "Double-Happiness" cigarettes, one of the best brands in China at that time. "I wish you great joy!" he said. Before the celebration performances started, Mr. Guo and Mr. Bao'erhan invited Puyi and I to take a commemorative photo with them. Puyi was very happy indeed.

Puyi was still excited when we had lunch at the CPPCC HQ canteen. First of all he praised the food which was fried pork-balls, fish fried in batter and stir-fried sliced pork and steamed rice, saying how delicious it was, and then he talked with me about Mr. Guo Moruo.

"Mr. Guo Moruo is one of the greatest Chinese modern writers, an accomplished poet, archaeologist and social activist." Puyi said, asking me: "Have you ever seen the modern drama *Wu Zetian*?"

"I haven't seen it," I replied.

"It has been performed in public. I really appreciate it. It's very interesting. Mr. Guo Moruo wrote the script. He is also a well-known calligrapher and has been invited to put his calligraphic works on display in many places. Furthermore, Mr. Guo is an historian of great distinction and his wife, Madam Yu Liqun is one of the few female calligraphers in China."

Puyi told me that he once met Mr. Guo Moruo at a banquet.

Mr. Guo said to him with a smile, "You should help experts in the Qing Dynasty with their study!"

Puyi replied: "I'm sorry I don't know the Manchu dialect. It is impossible to study the history of the Qing Dynasty without knowing Manchu". He recalled that Mr. Guo Moruo had respected him highly and greeted him enthusiastically, whenever they met.

That afternoon, Mr. Tong Xiaopeng, the Deputy Secretary General of the State Council and the director of the Premier's office came to convey to us Premier Zhou

Puyi and I at Beihai Park

Enlai's congratulations, which made us very excited. Mr. Tong was fond of joking. Pointing at Puyi, he said: "Puyi, now that you are married, it seems that there's hope of seeing your Crown Prince this time next year! Ha! Ha!" Those present all burst into laughter and Puyi was beside himself with laughter also.

After Mr. Tong Xiaopeng left, Mr. Liao Mosha, the Director of the United Front Work Department of the Peking Municipal Committee of the CPC, came to see us with one of his deputy directors. Mr. Liao carried himself with dignity and was a noted writer, winning a high reputation in Chinese literary and art circles. He enquired, with friendly concern, about our life after marriage.

At noon on May 2nd, the CPPCC gave a banquet in honour of the Aisin-Gioro Royal Clan, with Puyi's seventh uncle and all of his younger brothers, sisters and brothers-in-law in attendance. The principle leaders of the CPPCC and the members of the Aisin-Gioro Clan dined happily together, to celebrate our marriage.

On the evening of May 3rd, the United Front Work Department of the Peking Municipal Committee of the CPC and the Civil Affairs Bureau of the Peking Municipal Government jointly held a banquet at the Fangshan Restaurant. The Fangshan Restaurant located on the Qionghua Islet, with a hill behind and a lake in front and being situated in Beihai Park, is popular at home and abroad for serving traditional Imperial-quality meals, in Qing Dynasty style. Mr. Liao Mosha and Mr. Wang, the Director of the Civil Affairs Bureau, personally proposed toasts to the bride and groom, respectively. By Chinese custom, it would be ungracious for the bride or groom not to accept a glass of wine, but I really couldn't drink wine. Mr. Liao assured me: "Don't worry; we'll escort you home if you get drunk." He held a glass of wine, insisting that I must drink it; we were locked in a stalemate.

It was Puyi who stepped forward bravely to rescue me: "She can't drink wine. She never drinks wine."

"That's unheard of! The bride must drink wine at her own wedding dinner!" Mr. Wang wouldn't back down, "And I have been holding this glass for a long time, what are you going to do about it?"

"All right, all right, I'll drink it instead of her." Puyi took the glass from the hand of Mr. Wang and drank it in one gulp. The second one who wanted to propose a toast to us then stood up. "Thank you!" Puyi said to him and drank it too. Heartily laughing, he drank the third glass, the fourth glass.... The sight caused the whole room to resound with laughter and applause, again and again. Director Wang heartily remarked: "Puyi knows how to take care of his wife! Shuxian is fortunate to find such a good husband." He turned to ask Puyi: "Did you treat your former empress and concubines as well as this?" Puyi confessed openly, "In the past I didn't know that husband and wife should

(From left) Pujie's mother-in law, Husheng (Pujie's daughter), Puyi and Zaitao

be equal and take care of each other."

Finally when exquisite pastries were served up, Director Wang announced: "Today's pastry was made by an experienced chef who cooked before in the royal kitchen in the Forbidden City." He suggested to Puyi: "How about inviting the chef out to see you?" Shortly a kind, stout older man, about seventy years-old came out to meet us. Taking Puyi's hand in his, he told us about his past when he worked in the royal kitchen of the Forbidden City. Puyi was delighted:

"I left the Forbidden City when I was 19 years old. For about forty years I haven't had the opportunity to eat this kind of delicious pastry. I never expected to eat it again today." He added: "It tastes even better than before!" The veteran chef then told Puyi, "Please tell me whenever you want to eat the royal pastry. I'll come to your home to cook it for you." Puyi thanked him profusely.

At that moment, a young girl, about twenty years old, walked up to the chef and made a deep bow to him, saying: "I'd like to learn from you how to make 'Royal' pastry." She was Miss Husheng, the young daughter of Mr. Pujie. Born in Changchun in 1944, she had grown up in Japan. In May 1961, she came to Beijing with her mother to see her father who had already got a special amnesty and then returned to Japan. This time she had come to China to join her uncle's wedding ceremony and to be reunited with her parents in Beijing. The old chef agreed to teach her. Later, for several days, he went to

The Last Emperor of China My Husband Puyi

Pujie ang his daughter Husheng in Guangzhou

Pujie's home personally, to teach Hushen how to cook the special pastry.

Also to congratulate us on our marriage, was the editor who had been assigned by the Masses Publishing House, to help Puyi edit the manuscript of *The First Half of My Life*. He held a banquet for us in the Western Dining Hall of the Cultural Club. Mr. Cha Cunqi, the fifth uncle of Empress Wanrong, was also invited to join us. He not only had an intimate understanding of Puyi's domestic affairs, but had also, for a long time, held the position of being his English translator. He and Puyi had formed a deep friendship. In the course of amending the book, they often worked together. He helped Puyi call to mind many historical events to include in the book.

As is well known, Puyi was cared for by his wet-nurse Mrs. Wang Lianshou, having been breast-fed by her until he was nine years old. After his "Grand Nuptials" in 1923, Puyi often sent people to fetch her to stay with him for a few days. Towards the end of "the Manchukuo" period, Puyi took her to Changchun and supported her until he left the Northeast. Sadly she was hit by a stray bullet and died in Tonghua, in August 1945. After Puyi returned to Beijing in 1960, he soon found her adopted son and his three children. On May 4th, we took Miss Wang Peiying, his wet-nurse's grand-daughter to the Beijing Botanical Garden. Puyi had considered the Botanical Garden as his second home, so he should return there after his wedding ceremony, according to Chinese traditional custom. (According to traditional Chinese custom, following the wedding ceremony, both bride and groom should return to their parents' homes with presents to show their gratitude for being raised well.)

When we arrived at the Beijing Botanical Garden at 10 am, Mr. Tian Yumin, the director, was waiting outside the gate to welcome us. Puyi introduced Miss Wang and I to Director Tian first, then he led us into the reception room. Director Tian expressed his congratulations on our marriage and asked how we were.

Director Tian invited us to his home for lunch. His wife had already cooked a lot of tasty dishes for us. We thanked her for giving us such a delicious lunch. Director Tian said to me: "Puyi is lucky to marry you. He can't do any housework, so you will have to do it all. We hope you take good care of him, treating him like your own elder brother." Both Mr. Tian and his wife were respectful, kind-hearted veterans of the CPC. They cared sincerely about Puyi. I fully understood what they were asking of me.

After lunch, Director Tian accompanied us to view the various plants in the garden, while Puyi told us their varying features. In the greenhouse, we saw a kind of plant as big as a tall tree. Puyi told Miss Wang and I: "It came from abroad and needs careful cultivation. Like 'mimose', it is a kind of pamper plant." He picked up a small iron spade and skillfully loosened the soil around it. He then explained, "The soil around it must be loosened frequently. I couldn't even use this kind of small spade when I first came here. Ha ha!"

Previously, I had been taken to visit Puyi's bedroom. It had only two single beds, several chairs and an office desk with a thermos flask and a few cups on it. I noticed that Puyi's bed still had the quilt and the cotton-padded mattress he had brought from the Fushun War Criminals Prison, the special prison for the politically important and high-ranking war criminals. Puyi had continued returning to the Botanical

Wang Lianshou (1886-1946), Puyi's wet-nurse

Garden, once a week, for manual labour, after he had been transferred to work at the CPPCC HQ. After work he liked to stay there during the night, and then he would return to the CPPCC HQ the next morning.

We had a joyful day that day, like a bride returning to her native home after her wedding ceremony. It was already 6 pm when we said our farewells to Director Tian and his wife, outside the gate of the Botanical Garden. When we arrived at the CPPCC HQ, it was already dark.

That evening, Puyi shared with me about the original impression he had of me at our first meeting: "I fell in love with you at first sight that very day! I had never before talked so easily with a lady for a whole afternoon. I was longing to marry someone I really loved and considered that we must have a common language. I felt that I would be sick at heart each time when I saw the lady if I didn't really love her. I appreciated the fact that you were sincere and dressed simply. (In the time of Chairman Mao, Chinese people were expected to dress simply.) Your troubled life experiences especially won my sympathy. I'm glad that you are a nurse as I like medicine too. I'm now an ordinary citizen, hoping to set up a home where the married couple both work, just like thousands upon thousands of citizens in Beijing. Neither of us will stay at home like parasites. Now that we are married, I'm sure that our life together will continue to be a happy one, admired by others."

Chapter Seven

Hopes of Having Children Vanish into Thin Air

The first week of our honeymoon passed quickly with busy activities. Every night, only two minutes after Puyi had fallen asleep, I would hear him snoring. Being aware that he was already fifty-six years old, I knew that it must have been hard for him to being so tired, so I wanted him to have a good sleep.

But I felt strange when the second week of our honeymoon started. Both of us still used separate quilts, because Puyi hadn't asked me to use a double one, like all the other newly married couples in China. I wondered if maybe this "Emperor" had supernatural self-restraint. When I had already gone to bed, he would still be sitting on the sofa, smoking cigarettes or reading a book. I was too shy to say anything, only keeping silent and drifting off to sleep, after a while.

One night I was suddenly awakened by a burning sensation on my face. I opened my eyes to find Puyi was observing my face, with a table lamp in his hand. I complained to him: "It's three o'clock in the morning and not only have you not gone to sleep, but you have a 100-watt light in your hand. Do you want to char my face?!" Hearing what I said he had no alternative but to go back to bed. But during the next few nights, he made a habit of observing my face with the table lamp after I'd fallen sleep. I was sure it was unusual and that a honeymoon shouldn't be spent like this.

Every day during the honeymoon, Puyi had been to Baitasi Hospital to have an injection. At first, I didn't know what kind of injection he was getting. Later I went to the injection-room in the hospital with him. I was able to ascertain that it was a hormone injection to stimulate a man's sex drive. I asked a nurse there, privately:

"Does Puyi often come here to have this kind of injection?"

"He has one every day," the nurse replied.

That night, I asked him: "Is there something wrong with you? Why do you get a hormone injection?" Being confronted with my inquiries, he started to cry and confessed that he was suffering from impotence which meant that he couldn't have a normal sex life with me at present. He confessed that he hadn't had a proper sex life for many years. He also explained that because of his physical labour in prison, he had

The Last Emperor of China My Husband Puyi

eaten a lot more at each meal, so putting on extra weight. This made him believe that he was in good health and therefore that he must be cured of his complaint. After returning to Beijing in 1960, Premier Zhou Enlai had personally given the order that Puyi be given a thorough health check. The doctors included Mr. Shi Jinmo, Mr. Yue Meizhong, Mr. Zhang Rongzeng, high-ranking traditional Chinese doctors, who had been invited to cure his impotence. He felt that he had already recovered and could get married, but now he knew that the problem was still present and here had been no improvement in his condition.

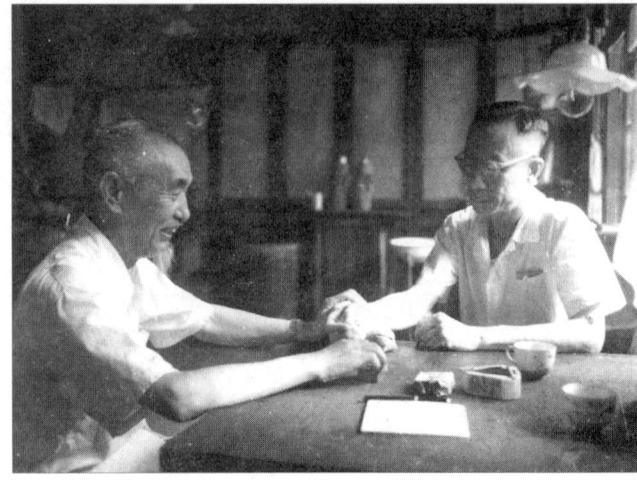
Famous traditional Chinese Doctor Zhang Rongzeng feeling Puyi's pulse

"Why didn't you tell me the truth before we were married?" I asked him angrily.

"I was too embarrassed to tell you. I worried that you wouldn't marry me, if you had known about it in advance. And at the same time I thought I could leave things to chance and that maybe I had already recovered without even knowing it." His words sounded sincere.

"You have a physiological problem. I sympathize with you, but you shouldn't have cheated me."

"Shuxian, I'm sorry about that. Maybe I was too selfish, but I never intended to cheat you. I really love you and I don't want to lose you. I beg you never leave me."

"Now, there's no point in getting unduly upset, but I'm still in my thirties and I wanted to bear children myself!"

"If you love children, we can adopt one!" While saying this, Puyi fell with a thump to his knees in front of me, pleading, "Although people around me introduced many women to me, I didn't really like any of them. I was overjoyed to encounter someone like you. I love you with all my heart and I will do my best to take good care of you, and make you happy throughout our lives. I shall never let you be upset by any unkindness on my part. If you have any other demands, like having a 'gentleman friend', I wouldn't stop you, so long as you still love me. My only request is that you never leave me or divorce me. Is that too much to ask?"

I had lost both my parents when I was very young and it was only when I met Puyi did I feel a dear husband's affection and love. He had been sincere, kind and had taken good care of me ever since we met. How could I possibly leave him? His sincere words had already softened my heart, leaving me only with sympathy and love for him.

I comforted myself: "It is good fortune that has brought us together; I must accept this!" With tears streaming down my face, I helped Puyi to his feet and endeavoured to console him by saying: "You once said that if we cannot be lifelong companions in marriage, let's be everlasting friends! Please don't cry, I won't divorce you. I know it pains you to suffer from this problem. Who can guarantee that one won't have some kind of physical problem at some stage in life? I don't think sexual pleasure is the only factor in a couple's life. From now on you can be like my 'elder brother'! I'll be happy with you so long as you love me. You said I may have a gentleman friend, but I must inform you that I really don't want a gentleman friend. I would never do anything like that to hurt you! Before we got married, didn't the CPPCC HQ send officials to our hospital to investigate my background? So, you should know what kind of person I am. You needn't be concerned that I would look for another."

I had made up my mind to sacrifice this part of marital happiness and to stay faithful to Puyi all my life. After that night, Puyi started calling me "little sister". The crisis soon passed and Puyi recovered his good spirits. He was aware that he owed me great love and affection, so he went to great lengths to take better care of me in our daily life. He seemed to want to make up for his own physical inadequacies.

I didn't personally want to report Puyi's "unmentionable disorder" to the superiors of the CPPCC, but finally one of them found out Puyi's secret anyway. He invited me to meet him to talk about it:

"We know about Puyi's problem and are sorry for you. We hope you won't divorce Puyi. Please take everything into consideration, including the possible political impact.

Puyi holding Ye Qianyu and Wang Renmei's son

The Last Emperor of China: My Husband Puyi

Why not act as a companion who cares for Puyi? In future you may come to ask our help whenever Puyi and you meet with any difficulties in your daily lives or work. We are doing all we can to find the best doctor to cure his problem. I'm sure that he will eventually recover."

The superiors of the CPPCC really paid great attention to Puyi's condition. They invited many famous doctors and experts to find a cure for Puyi. After trying it out for a while, they would ask Puyi about the result.

"Puyi, how has the treatment been?"

"I'm much better!" he would reply, because he didn't want the superiors to worry too much about him. Actually his problem hadn't improved at all. I myself didn't cherish any hope that his difficulty would be cured. I just wanted to carry on living together with him. But I never expected that, many years later, the secret, that I didn't wish others to know about, would be made into a salacious story, by some people.

In Hong Kong, a former friend and colleague of Puyi, published articles in newspapers and magazines, to attract attention to Puyi's impotence. According to his articles, Puyi had once given the impression that he acquired this condition because he had been too licentious in his teenage years, when he had lived in the Forbidden City, mentioning that the eunuch servants on night duty wanted the naughty boy to go to bed early, so that they themselves could go to sleep too. They

Puyi as a teenager before he began to wear glasses

would therefore push some maids into Puyi's "Dragon Bed*", to please him and keep him in his bed. Puyi had said that he was a little boy then and knew nothing about sexuality. Those maids were much older than him, so he "did as he was told". Very often, more than one maid would climb into his bed introducing him to the "delights of sex". They only let him sleep when he was exhausted. The next morning, he was always groggy, his head was giddy and the sun was too bright for his eyes. Puyi complained about this to the eunuch servants and they found some medicine for him to eat. At

---

* In China, an emperor's bed was called "Dragon Bed".

night time he could deal with the maids pestering him for sex, but he gradually lost interest in it. After Puyi got married, he often couldn't enjoy the normal sex life that he desired, with his empress and concubines.

When he had been the "Puppet Emperor" of the "Manchu kingdom", the Japanese sometimes arranged for him to attend their special religious ceremonies, which required him to walk a lot. This walking made him suffer from backache, which in turn had made it difficult for him to walk too far. He had to stop repeatedly to gaze around, or to intentionally talk to the people around about, asking them questions, thus easing his pain by taking short periods of rest.

Puyi and I at the Golden Water Bridge, 1962

I once consulted a few famous experts who studied on Qing history about this. They told me that after the fall of the Qing Dynasty, the "Small Court", then in the inner section of the Forbidden City, still practiced the multiple court systems. They believed what the journalist had reported could possibly have happened there.

Moreover, the journalist "friend" had said that he had made up three kinds of "secret treatments" for Puyi, besides the taking of oral medicine. There was also bathing in water boiled with medicinal herbs. He indicated that, in cooperation with both external and internal cures, his methods had effectively sustained Puyi's sexual life for a certain period, making him very pleased.

In fact, Puyi had suffered from impotence for several decades. He had been to see distinguished doctors from many fields, taking different kinds of Chinese and Western medicines, but all in vain. After getting married, we were always together and I never saw him taking any medication.

Later, Puyi told me several times that when Mr. Tong Xiaozhou came to congratulate us and hoped that we would have a "Crown Prince", how he had longed that it would come true! But at the same time, Puyi worried terribly about it and the worry finally changed into shame, which was too embarrassing for him to speak about. He knew that he would never have his own child.

Mr. Zhou Zhenqiang, one of the many who cared about Puyi, always felt obligated to me. Even when we toured in southern China, he still apologized to me: "Oh, I've hurt you so badly...."

But I responded: "How could I blame you! I was willing to marry Puyi. I'm happy being with him." What I said to him was the truth.

Actually Puyi understood it was impossible to cure his impotence. He told me that after his "Grand Nuptials" at the age of 17, he had had no sexual relations with Wanrong and Wenxiu. Later he married Tan Yuling and Li Yuqin as his "trophy brides".

In the 1950s (having "separated" in 1945 when they had lived in Tonghua), Li Yuqin went to the Fushun War Criminals Prison to look up Puyi, having obtained special ratification for conjugal rights. But even on that night, after having separated for more than ten years, Puyi told me that all they did was to talk for hours about life after they had parted from each other. Nothing else happened.

Li Yuqin (1928-2001), Puyi's fourth wife, "Fortunate Concubine", she mailed this picture to Puyi in 1955 when he was in Fushun War Criminal Prison.

On this matter, I understood him and sympathized with him deeply. I consider that besides sex, a married couple should enjoy rich lives, even without sex they can build up and enjoy profound affection between each other. Puyi and I loved each other in this way. Of course, it had been a great sorrow to us both that Puyi and I suffered in this way.

Chapter Eight
Teaching Puyi Domestic Chores and How to Live a Normal Life

I got up at 6 am the morning after our wedding ceremony. Puyi was lounging in bed and didn't want to get up. I reminded him that guests would be coming round to offer their congratulations on our marriage. After eventually getting up, he folded up his quilt and called me over to see his good work. Maybe he wanted to show me that he could do housework! What a good job he thought he had done! The quilt was simply rolled up into a bundle. I unfolded the quilt and taught him how to do it correctly. He watched me and tried to copy me several times, but still couldn't do it properly.

For some decades, Puyi had been used to the life of having only to open his mouth to be fed and holding out his arms to be dressed. He had had no opportunity or ability to live independently at all. Once, he had proudly told me that he had learned to take

Fushun War Criminal Prison, which is now a museum

The Last Emperor of China **My Husband Puyi**

Puyi liked wearing a dark blue Mao jacket, and a sleek hair style.

care of himself during the course of the ten year re-education in prison. But later on, I saw for myself that he did domestic chores very awkwardly, making many ridiculous mistakes. I never would have imagined them, if I hadn't seen them with my own eyes. He had dressed neatly, with a smart hairstyle, when we were dating, which gave me the misconception that he could take good care of himself.

After we got married, I heard that as early as his time in the Fushun Prison, Puyi had been renowned for not being able to take care of himself. Although he was determined to learn how to fold up his quilt, wash his clothes, tidy up rooms and even make repairs to clothes, he never managed to do them correctly. Before he became citizen Puyi, he had had no chance to learn how to cook meals or light the stove. Now, having his own home, he realised that he needed to know how to do these things. But attempting to do them was very difficult for him.

When he washed his face, the water would spill over the edge of the sink and his coat would get drenched by the time he'd finished. And when he ate meals, he would get rice, as well as oil, all over himself.

Once I asked him to bring in a bed sheet which had been hung out to dry in the courtyard, so we could make our bed. He stared vacantly at the bed and then bed sheet, not knowing which end was which, or what to do next. Another time when I was busy cooking in the kitchen and I asked him to get some eggs for me. He hurried to fetch three eggs, but dropped them all on the floor as he was trying to place them in my hands.

Not long after that, on a Sunday morning, Puyi and I went for a stroll around the streets. We stopped to have a western-style lunch at the noted "Moscow Dining Hall", so that later in the evening, I would only need to cook a quick meal at home. Later at home, before eating this evening meal, I had preferred to clean the

Puyi learning how to darn his socks in the prison

Puyi and I setting out to work, while living at 22, Dongguanyinsi Lane

kitchen first, so I asked Puyi to carry a pot of boiling soup to the dining room table. But he had no idea that he must put something under the pot's scalding base first. With a scream, he dropped the pot to the floor. Puyi was very embarrassed, blaming himself again and again: "I'm too clumsy, I hate myself, and I can't do anything right." Seeing the soup spilled all over the floor and splashed over his coat, trousers and shoes, I was very angry. He rushed to sweep and mop the floor and also to wash his clothes. I couldn't help being amused by his childish, ludicrous behaviour.

Puyi kindly offered to wash his clothes instead of me. But not only did he fail to clean them, but he also squandered our tightly-rationed soap, actually doing me a disservice. After eating meals, he often volunteered to clean the table and wash the dishes, but he always did it in a clumsy fashion. Once after eating breakfast, when he was cleaning the table, he failed to notice that there was a valuable imported wristwatch there. When he removed the table-cloth, the wristwatch was swept onto the floor and broke into several pieces. He became sullen and I attempted to console him, "It doesn't matter! It's no use crying over spilt milk, don't worry about it," I said. He replied: "I'll buy a new one for you, an even better one."

Another time, Puyi wanted to show me that he could light the coal stove. But one day upon returning home, I was alarmed to find thick, black smoke billowing out of the door. Smoke had filled the room and I thought the room was on fire. I glanced around the room quickly and found Puyi squatting in front of a coal stove, narrowing his eyes, and was blowing on the coal stove with his mouth! His two hands were stained with coal dust and beads of sweat were trickling down his forehead. Seeing me, he stood up and wiped the sweat away from his face, using both his hands. His face thus became streaked with black coal dust!

While he was single, Mr. Zhao Huatang, one of his colleagues, had offered to light

Puyi stayed in the home of his fifth sister after he returned to Beijing at the end of 1959.

the coal stove for him, every day. After setting up his own home, he decided to do it himself, but the room always became filled with smoke. When we tried to get rid of the smoke, we also lost all the heat at the same time, turning the room into an icehouse, especially in the cold winter. One day, a friend of ours came to our house and happened to see that Puyi was lighting the stove. Observing that he was all in a fluster, the friend immediately showed Puyi how to do it. While Puyi was very seriously taking the opportunity to learn the skill, the friend jokingly commented to Puyi: "It's understandable that you cannot light a coal stove. You were an emperor before and weren't required to do it!"

It was funny that Puyi often lost his way when he went out on the streets alone. A relative told me that one time in 1960, when Puyi had just returned to Beijing from the Fushun Prison, he was staying in the home of his fifth sister. As a way of convincing people that he was now an ordinary citizen, he went to sweep the street outside the gate one morning. But after he had turned into another street, he soon became lost and didn't know how to find his way back home. It was fortunate that one of his nephews went out, found him and then brought him back home.

I also once heard a Commissioner of the HAPE say that during the Spring Festival of 1962, Puyi and the other former VIP's who had received a special amnesty had been invited to join the Spring Festival Evening Party at the Great Hall of the People. Some of them went to see films, some Peking Opera and some others watched acrobatics. Puyi had hung about in several halls with the crowds, but finally lost his way. It had earlier been arranged that after the party was over, each of the small groups of them would assemble at the Chongwenmen Hotel. But by midnight Puyi was not to be seen. They all worried about him, so two groups went to search for him. Mr. Shen Zui and some other people came across Puyi while they were walking around the Great Hall of the People. Puyi himself was walking around there too, trying to find the way back!

After we got married, Puyi still liked to visit the Beijing Botanical Garden for two days of gardening. He usually went there every Friday morning and would return home at about 5 o'clock on the Saturday afternoon. But one Saturday evening he still hadn't got back by 8 pm. What was the matter? I tried to phone the Botanical Garden but nobody answered the phone, for most of the staff there had already gone back home. I called many places in the Botanical Garden and finally found one person on duty. He told me that Puyi had already left a long ago. I was very anxious and immediately reported it to the leaders of the CPPCC HQ. Mr. Shi Yong, the Deputy Secretary General of the CPPCC, consoled me by saying that maybe he'd lost his way and gone to the wrong place and that somebody would send him back.

He finally came back home at 11 o'clock in the evening, without having eaten! In fact he had missed the private car of Director Yu, which he had always travelled home in, so he had to take the bus. Unexpectedly, when changing buses, he had got on the wrong bus. Then, when he got off from the bus, he had become confused, walking around in circles for several hours. Finally, he was sent back by a kind-hearted passerby. The alert was over, but following that, the leaders of the CPPCC HQ never allowed him to go to the Botanical Garden by himself. They would arrange for certain people to escort him there and then he would return home in one of the private cars of a supervisor of the Botanical Garden.

Puyi at the Beijing Botanical Garden

I also helped him to remember the number of the buses that he should take in case he missed the private car. He wrote them down in detail in his small notebook. Later on, on two occasions, he purposely didn't take the private car, to prove that he was able to come back home alone and that he wouldn't lose his way.

Some small details in daily life proved difficult for Puyi. He confessed that he couldn't even button his coat up or distinguish between grass and flowers before. When filling a bowl, he often scattered the grains of rice everywhere. Fortunately, he had been willing to learn these things and had said to me many times: "I should have learned to do them myself from the very beginning!"

In the clinic of the Fushun Prison, he had learned to bind up wounds, measure blood pressure, make sterile bandages and perform other minor medical procedures. While working at the Beijing Botanical Garden, he had also mastered the skill of cultivating plants. Physical work helped him to gain confidence after he had already con-

The Last Emperor of China My Husband Puyi

At a welcome home party for overseas Chinese, October 3rd, 1961

sidered himself hopeless. He had become aware of the value of his existence.

There was an interesting story about how Puyi learned to welcome guests. Once, a colleague of mine came to visit us. Puyi remained sitting on the sofa, leisurely smoking cigarettes and sipping tea, but didn't stand up to welcome his guest or offer tea and cigarettes. After the guest left, I criticised Puyi: "It's not polite to treat guests in this way. He certainly took your behaviour as a snub to him. When guests come, you should stand up immediately to welcome them with tea and cigarettes and invite them to sit down, to show your politeness."

Several days later, a member of the CPPCC came to our home. Puyi stood up immediately and entertained him with tea, candy and fruit. The guest was surprised: "Mr. Pu! You are now able to welcome guests! Who taught you this?" He teased Puyi: "I need to reprimand you, for previously you didn't welcome me like this, when I came here to visit!" Puyi beamed: "Don't bother! I'm improving!" Ever since then, any guests who came to our home were warmly welcomed by Puyi. And if it was mealtime he would also invite them to have a meal with us.

Of course, he couldn't avoid making some mistakes when he did the housework. When he did make mistakes, he liked to say: "Don't worry! Don't worry! I'll learn to do it eventually." Whenever making any "new achievements", he would always show me, saying "how did I do?" Once he let me see the inside collar of a coat he had just washed, to check whether it was clean or not. I told him that it was good and praised him for doing it well. He looked triumphant. Another time, he baked pancakes for me to eat. He served me the good ones to get my praise, which was important to him, but hid the burnt ones and ate them secretly himself! Actually, how could he possibly hide it from me?!

He always worried that it would tire me out to do so much housework, after a full day's work at the hospital, so he would intentionally find some topics to chat with me about, in order to get me to sit down and have a rest for a while.

After getting married, we had spent our earlier time together in this way, contrary to the gossip, which had suggested that I married Puyi to attain a high political position and to enjoy a much better life. By then, Puyi was just an ordinary commissioner of the HAPE, with a monthly salary of only one-hundred yuan, while mine was only fifty yuan. How could we enjoy ourselves financially?

In those days Puyi and I each had our meals at the canteens of the CPPCC HQ and at my hospital, respectively. I had very good meals by paying 25 yuan a month, but

On May Day 1964, Puyi and I were listening to our new radio.

The Last Emperor of China **My Husband Puyi**

Puyi spent all of his salary on food. Six months later, I again asked him how he spent his salary. He said he spent it freely in buying meals, cigarettes and snacks between meals.

When he couldn't make ends meet he went to borrow money at the finance section. He was required to pay back the loan when he received his next pay. He couldn't break out of this vicious circle, always being in debt. Later, we decided to cook meals ourselves at home, to save money. First, we repaid all our debts and then scraped together the money to buy a radio and some other articles for daily use. We kept our salaries in the same drawer and each took a set of keys. Each of us would take money from it when we needed to. Puyi always told me when he took some and I would tell him what he should and shouldn't buy.

Because Puyi easily lost his way, the government often sent a private car for his use.

Because of our limited income, we had no money to hire a housekeeper. I had to do all of the housework myself. Our home was in Xicheng District of Beijing. Every morning at 6 am, I had to catch the bus to go to work at the hospital in Dongcheng District. After work was over, we often had professional meetings or political study sessions to attend. For two evenings a week, I would go to study part-time at a medical college. It would already be past 9 pm before I returned home. I then had to cook meals, wash clothes and tidy rooms until midnight. Puyi would change the clothes he wore every day, so I had to do washing every day. Arrangements were often made for Puyi to receive foreign guests and I had to help him with choosing suitable clothes, polishing his leather shoes, knoting his tie and buttoning up his shirt and coat.

I had a weak constitution initially and only two months after getting married, I found I was suffering from hepatitis and neurosis. During that time my body weight dropped quickly from more than 55 kg down to 45 kg. Soon afterwards, nephritis, cholecystitis and uterine haemorrhage plagued me, one after another….

Chapter Nine
Hangovers from the Previous Lifestyle of the Royal Family

From 1909 to 1945, Puyi was made emperor three times, and so cultivated unique customs and hobbies, different from common people. I referred to them as "hangovers from the previous lifestyle of the Royal Family".

Many people knew that Puyi was a "hygiene fanatic" when he was emperor. He would never touch door handles when passing through a door or money when doing shopping. Those who came to meet him had to be sterilized beforehand! Once in our room at a hotel where we stayed, I found Puyi squatting on the porcelain toilet pan. I asked him why he wasn't sitting on it. He remarked that he didn't want to sit on the same seat where all kinds of people had been sitting. I understood that it was because he thought it would be dirty and unhygienic.

In the time of the Manchukuo, Puyi had lived an irregular life, often going to bed after midnight and waking up the following noon. After returning to Beijing in 1960, the government had arranged for him an ordinary job, which meant he had to stick to a regular working timetable. But sometimes when I would wake up at about midnight, after a short sleep, he would be sitting on the sofa reading a book or would be still writing something at the desk, using a 100-watt table lamp. Then the next morning, it was difficult to wake him up and he was often late for his work, although his colleagues understood his background and never said anything about it. I warned him several times to change his bad habits of going to bed late and getting up late. After a while, he accepted what I was saying and changed his ways.

I noticed that Puyi had great self-control which he demonstrated in our common life. He wanted to correct his poor habits which were formulated over the many years in his previous unusual life style. One day in the autumn of 1962, in the auditorium of the CPPCC HQ, Mr. He Changgong, the Geological Minister and a leading member of the CPPCC, asked me kindly: "Are you used to life with Puyi?" I told him: "I didn't expect that Puyi would have such unique lifestyle habits. For a long time after getting married, I was upset by them, but I'm glad that he was willing to take my advice and change many of those in difficult ways."

The Last Emperor of China My Husband Puyi

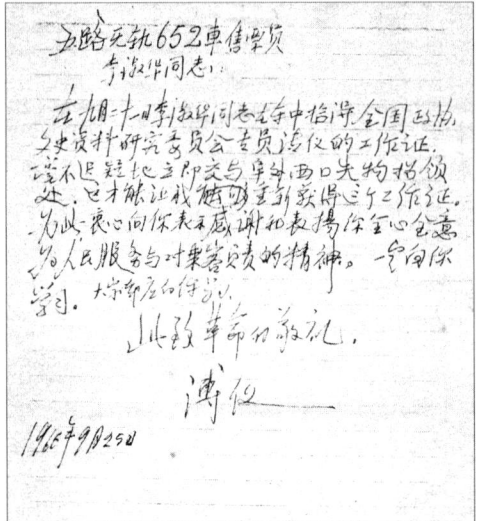

A thank letter from Puyi to a bus conductor for finding and returning his work card

But Puyi never did change some of his scatterbrained ways. He often lost all kinds of things. I considered this was because when he had been emperor previously, he didn't need to hold anything in his hands when he was out. So, whether he had a satchel or handbag, whenever he placed them down, he invariably forgot to take them when he left. While staying at the home of his fifth sister, in 1960, he went to a nearby service station one day to make a phone call. He left his black leather case there, which contained money and grain coupons. Fortunately, it was returned to him quickly by one of their observant assistants. Several of the commissioners who were colleagues told me that Puyi had lost many bags. It was lucky that there were no valuable objects in them, only his private study materials. Later, he accepted a suggestion from several others that he should write down his name, place of work and phone number in an obvious and clear place inside his bags, so that those who picked them up could get in touch with him. The method worked, and some of his lost bags were returned to him personally. But we knew that the principle reason for these kinds of gestures was that these were precious opportunities, for those who came across his bags, to visit him. They could have a look at the famous "Last Emperor of China", with their own eyes and have him thank them personally.

In March 1962, Puyi was invited to join the National Conference of the CPPCC as a non-voting delegate. All of its delegates were offered accommodation at the Xinqiao Hotel, one of the best hotels in China at that time and they were told they could take their wives or lady friends with them too. One day, Puyi gladly came to collect me from my home. But when our car was on its way to the hotel, Puyi sud-

Puyi's credentials allowing him to attend the CPPCC Conference

denly discovered that his work I.D. Card and the non-voting delegate card were not in his pocket. He was very anxious, for without the two cards, we couldn't go into the Xinqiao Hotel. We hurried back to my house to look for them and there they were lying on the floor! Puyi had dropped them when he was taking out a handkerchief from his pocket.

Puyi often forgot to take his meal coupons with him, for food at the CPPCC HQ canteen. After a while, the staff there realized that he didn't do this intentionally, so they offered to put it on his slate and told him to pay next time. It was unbelievable that after Puyi collected his first plate or bowl and took it to a table that he often forgot where the table was, when he went back from the counter for the other dishes. Then he would go to tell the staff that they hadn't given him the first plate! The kind staff understood him, so they would say nothing and just hand him another one. Finally, when all the people had left the dining hall, the staff would see that the original dish they had given to Puyi was still there on a table.

Once I teased him: "You could get rid of the other faults, but why it was so difficult for you to change your habits of forgetting things?" He smiled: "You needn't worry, when you lose anything, it will return to you someday." It sounded like a joke, but in fact, it was almost true of Puyi. He had lost many things, but all of them really did come back. Some he found by himself, some were sent back to him by others.

At the end of August 1963, we went to call on his third sister, Yunyin. On our way to the bus stop, we stopped first at the laundry to pick up our clean bed sheets. But on the bus, Puyi suddenly realized that he'd lost the bag with the sheets in it. We got off the bus at the next stop and walked back hurriedly to the bus stop where we had boarded the bus. At the bus stop, he was told that: "A moment ago, a pupil picked up the bag and handed it to a traffic policeman." The next day, the traffic-police brigade of the Dongsibei Street informed the CPPCC HQ, so that Puyi was able to get the lost item back.

The same kind of stories happened again and again. One day, somewhat agitated, Puyi went to the hospital to find me. He asked me whether or not I had seen his beloved golden French pocket-watch, which he had bought from the noted Wuliwen overseas firm in Tianjin after he left the Forbidden City. It was precious to him because it had been returned to him by the prison authorities when he finished his remoulding at the Fushun War Criminal Prison. He had previously donated it to the state. When I went back home that night, he told me excitedly that he had found it, rolled up in the bind.

In late autumn of 1963, we went to the auditorium of the CPPCC HQ to enjoy a performance. In case it got colder later on the way home, Puyi had taken my overcoat

The Last Emperor of China My Husband Puyi

Puyi liked to collect pocket watches. These are part of his collection.

for me. But he became aware that the overcoat was not in his hands, after we had boarded the No.7 bus. Getting off the bus at the next bus-stop and hurrying back to the original bus-stop where we had boarded the bus, we were very pleased to see that the overcoat was still there and both breathed a sigh of relief. Due to his concern, his forehead was covered in sweat. I consoled him: "How anxious you are!"

Puyi smiled: "You are telling me off again!" At that moment, another bus came and we got onto it straight away. But very quickly he again found he'd lost something—me! I had failed to elbow my way onto the terribly crowded bus, so it had driven off without me. Then he got off at the next stop and hurried back again to find me. When we finally arrived at the auditorium, the performance was already halfway through!!

I always worried that there was one object which Puyi would lose, but unexpectedly he looked after it well and used it up until his death. It was in June 1963, after we moved to 22, Dongguanyinsi Lane. Every day Puyi had to cross a vast lawn to get to work at the CPPCC HQ. I was afraid that he would be exposed for too long in the strong summer sunshine, so I bought him a dainty little black parasol. I kept reminding him never to put it down anywhere and to remember to take it with him all the time. He did as I told him. Later, I praised him for making progress. He commented, "It was my wife who bought it for me, how could I lose it?" Now the parasol is one of the keepsakes that Puyi left behind for me.

Chapter Ten

Mortals and Secularity

Puyi's and my life together didn't last long, but it left me with the most precious and unforgettable memories, as demonstrated for you by some incidents recalled from our daily lives.

Before we were married, whenever we met, Puyi would always be dressed in a trim Mao jacket and with his "brilliantine-daubed hair" carefully parted. This gave me the impression that he paid great attention to being well presented, along with all the different kinds of clothes he wore each time we met. Later, I knew that like many Chinese men did during their courtship, Puyi had done it only for appearances sake, following the urgings of Mr. Wan Jiaxi. In fact,

Puyi and I in the autumn of 1962

he was not particular about his clothes. He had several fine woolen "Mao" jackets, made to measure by the government, but only wore them on official occasions. In daily life, he wore two other jackets on alternating days. One was made of blue Khaki, issued by the government when he had just returned to Beijing in 1960. The other one was black, issued to him when he was at the Fushun War Criminals Prison. It had turned almost white from so much washing. In the almost six years of our common life, Puyi

The Last Emperor of China My Husband Puyi

had never spoken with me about making new clothes for himself. Instead, he always said he had enough clothes and we should remember that our country was still suffering from economic hardship. He returned half of his ration of clothing coupons to the government, hoping that they would pass them on to those who had more urgent needs. After we got married, several times he had said to me: "Little sister, we are not rich. Please don't buy new clothes for me. I have enough already." Apart from official occasions, he always wore shoes made from cloth.

Once, when we were wandering around in a department store, I had my eyes on a pair of shiny ox skin shoes and wanted to buy them for him. He obstinately refused my offer but instead insisted that we go to the "Children's Toys" section. He said to me: "Look at that big chubby toy child.

On June 1st, 1963, Puyi and I moved into our new residence at 22, Dongguanyinsi Lane, Xicheng District, Beijing.

How lovely he is! Why don't we buy it?" I didn't know whether to laugh or cry. If I didn't do it for him, he wouldn't even remember to buy a razor for himself!

In the Forbidden City various brilliant chefs had worked in the Imperial Kitchen and had used only the best ingredients to cook for Puyi. For every meal, he would get more than one hundred kinds of superb dishes. Many people believed that, after becoming a citizen, although it was impossible for him to have the same meals as before, he definitely ate much better food than ordinary people.

Actually, he was not too fussy about his food and mostly had simple meals. If he missed a meal when trying to dine at the CPPCC HQ canteen, he was quite often invited to eat at the home of Mr. Zhou Zhenqiang, one of the matchmakers of our marriage.

Madam Zhou was famous for her excellent cooking. We had no cooking equipment until we moved to live at 22, Dongguanyinsi Lane, in June 1963.

A year later, Puyi obtained a large fee from the publishing of his work *The First Half of My Life*. We were happy to have money to buy a dining table and several chairs, and so set up our dining room. Because our country still hadn't completely gone though its time of economic hardship, Puyi often said to me: "We should strive to cut back on how much we spend on food. It would amount to a huge quantity if everybody did this." Sometimes we had just a few leftovers after a meal. Puyi would never allow me to throw them away. He preferred to eat them for the next meal. "You're full, let me eat it," he always said. I often heard him say that "the grain was grown by the farmers' hard work, each grain of wheat is produced by the sweat of their brows".

Puyi preferred wheat-based meals, often asking me to cook a corn flour pancake or a kind of steamed sponge cake, made from a mixture of wheat and corn flour. At that time that was the daily food for the middle and lower classes of China. Puyi considered that corn flour was more nutritional, saying that it was "good for your health". I don't think that he actually enjoyed eating corn, sorghum and millet, which were called "coarse grains" in China, but he knew that, as an ordinary citizen, he must eat the same as everybody else.

In order to change our diet, we often went to have meals at the canteens of the Cultural Club and the CPPCC HQ, or the eatery nearby, where we bought only one or two dishes, such as a plate of fried fish or crispy spiced chicken. Occasionally, he drank a small bottle of beer. While eating at eatery, Puyi's only concern was whether or not the food was hygienic. Once he went to a nearby eatery, to buy *youtiao* (fried twisted dough sticks, which are a typical food for breakfast in China), but he saw a waitress taking money and grain coupons, then serving food with the same hand. He felt nauseated immediately and couldn't even eat his breakfast. That evening he recorded this in his diary as a noteworthy event.

One of Puyi's pleasures was to eat western food. He started eating it when he was in Tianjin between the years from 1924 to 1932. At least once a month, he would suggest that we go to eat western food at Moscow Dining Hall or the western food dining hall inside the Dong'an Bazaar. We limited how much we spent to five yuan each time.

Although he had bronchitis, Puyi was still a heavy smoker. He often suffered from a bad cough at night time while sleeping. I advised him to cut down on smoking, but he said it was impossible for him. So I suggested that instead of smoking so many cigarettes each day, he could smoke better cigarettes, that although were more expensive, contained less nicotine, which would be better to his health. Finally, he took my advice.

Puyi was grateful for the special care granted by the government and was satisfied

The Last Emperor of China My Husband Puyi

with the two residences arranged by them. Not long after we were married, Mr. Lian Yinong, director of the Secretariat of the CPPCC HQ, in charge of the residential service of the CPPCC HQ said to us: "You are now married and your present apartment is too small for you. I'm looking for a new one that will suit you." He questioned Puyi: "You once lived in the Forbidden City with so many huge houses, are you used to your present residence now?" Puyi replied to him: "It's not bad!" He explained that he was not free in the Forbidden City, in spite of the numerous splendid rooms, whereas now although his own residence was small, he lived in a vast world. They were two different worlds!

Our marriage photo, 1964

We had lived in a small house with only two rooms in the grounds of the CPPCC HQ for roughly a year. On June 1st 1963, we moved to a new home at 22, Dongguanyinsi Lane. It was an excellent western-style bungalow, with two sitting-rooms, two bedrooms and a big bathroom with a bathtub. It also had a kitchen, a storeroom, a room for the maid and a spacious covered veranda outside. In front of the house was a vast long courtyard, with pine trees, cypress trees, pear trees and flowering Chinese crabapple trees. They gave us a lot of shade in the summer. All of the rooms in this house were spacious and high and had more windows, so it was quite cool inside in summer. But in winter, we had to light several coal stoves to heat the main rooms. This meant we had to spend more money to buy coal.

After Puyi passed away, I couldn't afford to keep living there, so I asked the CPPCC HQ to let me move to a much smaller residence.

Chapter Eleven

Puyi – A Great Fan of Peking Opera

In May 1964, we had three French correspondents visit us at 22, Dongguanyinsi Lane. One of them was a young lady with long blonde hair. As soon as we were introduced she started to question me, making me feel nervous.

"What do you do at your hospital?"

"I'm a nurse," I stated.

"What do you do when you are at home?"

"I go for a walk with Puyi, or go to see a film or a Peking opera with him. Sometimes we stay at home, reading books or newspapers or we just chat," I explained.

"What's your favorite kind of entertainment?"

"Puyi loves Peking Opera and so do I. We often go to watch it together," I answered.

"Are you happy?"

"Very happy!" I stressed.

On that day, they recorded our conversations and took some photos of us.

Puyi and I had a very happy relationship and lived comfortably. Before marrying Puyi, in my mind, I considered that all the emperors kept solemn expressions all day long, like the clay Buddhas in the temples and that they couldn't do anything except issue orders and edicts. Puyi was not like this at all—he behaved like an ordinary person, loving life and having many hobbies.

Puyi was fond of reading books. Very often if I woke up during the night, I would see Puyi engrossed in reading. He particularly appreciated Chinese classics, like *Dream of the Red Chamber*, *The Romance of the Three Kingdoms* and some other famous works.

At the beginning of 1963, several times he expressed his desire to buy a radio. He said that a cheap one would be alright. After we bought one, he listened to the news and music every day.

Puyi's genius for Chinese painting and calligraphy was evident at an early age. The royal family engaged several excellent painters and calligraphers to teach him Chinese painting and calligraphy. As early as his teenage years, his calligraphy and painting

The Last Emperor of China My Husband Puyi

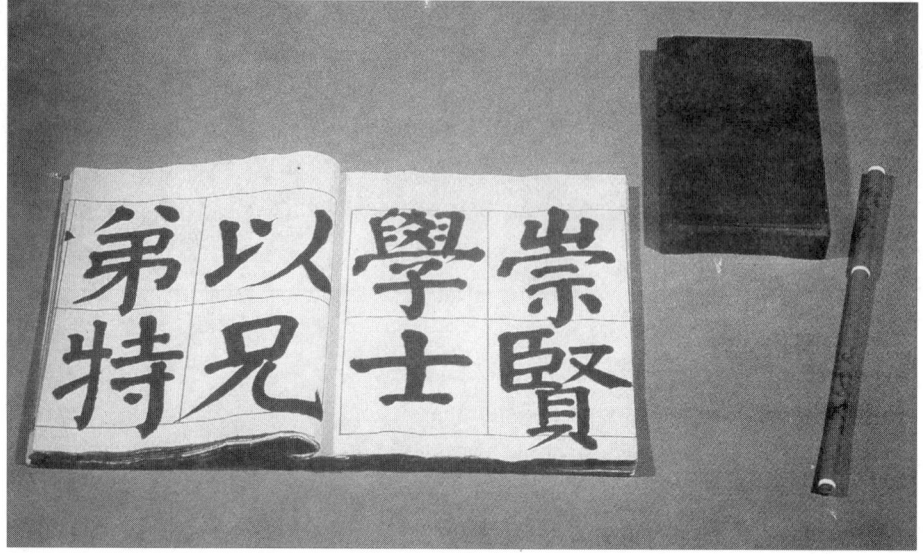

Puyi's childhood calligraphy

were being published in popular newspapers and magazines, winning favorable comments. I didn't see him paint a lot, but he liked practicing Chinese calligraphy when he was in a good mood. Our friends, relatives and colleagues would ask him to do some calligraphy for them, when they met him. When being received at our home by him, many foreign friends also expressed their wishes for Puyi to write some calligraphy for them. Puyi appreciated their trust and worked on it carefully. Puyi would never give anybody his calligraphic work if he was dissatisfied with even a single word of it. Before their wedding, a colleague of mine came to our home with his wife, to request Puyi draw a picture and write his signature on a folding fan. Puyi gladly did so. While in Fushun Prison, Puyi learnt to do *Taijiquan* (Tai Chi), a traditional Chinese form of exercise, which promoted effective development of both mind and body. Puyi performed it in our courtyard every morning. Once he was seen doing it by a foreign friend, who pleasantly invited Puyi to continue to do it for him while he took many pictures. After dinner in the evening, Puyi often called me to take a stroll with him. Many people knew that Puyi had enjoyed cycling earlier in his life at the inner court of the Forbidden City. He had even ordered that all of the bottom thresholds of the gates of the palace be sawn off, to make it easier for him to cycle. He took cycling as a kind of physical exercise and still liked doing it in his later years. I was worried about him, refusing his several invitations to sit on the carrier and ride straddle with him. One time he knocked down an old lady near our home, while cycling. He jumped off his bike and immediately apologized to the old lady, inquiring as to whether or not she was hurt. He was going to take her to a nearby hospital for a check-up. The old lady got up from the ground and was embarrassed when she found out that she had been hit by the "Little Emperor". She swiftly dusted off her clothes and reassured Puyi: "It doesn't matter, I'm fine." Puyi gave her his address, insisting that she must come and tell him if, during the next few days, she felt any pain. The old lady didn't come to find Puyi, but he still worried about her. He especially bought a box of famous Beijing pastries and took it round to her place. The old lady was greatly moved by Puyi's thoughtfulness and told the story to all the people she met: "I was born toward the end of the Qing Dynasty. I still remember when Emperor Xuantong (Puyi) came to the throne. I was told to 'kowtow*' to his portrait at home. But now, the Emperor has been to my home to see me, with some pastries. This would never have happened earlier!"

Influenced by him, I later on told him that I wanted to buy a bicycle too, so as to learn how to ride it in our courtyard. Then I could go shopping and to work by bike. Surprisingly, he didn't agree with this idea. He said, "If you do that I would be a bundle of nerves." I then realised that he would worry about my safety.

Puyi enjoyed chatting and, because of his very special background and life experience, he was welcomed by people from all walks of life. He liked to communicate with them and chat with all kinds of people, even naive children or illiterate old ladies. At home, he explained to me the complex protocols practiced inside the Forbidden City. He said that the various "kowtows" were ways of paying respect and were done to different kinds of people in different levels of society. He did them personally to demonstrate them to me. Sometimes you must kneel with both knees, first the left one, then the right one, with a straight back, whilst sometimes going down on one knee was acceptable.

Puyi enjoyed appreciating and singing *Nanniwan*, a graceful folk song.

Puyi's bicycle while in the Forbidden City

---

* Kowtow is a Chinese custom of touching the ground with one's forehead, especially in submission, to the power of the throne.

The Last Emperor of China My Husband Puyi

Puyi was always cheerful and talkative.

He enjoyed it because it was sung by Madam Guo Lanying, one of China's best sopranos at that time and the song was quite popular among the public. He told me with reverence, that our beloved Premier Zhou Enlai loved it and often sang it. In March 1963, Puyi wrote down the words of the Chinese national anthem and *The International*, and made a big effort to learn them. I heard him humming them along with the radio, although he was not good at singing! One year, when the CPPCC HQ organized a song contest, Puyi enthusiastically joined a choir.

In daily life, Puyi was talkative and cheerful and rarely became angry. I often heard him burst into laughter while talking with friends. Therefore he looked younger than his age. Even when he passed away, at the age of 61, he still had pitch-black hair with not a single grey hair. Because he liked to jest with me, one evening I decided to play a joke on him by taking away his spectacles, while he was washing his face. He was very short-sighted and I hid myself behind the door. He couldn't find his spectacles afterwards and had to stretch out his hands, fumbling in the dark. He dared not take one step, only begging me to give them back to him. I pressed them into his hands and teased him:

"You were a feudal emperor before, now you are a 'good for nothing'. Without glasses, you can't even walk. I'll divorce you!" He was frightened and went pale immediately. To my amazement he rushed into the kitchen and picked up a knife, to slit his throat! I dashed to grab his hands and explained to him that I was only joking with him, and not to take me so seriously! He suddenly began to smile, "I was teasing you too!" Then he laughed heartily, but I was "scared to death"!

As the Chinese former emperor, Puyi received many invitations to attend various cultural activities, like song and dance parties, official celebrations and Peking Opera. Puyi was always glad to take me along to join them. One of them left with me an unforgettable impression. It was a party to appreciate the wonderful full moon on the Mid-Autumn Festival, which was held in the CPPCC HQ, on a vast platform on the top of its office building. For me it was the first time to take part in such a magnificent

Mid-Autumn Festival, 1962, Puyi and I were invited to attend the "Appreciating the Moon Party" held by the CPPCC HQ

official activity and to see so many noted public figures in a happy and relaxed mood. Alongside the long table arranged with fine moon cakes, cigarettes and tea, all the guests chatted excitedly, wrote calligraphy and painted pictures to show their feelings for this traditional Chinese Festival. A reporter from the Xinhua News Agency approached Puyi respectfully, asking him to give his reflections on the Mid-Autumn Festival. Puyi remarked: "Last year and the year before last, I attended the party alone to appreciate the full moon, while this year I am able to enjoy the full moon with my wife." The reporter turned the microphone of his tape-recorder towards me. I said: "For the first time in my life, I am having the opportunity to take part in this grand party to enjoy the full moon. I'm enthralled by this idyllic scene."

And the celebration party for the March 8th Women's Day of 1963, was impressive too. Several of Puyi's sisters were also invited to join it and we went to the conference room together. His colleagues teased him: "Mr. Pu, why are you always with your bride? Today is Women's Day!" Puyi smiled and replied plausibly, "It's the first time for her to celebrate Women's Day at the CPPCC HQ, so I should accompany her." That day Madam Deng Yingchao, wife

The "Appreciating the Moon Party" held by the CPPCC HQ. Puyi, Zaitao, Pujie, Sagahiro, Husheng, 1962

of Premier Zhou Enlai and Madam Xu Guangping, wife of Lu Xun, both came by invitation and they made excellent speeches. Finally, there was some wonderful entertainment performed by the most famous Chinese artists. Puyi asked me, "Did you ever join such celebration activities like this before?" I responded, "We had a celebration meeting for Women's Day in our hospital each year, but not as grand as this. There were no VIPs there!"

Puyi loved Peking Opera very much. He would definitely choose to enjoy Peking Opera if we received several different invitations at the same time. Each time, after its opening played by gongs and drums, he would close his eyes and savour every note. At the same time I would hear both his hands and feet tapping to the beat of the singing of the players on the stage. He hummed and looked completely absorbed by it. After we returned home, he would still be excitedly imitating the players' performances. One of Puyi's hobbies had been to collect Peking Opera masks. He would buy one or two of them, whenever we went to the department store. Slowly he had collected each of the masks for the various roles, which had filled a big box in our home.

Once when we talked of the Peking Opera, Puyi told me that in his earlier years, he had two opportunities to enjoy the excellent performances of Mr. Mei Lanfang, the "great master of Peking Opera". The first one was on October 2nd 1923, when High Consort Duankang, the former Emperor Guangxu's Jin Concubine and Puyi's aunt, celebrated her 50th birthday. As the "icing on the cake", the Royal Family had invited three "masters", Mr. Mei Lanfang, Mr. Yang Xiaolou and Mr. Shang Xiaoyun, to play Peking Opera in the Forbidden City. Mr. Mei had performed *A Startling Dream of Wandering through the Garden* and *Conqueror Xiang Yu parts with his Concubine*, which had won everyone's heartfelt applause. Besides rewarding three of them a snuff bottle made in the reign (1736-1795) of Qianlong. Puyi had especially rewarded Mr. Mei with a sumptuous meal and 500 silver dollars. But, it provoked gossip among the former senior Qing Dynasty officials who were still following him. They said that all the performers were from "the humble people" and that Puyi shouldn't have given him such a magnificent reward.

Another occasion occurred later, when Puyi lived in Tianjin. He went to the renowned Kaiming Theatre with Wanrong, his empress, to appreciate *Xishi* played by Mr. Mei Lanfang. Unexpectedly, because of this, one of his former senior officials angrily presented a formal letter to Puyi. It read:

It was our dereliction of duty, which made Your Majesty lose dignity by attending the theatre personally. As a result of this error, I have no alternative but to step down from your service.

Again and again, Puyi attempted to appease him and to urge him to stay by his side, finally rewarding him with two valuable animal skins. His mood quickly changed from anger to gladness and he

At the birthday party of the high consort Duankang, Mei Lanfang, the Peking Opera master, was invited and paid to perform in the Forbidden City, October 2nd, 1923.

praised Puyi's "brilliance". After that occasion, Puyi never went to the theatre anymore. Later when the Swedish Crown Prince went to visit Tianjin, he expressed his wish to meet with Puyi, but Puyi refused him. As he had seen the Prince's photo with Mr. Mei Lanfang, he considered that the Prince had detracted from his status by doing this.

"In the old society (before 1949), all of the performers had been despised as 'humble class', no matter how excellently they performed," Puyi sighed, "but in the new society (after 1949), it is completely different!" He cheerfully told me of his meeting with Mr. Mei Lanfang at the beginning of 1960, when both of them joined the CPPCC Conference. Puyi said that during the past thirty years, both Mr. Mei and Puyi, had experienced great fluctuations in their lives, whilst now they were able to recollect the past standing side by side. How excited they were!

On October 3rd 1961, Puyi had an unforgettable chance to meet with Mr. Ma Lianliang, another master of Peking Opera, when both of them were attending a wine party held by the CPPCC. Their friendly talkativeness attracted a lot of reporters and they were glad to stand on the steps by the gate of the dining hall for a souvenir photo. Later I saw the photo and Puyi explained to me that Mr. Ma Lianliang had won a considerable reputation at home and abroad and that he was very polite to him. Puyi said that he had great respect for him.

Chapter Twelve

Accompanying My Husband Back to the Place Where He Ascended the Throne as Emperor

The Forbidden City was the place where Puyi lived from the age of three until nineteen. Naturally, he had quite an attachment to it. He returned there with me many times and he seemed to be filled with a whole range of feelings whilst we were there.

Puyi liked to enter the Forbidden City through the "Gate of Divine Military Genius". In front of it, he usually stopped and looked at the exterior of this great construction, created by the ancient Chinese People. He first settled his gaze with fondness on the moat which encircled the Forbidden City, then turned to the exquisite corner tower and

A birds-eye view of the Forbidden City from the top of Jingshan Hill

its tall surrounding scarlet wall. He would finally fix his eyes on the magnificent Gate of Divine Military Genius with the five huge characters "故宫博物院" above it, meaning "Palace Museum".

He said to me with deep feeling: "The Forbidden City was built five hundred years ago, from 1406 to 1421, during the Ming Dynasty (1368-1644). Its construction, under a grandiose scheme, involved the collection of very large quantities of the best building materials, from all over the country, as well as the diligent work of many thousands of skilled labourers and outstanding artisans. In both the Ming and Qing dynasties, the Forbidden City was the residence of 25 Emperors who wielded absolute power. They all married numerous beautiful wives and led a life of luxury and dissipation. I was the very last one." Puyi added, "By chance, I became the host of the Forbidden City and, mistakenly, I believed that it was my private property."

While sitting on a bench in the Imperial Garden, Puyi told me that in his boyhood, his favorite hobby had been to enjoy feeding ants. He ordered eunuchs to find corn flour and scatter it by an anthill to draw the ants out to eat it. A game he liked was to play "hide and seek" with the eunuchs, each one being blindfolded by a piece of cloth, as they tried to catch each other.

If a eunuch caught Puyi, he would be awarded a piece of pastry to eat. But when Puyi caught a eunuch, he would punish the eunuch by making him stand on the same spot for half an hour. In the winter, when it snowed, Puyi always excitedly called the

Puyi looking into the outside world from the roof of the palaces in the Forbidden City

eunuchs together to make snowmen.

Puyi sighed: "I was taken into the Forbidden City at the age of three, by an edict of Empress Dowager Cixi (1835-1908), and stayed until the age of nineteen. I lived in such a small space with a huge wall around it. Slowly I became dissatisfied with playing 'hide-and-seek' and became bored of the dull life there, hoping that I could 'grow wings' so as to fly out of the Forbidden City, like escaping from a prison. Even now I still hate Empress Dowager Cixi, when I think of how depressed I was at the time."

"I was terrified when General Feng Yuxiang drove me out of the Forbidden City in 1924!" While saying this, Puyi pulled me towards the goldfish pond. He told me, in a hushed voice, what had taken place there about forty years before. General Feng had sent troops, led by Lu Zhonglin, to surround the Forbidden City, ordering Puyi to move out within twenty minutes. After negotiation between the two sides, the time limit was extended to three hours. In the meantime, in order to force Puyi to move out as quickly as possible, Lu Zhonglin ordered his army to bombard the inner court of the Forbidden City where Puyi and his family lived. One of the shells exploded in the goldfish pond. Puyi was scared out of his wits and couldn't even stand up. He smiled: "It was lucky that the shell didn't hit the roof of the palace where I was. Otherwise, I would definitely have been killed! So I have never believed that 'Buddha blesses the Emperor!'"

At the "Palace of Earthly Tranquility", known as "Kunning Palace", Puyi showed me the room on the eastern side. It had been the wedding chamber for the Emperors of the Qing Dynasty and their "Em-

A picture of Puyi with the Empress Dowager Longyu, 1911. She attended to state affairs from behind a curtain.

presses to be", after they had celebrated their "grand nuptials". The brides and grooms usually stayed there for two nights and then moved back to reside in their living quarters. Puyi revealed: "But I didn't stay here on my 'Grand Nuptials Day'! However, I couldn't contain my curiosity and finally raised the red veil which covered the head of Empress Wanrong, to look at her face. Seeing that she was very beautiful, I felt satisfied and so then returned to the 'Mind Nurture Palace' (Yangxin Palace) and enjoyed

The Last Emperor of China My Husband Puyi

practising calligraphy and drawing pictures. I didn't go back to 'The Palace of Earthly Tranquility' that night, I left Wanrong there alone."

Next, Puyi told me the story of the eating of "son and grandson cakes". He told me that according to the customs of the Manchu, the bride and groom must be accompanied on the first night after the wedding ceremony by a middle-aged maid of "perfect happiness" (*quan-fu-tai-tai*, whose parents were both still alive and who had at least one son and one daughter) to get instructions from her about how to eat "son and grandson cakes". After Puyi and Wanrong were escorted to the "Palace of Earthly Tranquility", their maid held a plate of "son and grandson cakes", asking them if they preferred a ripe one or an unripe

Puyi's bedroom in the Mind-Nurture Palace in the Forbidden City

Puyi's bedroom in the Mind-Nurture Palace in the Forbidden City

92

one. Puyi had quickly answered that he wanted a ripe one. He picked one up to eat and let Wanrong eat some too. The maid was horrified and she reported this to Puyi's family. The colour drained from their faces, because the Manchu had a superstition that "unripe", pronounced "*sheng*" in Chinese, had the same pronunciation as "bear", meaning "to bear children", while the word "ripe" pronounced "*shou*" in Chinese, implied that they would not have any descendants. This was a very bad omen.

In the "Mind Nurture Palace", Puyi led me into his bedroom of that time. He bent down to look closely at the bedding and nodded:

"This is the quilt that I used!"

"It's about fifty years old, how durable it is!" I exclaimed.

"That is the place where I slept." Puyi pointed to the wooden "Dragon Bed".

"Was it comfortable sleeping here? Did Empress Wanrong sleep here too?" I was interested to know.

"Sometimes I went to stay with Wanrong in her room," he replied.

"Did you go to stay with Wenxiu too?"

"I didn't like to go there, and if I went, I stayed there only for a little while and then left."

He whispered in my ear: "My relationship with both of them was platonic only." Puyi confessed to me that he had been vexed all of his life about his sexual difficulties.

At the palaces where the four High Consorts had lived, Puyi carefully looked at the original furniture and daily necessities, seeming to want to remember anything he could from them. He told me: "The four High Consorts were the concubines of Emperor Tongzhi (1856-1874) and Emperor Guangxu (1871-1908). I was told to call them, 'Revered

Puyi's birth mother with Pujie, his younger brother

The Last Emperor of China My Husband Puyi

Mother'. I disliked their control and often lost my temper with them and bickered with them: 'I believed that I was the Emperor, so who had the right to control me?'"

Puyi talked of his real mother, Madam Guaerjia, with deep feeling. She was the eighth daughter of Mr. Ronglu, an academic, Governor of Hebei Province and Beiyang Minister. She

Puyi's schoolroom in the Palace of the Cultivation of Happiness (Yuqing Palace) in the Forbidden City

was also quite famous for being quick-witted, strong-minded, dressing fashionably and "spending money like water"! Her marriage with Puyi's father was personally arranged by Empress Dowager Cixi. In the autumn of 1918, Puyi lost his patience with High Consort Duankang's restraints and quarrelled with her openly, which made her "lose face". The furious Duankang couldn't say anything to Puyi but summoned his mother and grandmother to her residence, to rebuke them. Finally, Puyi's mother had to promise her that she would persuade Puyi to apologize to her. Puyi said to me: "My mother had never been scolded like that in her life. She had a very headstrong personality and this shock was too much for her. After returning home from the Forbidden City, she committed suicide, by swallowing a fatal dose of opium." Puyi was very sad when telling me about this.

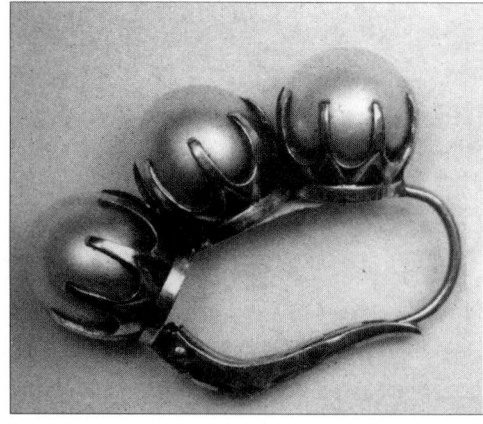

Empress Dowager Cixi's jewelry

Empress Dowager Cixi's jewelry

While visiting the "Imperial Kitchen", Puyi told me that sweet pastry had been his favourite snack ever since he was a child, therefore the "Imperial Kitchen" used to daily bake a range of excellent sweet pastries for him. Actually, he could eat only one or two. The rest were just for show, then given to the eunuchs.

When we were close to the "Palace of the Cultivation of Happiness" (the Yuqing Palace), Puyi pointed out to me where his study had taken place. Because there were many tourists around us, Puyi had to lower his voice: "I was too fond of playing then and didn't like reading books. I was the Emperor, 'the Lord of Ten Thousand Years'. All my tutors could do was to just let my chief eunuch stand outside my bedroom when I got up in the morning, to read out the previous day's lessons several times, hoping I could hear some of them and remember a little." Puyi burst out laughing when he mentioned some of the mean tricks he played on his old tutors: "When the tutor dozed off, I would quickly roll a piece of paper and poke it up his nose."

In the Treasure Hall, which included three rooms, Puyi instructed me concerning its background and about the uses of all the artifacts there. In particular, he explained in detail each one of Emperor Dowager Cixi's jewels. "Empress Dowager Cixi used to dress herself up with her favorite jewels when she received foreign ambassadors and envoys. She said that she did this to demonstrate to them the financial capabilities of China, so as to impress them."

Puyi intentionally lowered his voice when he said this, to avoid being heard by the tourists near us. But the inside information he was giving naturally allured several of them. They walked closer to inquire of him: "How do you know these things so clearly?" More and more people began to surround him. Puyi promptly replied: "I don't know!" then broke away from the crowd.

Chapter Thirteen
Visiting Historical and Cultural Sites Together with Puyi

Puyi and I were fortunate to live in Beijing, one of the six ancient capital cities of China. As early as 400,000 years ago, people already lived in Beijing and as a city, Beijing is more than 3,000 years old. The Jin Dynasty (1115-1234) was the first one to build its capital in Beijing. Later, the Yuan Dynasty (1206-1368), the Ming Dynasty (1368-1644) and the Qing Dynasty (1644-1911) also chose Beijing as their capital. The Ming and Qing dynasties left the world famous huge royal palaces, beautiful gardens and many items of precious heritage. Puyi was very fond of touring the parks in Beijing which had been converted from what were once royal gardens. On Sundays, we usually got up and left home very early to go to parks and historic sites to avoid the numerous visitors who might come to visit us throughout the day. We liked to have our meal at the Cultural Club at noon and in the afternoon we would stroll up and down the streets or have a look at department stores.

Opposite the "Gate of Divine Military Genius" of the Forbidden City is the Jingshan Park, one of the former royal gardens, a place Puyi and I often frequented. When Puyi and I went there for the first time from the main gate, Puyi turned round to look at the Forbidden City, before entering into it. He said to me: "I visited Jingshan Hill several times when I lived in the Forbidden City, but back then I had no freedom to walk across this road. I was carried across on sedan chair*!"

Puyi and I at Tian'an men Square, 1962

* An enclosed chair carried on poles by men. The Chinese Emperors' sedans were huge and delicately decorated and carried by at least sixteen men.

Entering the Main Gate, we saw the "Chamber of Beautiful Expectation". Behind it stood the 43 metre-high Jingshan Hill. In front of it, I followed Puyi, walking eastwards up the slope along the scarlet surrounding wall. We turned north at the end and walked only a few steps before coming across an old locust tree. Puyi whispered to me: "You must have heard the story about Emperor Chongzhen hanging himself from a tree, at the Jingshan Hill? In the Yuan Dynasty, there was only an earth hillock here called 'Blue Hill'. A huge pile of coal was stored at this place, for the construction of the Forbidden City, at the beginning of the Ming Dynasty. The locals called it 'Coal Hill'. Later, the earth, which was dug out during the creation of the moat around the Forbidden City, was ordered to be heaped up here. It slowly formed the five peaks. In the Qing Dynasty, the royal family built several pavilions on Coal Hill and a few memorial halls behind it, to house the belongings of the deceased emperors and empresses. It was then renamed from 'Coal Hill' to 'Jinshan Hill'. In 1644, when the great peasant uprising army, led by Li Zicheng, broke into the city of Beijing, Emperor Chongzhen, the last one of the Qing Dynasty, first killed his Empress and concubines with his own hands, then escaped from the Forbidden City to this location. But finding himself surrounded and coming to the end of his tether, the 33-year-old emperor hung himself from this locust tree. It proved that those feudal emperors, who cruelly oppressed the people, had to finally meet their own destiny." Puyi sighed with deep emotion, "I was fortunate to experience New China led by the Communist Party of China, otherwise, maybe I would have been forced also to hang myself from this tree!"

Finally, we climbed up to the top of the Jingshan Hill. Holding the railings of the Everlasting Spring Pavilion, we enjoyed the hazy panorama of Beijing covered by huge green pines and old cypresses. This charming view, looking down over Beijing became fixed in our minds.

Down from the Jingshan Hill, we walked out of the park via the East Gate. Puyi pointed to a bungalow inside it, telling me: "I lived in it for a while after I returned to Beijing in 1960, to do physical labour, which included watering flowers and planting grass in the park."

He added: "Later I heard that the authorities had already assigned me to do physical labour at Jingshan Park and the Forbidden City but that Zhou Enlai had said that it was unwise to do so. He said that tourists would easily recognize me. So instead I was sent to the suburbs, to labour at the Beijing Botanical Garden. How thoughtful the Premier's consideration was for me!"

On a sunny Sunday, not long after we got married, Puyi and I invited Mr. Zhou Zhenqiang, one of our matchmakers and Miss Yu Lingjun, one of Puyi's nieces, to tour the Beihai Park (the North Sea Park), one of the most attractive parks in Beijing. Enter-

The Last Emperor of China My Husband Puyi

ing the park, we stood by the lake protected by the white marble railings, appreciating the delicate green waves on the surface of the lake, the pavilions with their glazed tiles and ornate beams and columns, as well as the pretty White Dagoba at the top of the Qionghua Islet. Puyi happily offered to tell us how Beihai Park, which he had become familiar with, had begun to be built.

Puyi said that as early as in the Liao Dynasty (907-1125), a second imperial residence was built here. When the Jin Dynasty (1115-1234) took over power, they had constructed the Imperial Palace here. The Qionghua (Jade Flower) Islet was made from earth dug out from around the lake. The rocks piled on the Qionghua Islet were brought here from far away Kaifeng. During the Yuan Dynasty (1206-1368), the Guanghandian Palace (Palace in Broad Cold) and many other palace buildings were erected on

Puyi and I wandering about in Beihai Park

the Qionghua Islet. Kublai Khan received Marco Polo when he was relaxing here. The world-famed White Dagoba at the top of the Qionghua Islet and the Buddhist Temple around it were both built in 1651, with orders from Emperor Shunzhi a few years after the Qing Dynasty was established. This was a gesture of his devotion to Buddhism and a desire for the unification of China's various nationalities.

The "Tower of the Ten Thousand Buddhas", at the northwestern corner of the Beihai Park was built in 1771, in honour of the 80th birthday of Emperor Qianlong's mother. The tower contained 10,000 niches, each holding a gilded "Amitayus Buddha" ornamented with many jewels. It was a great shame that they were looted when the "Allied Force of the Eight Powers" invaded Beijing in 1900.

When we arrived at the "Double-Sided Nine Dragon Screen", holding Miss Yu Lingjun's hand, Puyi told us its history. Built during the Ming Dynasty in 1602, the screen was made from 424 multi-coloured glazed tiles, the screen was 6.65 metres high,

25.86 metres long and 1.42 metres thick. It vividly shows nine dragons playing in the waves, representing the paramount power of the Chinese Emperors. Tourists marvelled at the great artistic merit and the beautiful modelling of this ancient art object.

We had a short rest at a tea-house by the glistening lake. While sipping tea, Mr. Zhou Zhenqiang joked with Puyi asking him if he could come here to drink tea freely when he was emperor. Puyi told him: "At that time, I came here in a regal sedan chair. It was carried along the special road covered by a royal yellow carpet, with soldiers sounding the clarion by beating gongs, to clear the way in front of my sedan chair. I was not free then! Now I may come here with my wife and friends, to have a tour, sip tea and eat pastries. How free I am!" Afterwards, we got on a wooden boat, rowing to Qionghua Islet. Finally, we climbed up to the top of the hill, standing under the White Dagoba to get a birds-eye view of Beijing. Puyi was excited, saying to us:

"Before I would be tired after walking a few steps, while now, after so much climbing, I don't feel tired at all."

The Guangji Buddhist Temple was one of the leading Buddhist Temples in Beijing, but was not open to tourists then. Its Abbot, Master Juzan was the Deputy-director of the Chinese Buddhist Association. He and Puyi were close friends, for both of them were members of the Outstanding Committee of the CPPCC and in the same group for political study. When Puyi read from newspapers that a relic tooth of Sakyamuni, the founder of Buddhism, was treasured at the Guangji Temple, he expressed to Master Juzan his desire to see it with his own eyes. Puyi was grateful to Master Juzan as he immediately invited him to his temple.

On one Sunday, in the beginning of spring 1963, Puyi and I went to visit the Guangji

The Mahavira Hall inside Guangji Buddhist Temple

Temple, where Master Juzan, wearing a grey Buddhist robe and accompanied by his disciples, was standing at the gate to welcome us. He enthusiastically ushered us into the lounge of his residence in the western courtyard of the temple. It was not large, but had two rather conspicuous upright bookcases filled with the Buddhist scriptures, in various editions, and many books on philosophy. Master Juzan, was of medium height and glowing with health. He was apparently also an accomplished scholar. "Fragrant tea" was served us and Puyi sipped a mouthful declaring: "Good tea!"

We chatted for a while, and then Master Juzan stood up, with a bunch of keys in his hand, to take us around his temple. First, we went to the main Prayer Hall, the place where the Buddhist believers worshipped. Like those in the other Buddhist Temples, it had a huge clay statue of a seated "Sakyamuni" at its centre. Several clay minor Buddhas were standing nearby and the eighteen arhats were further away, standing on both sides in two lines against the walls.

Master Juzan introduced each of them to us. I didn't believe in Buddhism, but Puyi did. I knew that he had worshiped every day in the Imperial Palace, in Changchun, during the period of the Manchukuo. Then we were taken to the hall where Master Juzan would give lectures on Buddhist teachings, to his disciples. On the second floor of the hall the "tooth relic of Sakyamuni" was stored in a delicate shrine. For a long time, Puyi gazed at the tooth, about two-thirds the size of a thumb in length.

The tooth of Sakyamuni was said to be found by a monk, in Xinjiang, in the fifth century A.D., Master Juzan explained to us.

"The monk looked after it himself at first, but lost it later when his residence was looted. The looting occured because the news was revealed to the public that the tooth was kept there. In the successive years, it was housed by the royal families of different dynasties. In the Liao Dynasty, an emperor had especially constructed a pagoda in a temple, in the West Mountain in Beijing, to house the tooth relic. After the pagoda was burnt down by the Allied Force of the Eight Powers in 1900, people were then able to see the tooth inside a sandalwood box in a stone case. In the 1920s, when Beijing was ruled by warlords, the relic tooth was sent to a pawnshop but later redeemed by some monks. In 1953, the Chinese Buddhist Association decided to house it in the Guangji Temple."

Finally, Puyi and I followed Master Juzan back to his lounge. While sipping tea, he extended a warm invitation to us to have lunch there, adding that they had some very skilful chefs to cook vegetarian meals, but Puyi gently declined. A little later, Master Juzan and his disciples waved us off from the gate of the temple, gazing at us affectionately until we had walked far away.

Many times we toured the Summer Palace, which had been built in 1889. One visit in June 1963 was impressive. Beforehand, Puyi had mentioned that he wanted to go to a restaurant there, where they would let clients personally select a live fish from the tank, and then they would cook it according to their tastes. He suggested we had our meal there, so we made sure to reach the restaurant before lunch time.

While enjoying the excellent fish, I asked him: "How did you know about this restaurant?"

"I came here after I returned to live in Beijing," he replied.

"Did you often come here when you were young?" I queried.

"The Summer Palace was the private garden of the Qing Royal family when I lived in the Forbidden City. At that time, Mr. Reginald Johnson, my English teacher, was sent here by me to manage it and several times I came here for a tour myself by bus."

After lunch, we rambled around the East Hill to view the magnificent traditional Chinese building structures. Inside the "Hall of Jade Ripples", by the Kunming Lake, Puyi showed me a wall made of blue bricks. He told me that during the later Qing Dynasty the conservative Empress Dowager Cixi turned several rooms here into a prison, to confine Emperor Guangxu, her adopted son, because she had hated him for supporting a movement to reform the Chinese feudal system. Since 1889, each year at the beginning of spring, Empress Dowager Cixi had come here, in a huge luxurious sedan chair carried by sixteen men to stay in the Summer Palace until October, when she would return to the Forbidden City.

Then, Puyi took me to see the famous oil painting of Empress Dowager Cixi, painted by a female American artist. And in the "Hall of Happiness and Longevity", the residence of Empress Dowager, Puyi looked at the elegant display and said to me: "She ignored the danger the country was facing, but led a sumptuous life here, with a service staff of several thousand, to attend to her life's daily needs. The money spent on a single meal of hers would have been enough to feed 5,000 peasants a day."

We then went to Longevity Hill. Puyi climbed to the top of it with great excitement and waved down to me from there. He came down quickly, because I didn't have the energy to do it, and so I just waited for him at the bottom. We walked leisurely along the "728 metre-long Corridor", which runs alongside the Kunming Lake; the surface of the lake ruffled by the spring breeze. We reached the Marble Boat where Puyi pointed to the magnificent buildings, built in ancient Chinese style. "In 1888, in order to construct a satisfactory private garden for herself, Empress Dowager Cixi, in spite of the protests and indignation from all in her circle, adamantly decided to restore the 'Garden of Clear Ripples', built by Emperor Qianlong in 1750. To do this, she used funds intended for the development of the Chinese Navy. These funds amounted to thirty million taels of silver (937,500 kg). She renamed it 'The Summer Palace'."

Puyi and I with Pujie and his wife touring the Summer Palace in June, 1963

Puyi continued: "Even after she died in 1909, Empress Longyu, Cixi's daughter-in-law and niece, ordered countless small paper boats and paper children to be made, at a cost of more than ten-thousand *taels* of silver, and had them burnt on the Kunming Lake to demonstrate her filial respect for her mother-in-law. This caused many complaints to be voiced that 'Cixi not only harmed people when she was alive, but still made people's lives a misery after she died, so that it was hard for people to survive' ."

We had a very interesting time that day and didn't leave the Summer Palace until 4 pm.

Puyi loved animals so he took me to the Beijing Zoo several times. Each time, before going there, he personally went to buy fruit and biscuits and cut them into tiny pieces. When he fed the bears, they would take the food while standing on their hind legs. The bears happily "bowed to him" with their two paws together, like people, seeming to show their thanks. Puyi laughed heartily when he saw this.

From 1962 to 1966, running the risk of being recognized by tourists, Puyi took me to many historic sites, such as "The Fragrant Hill", "The Eight Great Temples of the Western Hill", "The Temple of Heaven", and "Liulichang Cultural Street". Several times in the Forbidden City, his expert and realistic explanations aroused suspicious looks from other tourists. He then realized that he would have to leave there quickly, just before he was likely to be recognized.

But Puyi couldn't leave so easily when he was having meals at restaurants. While living at 22, Dongguanyinsi Lane, Puyi usually got up after I had left for work. Then he would go to a nearby eatery to drink soya-bean milk and eat *Youtiao* for breakfast. Originally, the waiters there were happy to find a seat for Puyi and didn't make him wait in the line outside, but very soon they stopped welcoming Puyi anymore and ordered him to wait in the line, because more and more locals went to that eatery to have their breakfasts too, to see the "Emperor Xuantong" with their own eyes. This had greatly increased their workload and as workers of a state-run eatery, they couldn't get any more income from it. Clever Puyi understood the concern and stopped going to that eatery. And as a result, the clients of that eatery promptly reduced greatly in number.

On a Sunday afternoon, in a small restaurant in Wangfujing Street, when we were eating dumplings, an old man nearby recognized Puyi as being "Emperor Xuantong".

"Ah, is this the Emperor?" the old man said, although initially afraid.

"I'm Puyi! How did you recognize me?" Puyi queried.

"Who doesn't know Emperor Xuantong? Why do you come to such a small

Puyi and I at Fragrant Hill

restaurant? I think you should go to a big one."

"Why can't I come to a small restaurant?" Puyi asked.

"I see that after experiencing remoulding, you are a common citizen now. But I'm sure you wouldn't have come to such a small restaurant in the past!" said the old man.

"You are right! Before I was emperor and had no freedom to go wherever I pleased," Puyi stressed.

The clients in the restaurant moved closer to listen to their conversation.

Old man: "Do you still do any physical labour?"

Puyi: "I often go to the Botanic Garden to cultivate flowers."

Old man: "Where do you live now?"

Puyi: "I have my own wife and home!"

Old man: "I heard that you like painting?"

Puyi: "I learnt it when I was a boy, but I don't do it now."

Old man: "I lived in the East City. I like painting and keeping gold fish at home. My wife and I welcome you to come to our home."

Puyi: "Thank you for your kindness."

Old man: "Do you play Chinese chess?"

Puyi: "Yes!"

Old man: "I like it too. How about coming to my home to play chess with me?"

Puyi shook hands with the enthusiastic old man and all the clients there, before we left the restaurant.

Chapter Fourteen

Our Sincere Love

Some people didn't understand why Puyi, the former emperor of China, married me, a nurse. His colleagues in the CPPCC HQ and my colleagues in the Guanxiang Hospital all admired his devotion to me and it was interesting that Puyi preferred to be with me all day long. If he was free, he would always accompany me whenever I went shopping, and if he couldn't go with me, he would still walk me to the bus stop. When I returned home from the hospital by bus he would often be waiting for me there at the bus stop. At meal times, if I was still out he never ate his meal, but would wait for me to return so we could eat together, no matter how late

Puyi and I setting out to work

it was. These kinds of events were often recorded in his diary and it's interesting to note that even at home, he liked being around me. When I washed my face, he would watch me from beginning to the end and when I cooked in kitchen, he often stood on my side, being ready to help me. Sometimes I was made to laugh by his clumsy actions and I couldn't help affectionately scolding him: "Why are you always following me? Are you afraid I will run away?" He wouldn't say anything, only chuckle, with happiness and with satisfaction on his face.

When I had night shift at hospital, Puyi always felt uneasy. He would phone me for a chat, or come to my duty office with my coat, an umbrella, some fruit or pastry, and stayed there until the time of the last bus. Later on, the authorities of our hospital became aware of this and so kindly stopped scheduling me for the night shift. From 1964 to 1966, all of the doctors and nurses in the major cities in China had to join the travelling dispensaries organized by the government and take their turn working in rural areas for at least six months. But I was made an exception. I knew that this was because they hoped I would stay at home and take care of Puyi.

Several times, Puyi came to our hospital to be with me when I was on the day shift. Once a colleague of mine with a loose tongue told patients that he was the famous Emperor Xuantong. All of them came to surround him immediately, greeting him and talking with him, but this upset the normal work pattern. After we returned home I said to him: "I'd 'kowtow' to you a hundred times in order to beg you never to go to our hospital again! It's not me who isn't welcoming you to go, but because the patients flock around you as a very special visitor. It destroys the normal work routine of the hospital." Puyi answered me: "All right! Little sister, I'll never go again." At weekends around that time, the CPPCC HQ often gave Puyi free tickets for various kinds of entertainments. But if I was too tired after a hard week's work and had no energy to go with him, Puyi wouldn't go either. I knew that he was "a fan of Peking Opera", so I encouraged him to go and enjoy it on his own. But he said: "I don't want to leave you at home alone." On one Saturday evening, Puyi asked me to go with him to a concert at the CPPCC HQ. I told him that I was too tired to go out anywhere. He advised me: "After a full week at work, you should enjoy yourself. It's not far away, let me take you by the arm." Puyi always wanted to take me with him when going to a show. Once at a dance party, a lady invited him to dance several times. Puyi didn't want to dance with another lady, when I was there too, but it was impolite to refuse her. Finally, we had to leave so he took me to another dance party at the Nationality Palace. He had a special official pass, so we could go to many different halls and theatres.

After we were married, I still tried to continue studying at a medical college every weekday evening following my day's work. So, it would be 9 pm before I got to return home in the evening. Puyi supported my study and would wait patiently for me at home, so that we could spend time together. But he was unhappy if I carried on reading medical text books after dinner. He would close my book firmly and say: "You are out all day, I'm glad to be with you now. Please don't read books now!" I knew he did this because he was worried I would be too tired. He just liked to chat with me and he was always happy when we were together.

Sometimes, I was too weary to say anything when I returned home. I would just sit on the sofa to rest. He would come and sit by my side, trying to coax me by asking: "Why are you unhappy? Is something bothering you?" "Nothing is bothering me. I'm just a little tired." Immediately, Puyi would get up to make me some tea and peel some fruit for me. He would then comfort me, gently saying: "Help youself! Have a rest and you will feel better." I could feel his care for me.

At banquets, if he discovered that I was too nervous to pick up the food with chopsticks, he would move it across to my own plate for me, while everybody watched. It made me embarrassed and I would give him a little kick under the table, as a signal to stop. It made his heart ache that I did all of our housework, on top of my normal work in the hospital. He insisted that we hired a housekeeper to help out. I finally agreed with him and we found one who came in daily for half a day's work.

Our home was very far from the Guanxiang Hospital, where I worked. If it rained or snowed, Puyi would always meet me at hospital at the end of my shift and escort me back home, regardless of the long slippery road.

In summer of 1963, a freak rainstorm struck Beijing and all of its streets and lanes were flooded. In some places, the water was more than a metre deep, which stopped the normal flow of traffic. That morning I went to work barefoot, with my trousers rolled up. Puyi was anxious all day long. In the afternoon, he hurried to the hospital with an umbrella to take me back. But I had already left and returned home another way. When I was walking home, I heard some people saying, "Someone has fallen down a drain. His umbrella is lying next to the opening!" I hoped it was not Puyi! That was all I was thinking about until I got home and opened the door of our room. Puyi was not at home, as I had guessed. So, I rushed back out into the downpour to search for him.

At last, I saw him in a street standing some distance away. He was drenched to the bone and called over to me cheerfully: "Be careful of the manhole, it has no cover!" Having missed me at the hospital, he had worried about my safety and believed that I must have hid somewhere to shelter from the rain. On his way back, he found a manhole full of water that had no cover, and so was obscured to pedestrians. Knowing that it was the way I passed every day, he feared that I would fall down the manhole and so decided to stand by it, in the downpour with his umbrella open, to wait for me and warn me of the danger. Puyi recorded the matter in his diary of August 14th 1963. It had only eight characters in simple Chinese, meaning: "It rained in the evening. I went to hospital to take my wife, but she had returned home already."

Once, after work was over in the hospital, we were informed that our regular routine meeting had been cancelled. I was glad to take this opportunity to go downtown, to get my hair cut on Wangfujing Street. Usually Puyi would phone several times to speak to me when I had a meeting in the hospital after work. Therefore he soon knew that I had no meeting that evening. But by 9 pm, I still wasn't home. Puyi was very concerned about me and phoned many places to look for me and even asked Mr. Wan, his fifth brother-in-law to help him look for me. Mr. Wan told him that Beijing was too big and that he would never find me! Puyi didn't give up, he searched for me all over and phoned many police substations to make enquiries. Finally he was convinced that I had had an accident.

When I returned home after 10 pm, I saw him sitting on the sofa in tears! I was surprised and asked why he was crying? Seeing that I was safe, Puyi smiled through his tears: "You ask me that! Where were you?" I never expected that Puyi would be so worried, just because I returned home late. After that, if I was coming home late, I would let him know beforehand.

Another time, I made Puyi angry. At the invitation of the China News Agency, Puyi and I were taken to the Beihai Park to be pictured by the media. I was exhausted when I got back home and my foot had become blistered. Just a short while later, the CPPCC HQ sent a car to our house, to take us to receive the foreign guests. I told them I was too tired and couldn't go. Puyi went on his own but criticized me angrily when he came back home: "You always like to do what you want to do! You don't listen to anybody!" He lost his temper, "It isn't the right way to behave!"

I explained that my feet were blistered and painful. I asked him in response: "Why didn't you tell me you wanted me to go with you, then?"

"There were others present. I couldn't criticize you publicly. Although you were tired and your feet hurt, you should have still gone with me."

I cried. He softened his manner and comforted me, saying: "Forgive me, I have a hot temper and can be a little rough." Since we had become married, Puyi hadn't usually spoken to me in such a tone. He always reminded me in mild tones whenever I made a mistake. But this time was an exception. I understood that this was because I had made a serious mistake. I hated myself for that, so I cried. At the same time, I sensed that Puyi loved me sincerely.

With the precious historic photos he had treasured and the photos he had taken in Fushun Prison, Beijing Botanical Garden and at our home, Puyi compiled a photograph album. One day while looking through it together, we had a conversation about a photo Puyi took when he was living in exile, at "The Quiet Garden" in Tianjin.

"I took this picture in Tianjin after I left the Forbidden City. Can you guess how old I was then?"

"You look so young! I think you were not even twenty years old then?"

"Look at the pin in my tie. It's a diamond one. Have you ever seen real diamonds?"

"Of course I have. But I've never worn a diamond brooch."

"If you had married me then, I would have given you a variety of diamond brooches. Now I have nothing, so can't give you anything. But if you had married me then, you

Puyi in Tianjin after leaving the Forbidden City (1924-1932)

would have suffered, only serving as my accessory and plaything. At that time I had no idea what real love was and what a real couple should be. I would only chat or joke with my empress and concubines when I was in a good mood. I love you from the depth of my heart! I know I should respect and take care of my wife. I'm glad that we have set up a happy home. Anyhow I wouldn't have given you real love in those days when I could have been able to give you a diamond brooch!"

What Puyi said was true, as had already been completely proven by our sweet and harmonious married life.

My health was poor, so I easily caught colds. Puyi recorded in his diary how he took good care of me when I suffered from colds. Once I had a high fever during the night, so Puyi got up several times in the night, touching my forehead to see whether my temperature had already dropped, attending to my needs and bringing medicine with boiled water.

In the daytime, if he saw me sitting by an open window, Puyi would promptly come to close it, in case I was in a draught. Once I had a heavy cold when Puyi himself was hospitalised. He couldn't come back home but would inquire about my illness over the telephone, several times a day. He also phoned Pujie, his younger brother, asking him to take care of me instead of him. In January 1963, I had to stay in hospital to receive treatment for a typical "women's problem", when Puyi was taking part in the National Conference of Literature and History. He was much occupied with the busy itinerary, but still made sure to squeeze time in to visit me in the hospital.

Having been terrified by the deaths of several severely sick patients who had been staying in the wards close to mine, I went through the formalities of leaving the hospital, although I hadn't completely recovered. The doctors there advised me to stay for further treatment: "Puyi wouldn't let you go, he will blame us for this!" they said.

I was fortunate to meet Puyi on a bus on my way back. He was surprised: "Why are you here? Am I having a dream? How can you leave hospital before recovering?" He tried to drag me back to the hospital, making the passengers on the bus laugh. He advised me, "You won't get the attentive treatment at home that you would receive in hospital. I'm at a conference now so I can't take care of you." I insisted on going back home, so Puyi had to take me back to our home at the CPPCC HQ. He wrote about this in his diary that day. Puyi was uneasy about me while at the conference held at the auditorium close to our home and kept coming back home to check on me.

Puyi tried his best to find some very distinguished Chinese doctors and earnestly pleaded with them to cure my serious disease. At that time, all of them were aged men, seldom receiving patients, but they consented to Puyi's request, without hesitation. The highly respected Dr. Pu even asked Puyi: "Do you need me to pay a home visit?" Puyi thanked him, but declined the offer: "No! I'm very satisfied with your kindness already. How can I let you pay me a home visit?"

Puyi's friends joked with him: "Because you were emperor before, so Dr. Pu offered you a home visit." Later, Puyi and Dr. Pu became very good friends later on. Puyi preferred to go to see Dr. Pu when he was ill, thus he slowly got a useful collection of Dr. Pu's valuable prescriptions.

But there was an exception. In August of 1963, I was in bed with a cold. Puyi went to invite the seventy-year-old Dr. Zhang Rongzeng, a very popular Chinese doctor in China, to pay me a home visit. Afterwards, I cautioned him: "Dr. Zhang is very old, it is not right to invite him to our home!"

"You have a fever. I'm afraid it will get worse if you go out," he replied, defending his actions.

"I'll have an injection in the clinic first, and then go to see him." I stated. Puyi agreed with this point of view and ever after, we always went to see Dr. Zhang in his clinic and never requested him to pay us a home visit again.

Love is easily tested by illness. When I was ill I felt his deep love for me.

Now, whenever I recalled our sweet life together, I still regret that we had no children. "Why don't we adopt a child?" Puyi suggested to me many times. Some of our warmhearted friends offered to help us adopt a child, informing us how to go about it, and Puyi wrote down what they said in his pocket notebook.

Puyi loved kids very much, often dreaming that he had a child already. There were many kids in the grounds of the CPPCC HQ, so when Puyi took a walk in the grounds, he liked to chat with them, tell them stories and even play "hide and seek" with them. Madam Zhao, one of our neighbours, praised Puyi by saying that although Puyi was fifty years old, he didn't look old for he had a "child's heart"!

After we moved to 22, Dongguanyinsi Lane, Puyi still liked to invite neighbour's children to our home. He happily taught the kids how to fold paper planes, paper boats and arrows and would go to buy them coloured pens and wax crayons, to teach them how to draw pictures. He often entertained children with fruit, sweets and pastries and ate together with them happily. After becoming familiar with him, some naughty boys began to call him "Little Emperor". Puyi didn't get angry at it, but gently stroked their heads, telling them: "I was not happy being an emperor. I was shut in the palace and couldn't go out, like a bird in the cage. You are lucky to live in the new society you can go to school and play with your little friends freely. This is real happiness!" At first the kids didn't believe him. They asked him, as an emperor, "How could you say you were unhappy?" Puyi would tell them patiently about his feeling of depression in the Forbidden City. When Puyi went out, kids often surrounded him, begging him to tell them a story!

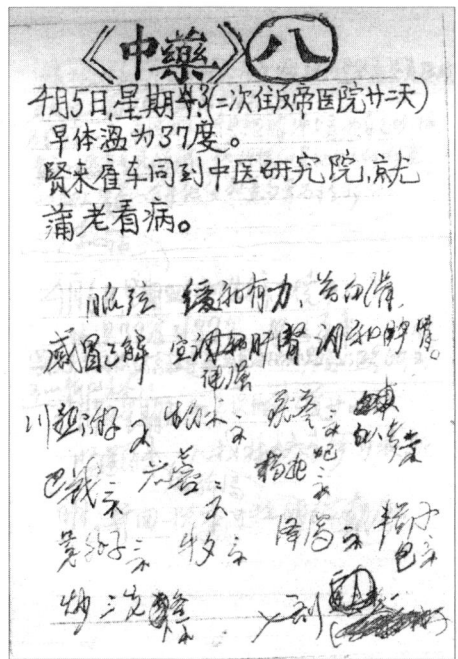

Puyi copied into his diary the prescription Doctor Pu Fuzhou wrote out for him.

One day, I returned home before the usual time, but was taken aback when I opened the door of our room. It was filled with boys with masks. They were playing fighting games, with wild abandon. One of them, wearing the mask of a warrior, stood out as much, much bigger. Seeing me walking into the room, he hurriedly took off his mask: "Oh no! You saw me this time...." The big child was Puyi.

Only then did I understand why sometimes I had found our room a little bit chaotic when I returned home from work. That was because our home had become a children's club! To cover his immaturity, Puyi always tidied up the messy room before I got back home. But I could still tell that the sofa had been moved, that there were paper scraps and maybe a lock of moustache from a mask on the floor. I would also find paper boats and arrows under the bed and table. I knew Puyi loved children, so I never bickered with Puyi about it.

I'll never forget Children's Day 1963, because we moved house that day. Puyi and I saw group upon group of children in splendid clothes. They were taking part in the various celebration activities. Puyi envied them, remarking to me: "Today is Children's Day, how happy they are!" Suddenly, he seemed lost in thought, asking me: "Did you celebrate Children's Day when you were little?" I told him with regret that I never did.

"I was trapped inside the tall walls. I didn't even know that Children's Day existed." Puyi sighed, saying to himself: "Our childhoods were wasted, what a pity!" Hearing what he had said, I understood more clearly why Puyi loved children.

In his childhood, Puyi couldn't see any kids within the Forbidden City. Only on very rare occasions, were his younger sisters and brothers taken into the palace to play with him. Later, Pujie, his younger brother and two other boys were summoned into the Yuqing Palace (his place of study) to be his fellow students. However, they were always aware that the little boy who studied with them was the paramount Emperor Xuantong, while they were his subjects, so they always appeared obedient, even acting in a cowardly way towards him when they were together. In Tianjin and Changchun, Puyi had some boys living together with him, serving as pageboys. But they were more than just his pageboys; they were actually his slaves. Nowadays, in the "new times", all of the young members of the Aisin-Gioro Royal Family have their own careers, and can support themselves. Among his many nephews and nieces, there include doctors, nurses, teachers, drivers, mountain climbers, Communist Youth League members, young pioneers, and even the Beijing motorbike-racing champion!

A scene from the film *Fire Dragon* where Puyi was playing a game with some boys

Puyi loved children.

    Miss Jin Aiyao was one of Puyi's nieces. Although born into the Royal Family, she became a member of the Communist Party of China very early. In 1950, she joined the Chinese Volunteers when the Korean War broke out and was awarded a medal in the world famous Shangganling Campaign. With feelings of love and reverence and holding her hand in his, Puyi said to her when he met her for the first time: "You are most beloved by the Chinese people (during the Korean War, Chinese volunteers were highly regarded by the Chinese people as 'the most beloved'), whilst I was the most despised. I'm no match for you at all. From today, 'uncle' must learn from his niece!" Puyi often mentioned this niece to me proudly: "From our Aisin-Gioro clan, a flock of 'phoenixes of the new era' have flown out." (The Chinese like to call the outstanding women "phoenixes".)

    Puyi loved children and wanted to adopt a child, maybe to make up for his lonely childhood? But then, both he and I had poor health, so I was afraid that we wouldn't have enough energy to bring up a child, if we really did go ahead with adopting one. So I had to advise Puyi to drop this idea. Now, I feel sorry for him whenever I think of this lost opportunity.

Chapter Fifteen

The Refusing of the Feudal Protocols

During the Spring Festival, 1960, Puyi and Pujie reuniting with Zaitao, their seventh uncle, after their release from prison

Puyi was very concerned about his seventh uncle Mr. Zaitao, and would often take me to see him. Although sometimes we were too busy and could stay there only about ten minutes, he had always inquired, with some concern, about his condition. He said to me that this was because Mr. Zaitao was his last remaining real uncle.

The Spring Festival of 1963 was the first one after we were married and we went to pay a New Year's call to Mr. Zaitao. The old man was thrilled to see us, but still called Puyi "uncle", according to the feudal protocol, which stipulated that subjects couldn't call the emperor directly by his personal name. When the loving uncle heard that Puyi could now do housework, he smiled to me: "Our 'uncle' really has received a successful re-education. Before he even needed others to wear his clothes! Now, he can fire a coal stove. Good for him!" Puyi smiled too: "Thank you, uncle!"

Filling the walls of Mr. Zaitao's home were many valuable calligraphic works and paintings that he had collected. While accompanying Puyi to view and admire them, he mentioned to Puyi that he would like "uncle" to write several calligraphic works for him. Puyi responded that he hadn't practiced calligraphy for ages. He went on to say that he didn't think his calligraphy was good enough to be shown in public. Although he said this, he still attentively wrote several sheets of calligraphy at home and sent them to his uncle, Mr. Zaitao.

Among Puyi's relatives, there were still some of them with ingrained feudal ideas and their funny expressions and deeds brought distress to Puyi. He once complained to me: "When I was emperor, even my parents had to kowtow to me when they saw me. Now, the feudal system has been overthrown for a long time, and all the people are equal. Why do some people still prefer the old feudal system to one of equality?" Once, Puyi had a meal with several of his distant cousins. During the meal, one of them had always nodded his head, saying "Yes! Yes!" to Puyi, like the former subjects did when they heard Puyi's talking to them. Another one once forgot himself, holding up his cup: "With both emperor and subjects present today, I'm very happy...." Puyi put down his cup and retorted: "We are cousins and the citizens of a new society. We are equal. Why do you still miss the feudal system? The former Puyi and the feudal times are all dead. You should be glad for the newly-born Puyi and the new times."

Another experience made Puyi even angrier. In the Spring Festival of 1960, at the home of Mr. Puren, his younger half-brother, Puyi met with a distant nephew of his, who was actually older than he was. The frightened nephew flopped down on his knees, calling Puyi "Emperor" and kowtowed to him. Puyi was too angry to say much, but furiously rebuked him: "China has been liberated for so many years? Why haven't you changed your feudal ideas?"

The "old man" who was still loyal to the Qing Dynasty and "the nephew of Emperor Xuantong" looked very much embarrassed, but refused to rise. Puyi angrily turned to leave, but was held by Mr. Puren, who hastened to smooth things over. The nephew seized this opportunity to explain to Puyi, "Now we are not Emperor and subjects, but we are still uncle and nephew! As your nephew, I should give you New Year respect and greetings!" Then, he kowtowed to Puyi again. Puyi jerked him up and criticized him gravely. Seeing that Puyi was so angry, the "emperor's nephew" felt snubbed himself and quickly found an excuse to slip away.

At the home of Mr. Zaitao, I heard a story about a young lady who had treasured the loving-kindness of the royal family. It moved me greatly.

At the beginning of 1961, Mr. Zaitao and his wife, desiring to be a matchmaker for

Puyi, held a banquet at the CPPCC HQ dining hall, to introduce the young lady to Puyi. With jewels on her head, a necklace around her neck and make-up on her face, the young lady appeared alluring. To attract Puyi, she spoke in a soft and steady voice and unnaturally put on an aristocratic face. After the banquet, Mr. Zaitao called Puyi and the young lady to the dance hall upstairs. Because it was impolite to refuse a lady's enthusiastic invitation, Puyi grudgingly had to dance with her for a short while. But she was very pleased and believed that it was a real honour to dance with the person who used to be the Emperor of China.

During the intermission, the young lady asked Puyi to give her his signature in calligraphic form. Puyi promptly replied that he was weary and couldn't do it for her. She looked a little bit disappointed. Afterwards, she frequented the Chongnei Hotel where Puyi then resided. Dabbling successfully in singing the Kunqu Opera, she sang it for Puyi to please him and offered to teach him. But Puyi had no interest to learn. When she knew that Puyi liked roaming about streets and parks, she often offered to do that with Puyi. After associating with Puyi for a reasonable period, she became impatient, so hastily and openly, expressed to Puyi her love for him.

Why did she pursue Puyi so desperately? There was a long story behind it. Her grandfather had been born into a poor farmer's family, during the reign (1875-1908) of Emperor Guangxu, in the Qing Dynasty. Her grandfather, with other destitute folk, had fled to Beijing, during a disastrous period of drought in their region. One day, while in the downtown area he saw the luxurious sedan of Prince Chun, the first generation prince and also Puyi's grandfather. The sedan had official attendants chearing the way with beating gongs. All the pedestrians would dodge in a flurry to both sides of the street. But her grandfather, a cowardly countryside boy, who knew little about life, fell to the ground in a panic, at a loss for what to do. An official attendant went up to whip him, but he was seen by Prince Chun when he glimpsed outside. He instantly took a liking for the clever looking and handsome boy and ordered that he be taken back to his mansion, to be a houseboy. Later, the boy was fortunate to be chosen to be a fellow student of Prince Chun's sons and studied diligently. Prince Chun recommended him to become an official and promoted him repeatedly. Later in life, because these promotions had also come with good wage rises, he was able to purchase coal mines, running them successfully, and so making a lot of money. So, the young lady's family had built up its fortune by the "royal graciousness" of the Qing Dynasty Emperor.

Although she never forgot "the infinite royal graciousness", it meant nothing to Puyi, who didn't care about repayment. Puyi had different criteria for choosing a wife and didn't think that the young lady was suitable for him. To avoid a phone call from her regarding a possible appointment, Puyi told the attendant at the Chongnei Hotel:

"If it's a lady's voice, please tell her I'm away."

Once her father came to Beijing, so taking the opportunity, she decided to invite Puyi to the "Moscow Restaurant" to join them for dinner. The concierge at the hotel had stalled her off with a vague answer, according to what Puyi had told him, but she was unwilling to give up and went to the hotel with her father, to find Puyi. She caught Puyi outside his room as he was coming out, but her earnest invitation got Puyi`s polite refusal again. Why didn't Puyi choose to befriend this young lady? "I appreciate honesty and sincerity. I don't believe we could have a harmonious life! She wouldn't love me sincerely." Puyi told me this when he mentioned the matter to me later.

Puyi had finished nearly ten years of remoulding and returned to Beijing from Fushun, on December 23rd 1959. He sojourned at the home of Madam Yunxin, his fifth younger sister and during the following two weeks, many of his relatives, friends and former subordinates went to call on him in succession. Later, Puyi complained to me that what embarrassed him was that some of them still treated him as "emperor".

Mr. Zhao Yinmao, one of Puyi's former chefs, was the first to come and see Puyi. He had worked for Puyi for over twenty years, from the time when he was a teenager until Puyi had been captured by the Russian Red Army. Under Puyi's command, he had been both severely punished when considered necessary but also had handsome rewards when appreciation was bestowed on him. People said that one of Puyi's rewards had enabled him to construct an ornate two-storied building in Beijing. To keep firmly in mind Puyi's gracefulness to him, he had installed a shrine with Puyi's picture on it in their lounge and often worshipped it. After the liberation, with his remarkable culinary skills which he learned at the Royal Kitchen in "Changchun Royal Palace", he easily found a stable, high-paid job as chef in a hotel attached to a government institution. Mr. Zhao Yinmao was beside himself with excitement when he saw Puyi, while calling Puyi "Emperor", and kowtowing to him repeatedly. Puyi pulled him up, as usual, but with anger: "I have already become a citizen. Why don't you call me by my name?" That day Puyi invited Mr. Zhao to have a meal with him, asking about his life after they had parted at Changchun (then the capital of the Manchukuo) in 1945. Eventually, when he saw him sometime later, Puyi managed to urge Mr. Zhao to call him "comrade". Mr. Zhao came to see us several times after Puyi and I became married. Sometime after, Mr. Zhao's original wife passed away, Puyi voluntarily went to his home, to gain his children's consent regarding his possible remarriage. The former servant and master had now become comrades.

On December 23rd 1959, according to the arrangement of the Beijing Civil Administration Bureau, Puyi left the home of his fifth younger sister and moved to stay at the Chongnei Hotel in Suzhou Lane, with some former Nationalist Party Generals. Also like

Puyi, they had been "remoulded" and had been granted a special amnesty from the government. After returning to Beijing, once again they were sent to visit factories, people communes, schools, and of course, to continue their re-education by having conventional political study sessions.

One day when Puyi was at the Chongnei Hotel, an attendant came to hand him a big envelope and told him that there were two old men downstairs wanting to see him. Puyi opened the envelope and was horrified to see two familiar huge red elegant cards, which had been popular in the Qing Dynasty and used to pay respect to emperors. The senders' names and official titles were written in the bottom left hand corners, to indicate to Puyi that they were from former senior officials of the Qing Dynasty. Filled with fury, he was aware that those who still treated him as emperor and like to kowtow to him, were not only his former entourage, but also the former courtiers and aristocracy of the Qing Dynasty, which had been overthrown as long as 48 years ago.

Premier Zhou Enlai heard about the matter the next day. It aroused caution in him, as he knew the ideological remoulding had been a painstaking and arduous task and had needed time. He said that they didn't expect that, after being remoulded, Puyi himself wouldn't want to be emperor any more, but the former courtiers themselves, perhaps still cherished their former illustrious status. They couldn't forget their Emperor Xuantong! On January 12th 1960, Premier Zhou received Puyi and his relatives. He reminded Puyi: "I don't think that all the people will be able to treat you as a common citizen. Maybe there are still some people who prefer to kowtow to you." Puyi immediately reported to Premier Zhou: "Not long ago, there were two old men who came to see me with cards bearing their former official titles of the Qing Dynasty. I had no idea about what I should say to them, so I didn't receive them." Puyi was annoyed to meet with so many people during the cause of one month, who had wanted to kowtow to him. Premier Zhou called those people "the untouched corner of society". He encouraged Puyi not only to avoid being influenced by them, but also to help them with their ideological remoulding.

Two days later, one of Puyi's distant nephews came to kowtow to Puyi at Madam Yunxin's home. He didn't expect that his behavior would anger Puyi. He had to run away quickly and never dared to come to see Puyi again.

After the Spring Festival of 1960, Puyi settled back to work in the Beijing Botanical Garden in the northern suburbs of Beijing. On a Saturday afternoon, on his way back to downtown, Puyi encountered one of the former eunuchs of the Forbidden City, who had served Puyi's daily life before. The old man had already heard that Puyi had returned to Beijing and recognized him instantly, paying his respects to Puyi. He didn't kowtow to Puyi, but his cringing appearance fascinated the curious sights of the pedestrians! Puyi hastened to support him, kindly explaining to him: "The former emperor is now a citizen, you don't need to kowtow to me anymore." This time Puyi didn't lose his temper as before, because he respected the old man who was senior to him and remembered what Premier Zhou had told him.

On a Sunday in July of 1960, Puyi returned to Madam Yunxin's home for a break. Madam Yunxin handed him a big parcel containing perfumed soap, toothpaste, towels, sweets, biscuits, etc. She told Puyi that a lady had sent it to her home a few days previously, on behalf of her father Mr. Chen Maotong.

Mr. Chen Maotong was the son of Mr. Chen Baosheng, who had been Puyi's most reverent and trusted tutor during his teenage years. Mr. Chen Maotong himself had followed Puyi to Changchun in the 1930s, working in the Puppet Government of "The Manchukuo". Now it was in 1960s that Mr. Chen sent the present to Puyi, conveying sentiments of gratitude from his father and himself. Puyi pondered it over, deciding to receive the sweets only, but returning the rest to Mr. Chen.

On August 7th, Puyi let Mr. Yuyan, one of his distant nephews and Miss Wang Peiying, his wet nurse's grand-daughter take him to Mr. Chen's home, according to the home address left by his daughter. Seeing Puyi coming to his home, Mr. Chen was pleasantly surprised at first, but then followed a young girl and a young man carrying the parcel he had sent to Puyi. He felt puzzled, but didn't know what to say. Puyi held out his hand first, and Mr. Chen shook it reluctantly. He was cautious, keeping silent for a long time.

"How are you these years?" Puyi first spoke.

"Just 'so so', one of my lungs has been troubling me for two years" Chen answered.

"Do you have a fixed job?" Puyi asked.

"After the liberation, I worked for a few years, but now I'm retired."

After exchanging a few words of greeting with Mr. Chen, Puyi swiftly switched topics. "Before, I committed unforgivable crimes to the motherland and our people. For these crimes, I didn't even think that capital punishment was sufficient for me, and yet the government didn't do that. Instead, I was given the valuable opportunity to study and change. I had never dreamt that I would be granted special amnesty by the government." When Puyi said this, Mr. Chen was perturbed, looking warily right and left, seeming to turn deaf ears to Puyi.

"The former relationship we had has finished. I don't hope to renew it. We should set up a new comradeship between us." Puyi put the parcel on the bed and told Mr. Chen: "I kept the sweets. Please take the rest for yourself. I have all the daily necessities. You yourself are not rich and needn't buy anything more for me."

"A gift for you? I don't have any idea about this!" Mr. Chen looked at Yuyan, then

Miss Wang in fake astonishment. He firmly denied that he had dispatched his daughter to send the parcel to Puyi. "Your daughter said that you had her send it to me. How can you say you didn't know about it?" Puyi became angry.

"My daughter is out of her mind! I really didn't know she had sent the parcel to you!"

"I don't care who sent it to me. Anyway I have no need for them. Keep them yourself." Puyi became angrier. Mr. Chen didn't say anything more, but still worried, was ready to defend himself. Puyi loathed his affectation, leaving his home quickly.

Afterwards, Mr. Tian, the Director of the Botanical Garden heard about the matter. He encouraged Puyi: "This time you didn't just refuse to see the conservative figures, but helped them with their ideological remoulding. You have progressed. But you must use an acceptable method to do it. Haven't you changed to be a new person throughout the ten years of remoulding? Do you know in the course of those ten years, how many people cared about you and desired to help you by every possible means?"

In his diary, Puyi wrote: "This time because of my blunt words, Mr. Chen didn't accept my help. I shouldn't have taken Yuyan and Miss Wang with me. I'm sure he misunderstood and believed that they were government agents. Therefore, he dared not admit that he had sent the gift to me. What I did not only couldn't help him, but appalled him. My goodwill functioned worthless. Henceforth, next time I must take care to use an acceptable method to do it.

Chapter Sixteen
Reunion with the Former Servants

After his return to Beijing at the end of 1959, many of Puyi's former subordinates, entourage and servants came to see him and he was excited when he reunited with those "ghosts from the past".

In the evening of November 13th 1908, three-year-old Puyi, as the heir to Emperor Guangxu, his uncle, was taken away from his native home in the Mansion of Prince Chun and sent to live in the Forbidden City. The very next day, he was announced Emperor Xuantong. After that, he couldn't see his real mother for many years.

Nevertheless, he was lucky to have Ms. Wang, his wet-nurse, to take care of him. Puyi said: "I grew up in my wet-nurse's bosom, suckled by her from one month until nine years-old and from then on I was as inseparable from her, as a baby is from its mother. When I was eight years old, my three high consorts resolved to expel her without my knowledge. I desperately wanted her back. Howling every day I would cry, "I want Momo, I want Momo", and I even did this in my dreams. I almost screamed my lungs out! Not long after my "Grand Nuptial" at the age of seventeen I had the power to send people to find her and often had her to stay with me for a few days at a time. Later, I took her to Changchun, to live with me until I had to leave there in 1945. I always took

Puyi's wet-nurse

her as my real mother, the only person I truly bonded with."

She was the first person Puyi wanted to see after he later came back to Beijing. He couldn't wait to find out her whereabouts. Eventually he found her adopted son, Mr. Wang Shuting, on the Houmenqiao Road, near the Drum Tower. Actually, before she was selected by Puyi's family to be his wet-nurse, she had only one daughter and her husband had already died of tuberculosis. To support her family she had to leave her little daughter with her old parents-in-law while she went into the Mansion of Prince Chun, to feed Puyi with her daughter's breast milk. Unfortunately, three years later, her daughter died of malnutrition. Puyi's family had kept the bad news from her, being afraid that it would affect the quality of her milk. Only after having been driven out of the Forbidden City five years later, did she discover about her daughter's death. Dejected, she had to adopt a son from her elder brother. He had lived in Changchun for many years with his adopted mother during the period of "Manchukuo". So he was very glad when he saw Puyi at his home. He had the unfortunate duty to tell Puyi the devastating news that their dear mother had been killed by a stray bullet, while fleeing from Changchun to Tonghua with the Royal Family, in 1946. Once again Puyi delicately wept for his wet-nurse. That day Mr. Wang Shuting graciously invited Puyi to have a meal with them at his home.

On later occasions, Mr. Wang's three children, two workers and a nurse often went to help Puyi with the cleaning of his apartment at the CPPCC HQ grounds and Puyi often visited Mr. Wang's family. He later took me there many times. When the three children got married, we happily showered them with gifts and after Mr. Wang died in 1966, Puyi still cared for his ill wife and three children.

Li Guoxiong, Puyi's personal servant for more than thirty years. Later, Puyi went to see him at his home.

In contrast, 'Big Li' (Mr. Li Guoxiong—he received this nickname because he was quite tall and strong), one of his former favoured servants, never came to see him. As early as in 1924, when Puyi still lived in the Forbidden City, twelve year-old 'Big Li' had been taken there to be his page boy. Later, Puyi took him to Tianjin and Changchun. Puyi very much appreciated his loyalty and had promoted him to be the Captain of his Court Honour Guards and later his Chief Steward. In 1945, both Puyi and 'Big Li' were captured, along with others, by the Russian Red Army and 'Big Li' continued to unquestioningly serve him in the Russian prison. Later he was extradited to China and remoulded in the Fushun Prison with Puyi. In 1957, 'Big Li' was released and returned to Beijing. Not long after, as a slave labourer he was forced to enlist into the "Production Team" and was sent to break stones on construction sites and do other back-breaking jobs in the state farms outside of Beijing, while under the strict surveillance of the police.

Due to the "remoulding", consisting of political study sessions and excruciating labour, 'Big Li' had already abandoned his loyalty to Puyi. He considered that his incarceration and suffering were not at all his fault, but because he had served Puyi for more than thirty years. Therefore, he loathed Puyi and he had expressed that he was unwilling to see him anymore. But, unexpectedly for 'Big Li', Puyi, then a commissioner of the CPPCC, with the help of Yuchan, one of Puyi's distant nephews, showed up at 'Big Li's' home in the slums of Beijing. Later 'Big Li' recalled this unhappy meeting thus:

Although he came to see me as a commoner, enthusiastically shaking hands with me, patting my shoulders and brushing the dust off my coat, I knew that they were for show, in order to make others believe he had changed completely. I hated to hear that he had been privileged by the government, assigned a satisfactory job and lived a comfortable life. With humble gestures, he told me that he missed me, but I didn't believe a word of it.

Puyi understood 'Big Li's' cold-shoulder attitude, in fact he was very sorry and felt that he owed 'Big Li' greatly. When Puyi and I got married, 'Big Li' didn't attend our wedding ceremony, even though he had received our invitation. Puyi had been to see him again, but failed to find him. His wife informed Puyi that he had already been assigned a stable job at the "Tianhe State Farm" in the far northern suburbs of Beijing and that he was forbidden from returning home during the peak farming season. After that Puyi sent others to convey greetings to 'Big Li'.

One day when Puyi accidentally heard that Mr. Zhu Jiefu, Deputy Chief of the Secretarial Section of the CPPCC HQ, was a distant nephew of Mr. Zhu Yifan, one of his three respected tutors, he couldn't hold himself back from looking for him. He quickly found Mr. Zhu Jiefu and eagerly inquired how things were with Mr. Zhu Yifan. A few days later, Mr. Zhu Jiefu brought Mr. Zhe Yujun, the fourth son of Mr. Zhu Yifan, to Puyi. Both of them were delighted to see each other, having mixed emotions of grief and joy.

In the late Qing Dynasty, Mr. Zhu Yifan was one of the well-known scholars and a *Hanlin* academician. In 1916, he was selected by the Qing Royal Family to be one of Puyi's tutors and quickly won their trust. He also became Puyi's private Chinese doctor. When Puyi left the Forbidden City to live in Tianjin in 1924, he was appointed the manager of the "Qing Royal Family Office" in Beijing. After the "September 18th Incident*", Mr. Zhu Yifan firmly opposed the Japanese invaders and refused to follow Puyi to Changchun, the Capital of "Manchukuo", to serve his Puppet Government. Prior to passing away in 1937, he had even refused Puyi's invitations to go to Changchun to visit him. Puyi was deeply grieved when it was reported to him that Mr. Zhu had passed away in Beijing. To show his respect to Mr. Zhu, Puyi had bestowed his family a considerable sum of money towards his funeral.

Zhu Yifan (1861-1938), one of Puyi's tutors in the Forbidden City

Mr. Zhu Yujun had told Puyi that he had four children and was middle-school teacher, living a happy life. All of his brothers and sisters had stable jobs and happy families. On this occasion, he revealed a secret to Puyi: Mr. Zhu Yifan, at the risk of his own life, once protected Mr. Zhu Jiefu, his nephew, who was involved in secret anti-Japanese operations in Beijing, by keeping his secret documents at his own home. Upon hearing this, Puyi revered Mr. Zhu Yifan even more.

The Chinese believe that "enemies are bound to meet on a narrow road". One day, on a crowded street, Puyi, who rarely went out alone, came face to face with Li Tiyu, his old rival. Li Tiyu, his former adjutant and driver, had had an affair with Wanrong, Puyi's empress, resulting in pregnancy, but the baby girl died at birth. Upon discovering the infidelity, Puyi had immediately driven him out of the Imperial Palace in Changchun. Almost 30 years had passed and neither expected to meet again.

Li Tiyu, thoroughly embarrassed about his serious offence in the past, bowed

---

* After secretly planning for a long time, the Japanese army in Shenyang carried out an attack on the Chinese garrison based there. By the next day, the whole of the city had been taken, and thus started Japan's invasive war on China. This event took place on September 18th 1931.

and genuinely expressing his apology to Puyi, saying, "I'm deeply sorry about that matter!"

"Let past be past. Don't apologize to me!" Puyi said calmly, "How have you been? What are you doing these days?"

"I'm doing odd jobs at the Kuanjie Chinese Medical Hospital. My family lives at Xikoudai Lane. Our life is 'so-so'."

"Good, now we are living in the same city again," said Puyi.

"I've thought about emperor often, but haven't had the courage to see you," admitted Li Tiyu.

Observing that Puyi was not angry, Li was slowly pacified. But soon, he was again "caught unawares" unexpectedly by Puyi saying,

"We are now comrades. Don't call me emperor anymore! I'll come to see you when I am free."

And Puyi soon acted on what he said. He went to see Li and his family at their home. When Li's wife was later suffering from a chronic disease and they didn't have enough money to treat it, he charitably gave them money, out of his shallow pockets. It moved Li deeply. Later, I heard that he had happily joined our Wedding Ceremony.

As early as 1916, Mr. Wang Jianzhai had entered the Forbidden City to work for Puyi. Later on he followed Puyi to Tianjin and Changchun, working as his accountant and secretary. In 1944, he had to leave Puyi and return home to the far eastern suburbs of Beijing to attend his ill mother. Knowing that Puyi had been released and had returned to Beijing, he came to see us at our home in 22, Dongguanyinsi Lane, which was very far away from his home. He recalled this visit in this way:

> When I rang the doorbell, a young girl opened the door. I asked her to report to Puyi that Wang Jianzhai, from the eastern suburbs wanted to see him. She entered his room, then promptly returned and asked me to come in, ushering me to the lounge, where I saw Puyi waiting for me by the door. He excitingly walked forward and hugged me, then let me sit down on the sofa. After having been his subordinate for so long, I dared not to sit down. Puyi coaxed me to sit down on the sofa and sat happily by me. With my hands in his, both of us were too excited to say anything. We wept a little together. When Madam Li came into the lounge, Puyi felt a little awkward. While wiping his eyes with a handkerchief, he introduced me to her: "This is Uncle Wang from the eastern suburbs of Beijing." Madam Li was of medium height. In a relaxed manner, she expressed her warm welcome to me. She said that it was cold in the lounge and invited me to sit down in their bedroom, where it was warmer. Then she welcomed me with tea, cakes and cigarettes.

Puyi looked much stronger and energetic — like a new man. He told me of his experiences after we had parted in Changchun, in 1944.

"That was a nightmare! It's too sad to look back. Only one year after you left Changchun, the Japanese surrendered. They forced me to immigrate to Japan. I also believed that I would have to live the rest of my life as expatriate in Japan, never to return. I'm very grateful to the Communist Party of China and the People's Government for forgiving me, a person condemned and hated by my people, for aiding Japanese Imperialists in enslaving the people in northeast China. The government allowed me return to Beijing to spend my remaining years in comfort." With thankfulness to the CPC, Chairman Mao and Premier Zhou Enlai, Puyi told me about his impressive remoulding and his happy new life after he returned to Beijing. He inquired, with care, about my family life, asking me if I had a bicycle or a semi-conducted radio, even asking me if I raised chickens at my home to lay eggs. Madam Li interrupted us: "Did Puyi ever beat you?" "He did, but it doesn't matter," I answered. Puyi was ashamed and said: "I'm very regretful for that. Now, I should apologize to you."

When it was close to noon, I stood up, to take leave of them. Puyi didn't agree, "You must get permission from Shuxian first."

Madam Li urged me to stay, saying, "You haven't seen each other for more than twenty years, please have lunch here, then you may chat longer." Puyi gently pushed me down on the sofa again saying: "Before you served me... today I'd like you to taste my cooking skill." He put on an apron and went to the kitchen to cook lunch with Madam Li. I wanted to help them, but Puyi wouldn't let me.

We chatted merrily while eating lunch and it wasn't until 2 pm that I left their home to catch the long distance bus in time. Puyi and Madam Li saw me off at the gate of their house. They invited me to come back again, anytime that I was free. After walking a few blocks, I turned around and saw them still standing there, watching me walk away. I was glad to be a part of their sweet family life, even if only for one day. All sorts of feelings had welled up in my mind. It was only the Communist Party of China that had the ability to remould Puyi, once a brutal, eccentric and callous person, into the one who had learned to respect and care about others. It was only the Communist Party of China that could successfully change a feudal emperor, who had needed others to help put on his clothes into a "labourer", who could earn his own living.

Chapter Seventeen

Puyi's Contacts with People from All Circles of Society

After being released, Puyi had finally gained his identity as an average citizen in Socialist China. He was assigned a job and began to meet people in a wide range of social circles. For the first time in his life, Puyi had equals. But, how did they treat Puyi and how did Puyi get along with them?

During Puyi's year of working at the Beijing Botanical Garden, he earned the respect and special attention from its superiors. Mr. Yu Dejun, the Director of the Beijing Botanical Garden, who had majored in Botany at Edinburgh University, was a famous horticulturist in China. He presented Puyi with his work *The Manual of the Botanical Garden*. With great interest, Puyi studied it attentively, taking notes, collecting specimens and obtaining a great deal of horticultural knowledge. Mr. Tian Yumin, the CPC Secretary of the Beijing Botanical Garden, had joined the Red Army when he was very young, but was later wounded in battle several times. He had been awarded for outstanding service during his military career. He had often invited Puyi to his home and lent him the books he liked from his personal collection. Sometimes he showed Puyi treasured antiques from the Qing Dynasty. Mr. Hu Weilu, being a soldier of the Red Army, as early as the 1920s, later became a high-ranking officer in the Chinese Police Force. He liked to stay at the Botanical Garden for health reasons and in the mornings, he and Puyi often practiced *Taijiquan* (Tai Chi) together in the garden and they liked to have their meals together

Yu Dejun, the Director of Beijing Botanical Garden, whom Puyi respected highly

The Last Emperor of China — My Husband Puyi

in the canteen. On the weekends, he would have Puyi driven home in his car. After a while, Puyi and the three leaders became intimate friends and they maintained regular communication, even after Puyi was transferred to work in the CPPCC HQ.

The entire staff at the Beijing Botanical Garden highly regarded Puyi and always "went the extra mile" to take care of him. Moved by their kindness, Puyi befriended many of them. Two young men, Liu Bao'an and Liu Baoshan, were assigned to the same apartment as Puyi, in order to attend to him as well as protect him. When Puyi was ill or suffered from haemorrhoids, they would accompany Puyi to hospital. They would also boil Chinese herbal medicine and buy and deliver meals from the canteen for him. In his own way, Puyi took care of the two young men, too. When the weather suddenly changed, Puyi would always move their blankets, which had been hung out to dry, back to their rooms so as to prevent them from becoming soaked with the rain.

I saw a large, well-preserved and colourful photo of a young PLA soldier, in Puyi's album. Originally, I took him to be one of Puyi's nephews, but later Puyi told me he was Liu Bao'an, his good friend, who had helped him tremendously when he was in the Beijing Botanical Garden. While gazing fondly at the photo, Puyi told me that Liu had been born into a very poor family in northeast China and had experienced a miserable childhood. He served both in the Chinese Libration War (1946-1949) and the Korean War (1950-1953). When Puyi left the Beijing Botanical Garden, Liu presented this photo of himself to Puyi and the two had said a very tough goodbye to each other. Puyi showed me the words inscribed inside its back cover:

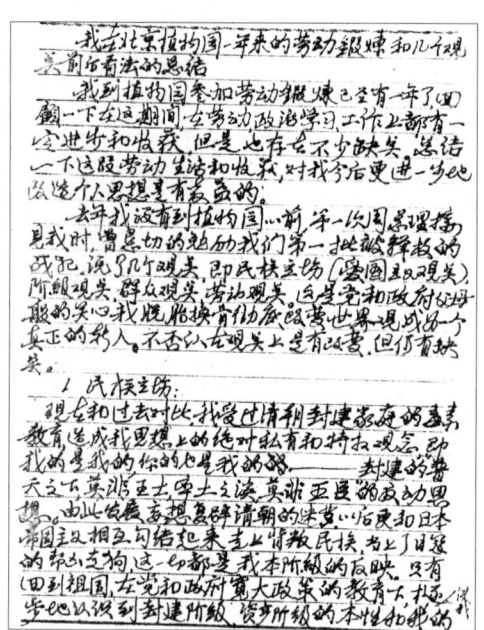

Puyi's personal reflections on his work at the Beijing Botanical Garden

To the respectable Mr. Puyi,

Although together only a short period, we have found a lasting friendship. I present you this photo as an everlasting momento.

Sincerely Liu Bao'an,
March 6th 1961

Shen Dechun (middle), Puyi's superior, who took good care of him

While working at the CPPCC HQ, Puyi had received genuine care from his superiors, of all levels. They often asked Puyi about his work and daily life and offered him their assistance. At the same time, Puyi was on good terms with all of his colleagues (many of them had been the former National Party Generals and major officials). Mr. Du Yuming had enjoyed joking with Puyi and also often argued with him about politics and other subjects. He praised Puyi as an honorable and forthright person. When Puyi was ill, his colleagues would come to see him with gifts and to extend their greetings. I was impressed by one jovial "get-together" with them. Each family had brought a dish that they made themselves. How wonderful it was! But I heard that during the first half of his life, Puyi had been somewhat crazy and had lived an eccentric way of life, making his servants suffer considerably. Between 6 o'clock in the morning to 12 o'clock at night, Puyi had expected his royal meals to be delivered immediately, whenever he chose to eat. Therefore, there had to be cooks readily waiting in the kitchen, anticipating his orders at all times! Moreover, they were criticized harshly or even fined by the unpredictable Puyi, for serving meals a little bit slowly or for improperly preparing them. Pampered Puyi, enjoyed teasing the eunuchs at will, reprimanding and beating them. Many incidents were accurately depicted in his book, *The First Half of My Life*. But now, Puyi had changed completely. He sincerely cared about people, regardless of class.

Mr. Zhao Huatang, a handyman who worked at the CPPCC HQ, tried his best to take care of Puyi, when the unmarried Puyi had lived in the apartment in the CPPCC HQ. Puyi would reciprocate this by returning his concern for the handyman and they slowly became good friends. When Mr. Zhao was ill Puyi would take some famous "Beijing pastries" to his home, to help him feel better.

Being in poor health, both Puyi and I had no energy to do our housework. So, we hired housekeepers. We always took them as our family members and helped them when they got into difficulties. Puyi always invited our former housekeepers back to join us when we cooked big meals. One of our housekeepers, Mrs. Du, sometimes didn't have enough money to pay her daughter's tuition, so Puyi would unhesitatingly pay for it. Even after his passing away, I helped her, despite my limited salary. Another housekeeper of ours fell down and hurt her knee while taking out the rubbish. Puyi and I attended to her in her own home. In her simple and dark room, Puyi behaved as though it was our own home.

Because Puyi had been the "Last Emperor of the Great Qing Dynasty", all the people, including the top leaders of the CPC and the State desired to see him in the flesh. He was often invited to join various banquets, conferences and social activities.

In the "second half of his life", Puyi was fortunate to receive the affection and esteem of Premier Zhou Enlai and was invited to attend many banquets held by him. He

Puyi and his colleagues Wang Yaowu (middle) and Yang Botao (left) in the CPPCC HQ

Premier Zhou Enlai heartily talking with Puyi and I, November 10th, 1963

The Last Emperor of China **My Husband Puyi**

Premier Zhou Enlai receiving Puyi and I in the Great Hall of People, October 10th, 1963 was grateful to Premier Zhou for his constant concern and was enthralled by the Premier's good nature and charisma. When talking about Premier Zhou, Puyi always expressed admiration for him. One day, Puyi came back home from a forum held at CPPCC HQ and told me with excitement that the forum that day was presided over by Premier Zhou.

"The Premier immediately greeted me affectionately when he saw me. I was so excited that I couldn't say anything. I was constantly considering how to repay his care to me! I couldn't think of any way I could show my appreciation for him, except maybe to show him the Forbidden City. Then I said to Premier Zhou that I know the Forbidden City very well and that I'd like to be his tour guide! I asked him if he could spare some time to visit the Forbidden City with me. Hearing my blunt suggestion, Premier Zhou was quite delighted, laughing heartily and the people around him all laughed too!" said a delighted Puyi.

On November 10th 1963, Premier Zhou Enlai, in Beijing, received some former Nationalist Party VIPs, who had received special amnesty. Afterwards, Premier Zhou held a banquet to welcome them and their wives. Premier Zhou, Deputy Premier Chen Yi, General Du Yuming and his wife, General Zhang Zhizhong and his wife and Puyi and I sat together around a table. I can still remember that we ate southern-style Chinese food that day. Enthusiastically, Premier Zhou Enlai stood up and tried to politely pass food from the shared plate onto mine. But his right arm failed him as it had been hurt after falling from a galloping horse during the war time. He said to me apologetically, "You may have to do it yourself." I am a Hangzhou native and the humorous Premier Zhou joked with Puyi, saying "Hangzhou is the home of beauty!" I smiled, "There is beauty everywhere and I don't think that I'm beautiful."

Premier Zhou turned to Madam Cao Xiuqing, wife of General Du Yuming, who had just been reunited with her husband, after spending many years in the U.S.A. "My wife is busy today and so can't join us, but she sends her best wishes to you. How about your life now after returning from America? Congratulations on being finally reunited with your husband, Mr. Du."

Puyi even often associated with some CPC and top state leaders. Amongst them were Mr. He Changgong, Deputy Minister of the Geology Ministry, Mr. Liu Lanbo, Deputy Minister of the Water and Electricity Conservation Ministry, Mr. Zhang Xiruo, the Director of the Foreign Cultural Liaison Committee, Mr. Liao Chengzhi, the Director of the Overseas Chinese Affairs Committee and his sister Madam Liao Mengxing. They had frequently run into Puyi during state affairs and activities and had often inquired about Puyi's work, life and health.

One day, Mr. An Ziwen, the Minister of the Organization Ministry of the Central

Committee of CPC, wanted to see Puyi while he was visiting Mr. Zhang Weihan, a committee member of the CPPCC, at his home. He sent a car to take Puyi and I to see him there. Mr. An enquired of Puyi about how to write historical accounts and compile them into books. Puyi reported to him in detail. Then Mr. An analyzed the International situation of the "Cold War" at Puyi's request. Puyi had already been diagnosed with kidney cancer, but he told Mr. An that he was confident he could beat the cancer and continually serve the people. Mr. Zhang Weihan invited us have a meal with them there but Puyi politely refused and so Mr. Zhang took us home. Before parting from us, Mr. An sincerely expressed hope that Puyi would take good care of himself, so that he could spend his remaining years in happiness.

Mr. Xu Bing and Mr. Liao Mosha were the CPC's major officials in charge of the work of the United Front. They had especially cared for Puyi and offered him help, before they were imprisoned during the Cultural Revolution. (Mr. Xu Bing later took his own life whilst in prison during the Cultural Revolution.)

In one of the albums Puyi treasured, there was a group of photos taken when the United Front department organized an outing outside of Beijing. Puyi pointed out a couple in a photo, telling me that the man was the internationally-known Chinese painter, Mr. Ye Qianyu. His wife Madam Wang Renmei had been a noted Chinese film star in the 1930s. She had played the leading role in the film *The Story of a Fisherman*, which had won the "gold medal" at the 1936 Moscow Film Festival. Later, Puyi introduced me to the couple. After this, we began to know each other well and soon became firm friends.

(From left) Lian Yinong (Puyi's colleague), Puyi, Ye Qianyu (a painter) and his wife Wang Renmei (a film star) at the Fragrant Hill

While taking part in the various activities of the CPPCC, Puyi gradually came to know many celebrities, such as Mr. Liang Shuming, a distinguished philosopher, who had a deep knowledge of both Western and Chinese philosophy, Madam. Xin Fengxia, a cel-

On June 10th, 1961, Premier Zhou Enlai entertained Puyi, Pujie, Zaitao, Saga Hiro and other previous Aisin-Gioro royal clan members

ebrated Pingju Opera singer and Mr. Chen Banding, an outstanding Chinese painter and a stamp engraver. Mr. Chen had once invited Puyi and I to his home, to look at his collection of ancient paintings. He proudly told us that he had been one of the students of Mr. Wu Changshuo, a Chinese master painter and stamp engraver, of the late Qing Dynasty.

Chairman Mao Zedong had entertained Puyi several times at his home. He joked with Puyi: "Once I was your subject!" At a banquet at Mao's home, Chairman Mao introduced Puyi to an elderly man, Mr. Qiu Ao, who was a respectable founding member of the Nationalist Party. As one of the close comrades of Dr. Sun Yat-sen, he had joined the struggle to overthrow the Qing Dynasty and had held many high posts in the Nationalist Party Government. He had become a personal friend of Chairman Mao in the 1950s and later Puyi's friend as well. He once invited Puyi to join a banquet at the famous Sichuan restaurant in Rongxian Lane, with Madam Li Shuyi, an old friend of Chairman Mao Zedong. They talked happily here about ancient Chinese poetry.

In order to revise his work *The First Half of My Life—from Emperor to Citizen*, the CPPCC held several discussions, inviting many popular scholars and experts to cri-

The Last Emperor of China My Husband Puyi

tique the work. Mr. Bai Shouyi, a famous historian and Mr. Lao She, a literary master, were among them. Actually, Puyi and Lao She had met each other at banquets held earlier by Zhou Enlai.

On June 10th 1961, Premier Zhou Enlai treated Puyi, Pujie, Saga Hiro and their relatives to a banquet. He asked Puyi and Lao She, who were invited along with the other chief guests, to sit on either side of him, saying excitedly: "Mr. Lao She was also a Manchu, who had worn a 'queue*' too, during the Qing Dynasty. At that time, he would have to kneel down in the emperor's presence. Now he could sit freely at the same table with him. How wonderful the change is!" What Zhou Enlai said moved Lao She deeply. He had said to himself, even after he returned home: "An emperor and an ordinary Manchu, eating at a banquet together. This world has really changed greatly."

In 1965, both Puyi and Lao She were invited to take part in the preparations for the celebration of one hundred years since the birth of Dr. Sun Yat-sen**.

One day, when they finished their work, seeing that Puyi's car, sent by the CPPCC HQ, had not arrived, Mr. Lao She kindly invited Puyi to get into his car, sent by the Literature and Art Association, and returned Puyi back to the gate of our house first. Puyi invited Mr. Lao She to have a short rest at our home. Because both of them were Manchu and natives of Beijing, they talked on many universal topics, from the fall of the Qing Dynasty to the great changes in Beijing during the following half century. I made tea for them, enjoying their conversation. Puyi apparently admired Mr. Lao She's literary talent, while Mr. Lao She cared about Puyi's book and taught him many writing skills.

We had no housekeeper then and Mr. Lao She asked Puyi how we dealt with our housework. Puyi told him that every morning he would personally sweep our courtyard, in order to "stretch himself". He said that he tried to do washing as well, but he looked at me smilingly, "Shuxian doesn't allow me to do it, she complained that I not only couldn't do it well, but wore the clothes out, by excessive rubbing." Mr. Lao She smiled. He praised Puyi, "You have already made great progress. It's good to learn how to do some chores. I'm sure you will do it well some day." Puyi showed Mr. Lao She the rooms and the courtyard of our house. Standing in our courtyard with tall pine and

---

* It's a long braid of hair, with a distinctive circle at the back of the scalp and shaved head, worn by Chinese men in the Qing Dynasty. The "Queue" is considered the symbol of the Qing Dynasty. Zhou said this here to mean that Lao She was born during the Qing Dynasty.

** Dr. Sun Yat-sen (1866-1924), a great Chinese democratic revolutionary, a native of Canton, who had led the Xinghai Revolution to overthrow the corrupt Qing Dynasty. He was also the founder of The Republic of China, so called China's "National Father".

cypress trees, flowers and lawns, Mr. Lao She remarked how graceful our house was and how fresh the air was.

Because of his very special historical status, Puyi was often recognised by people he didn't know himself and many wanted to make friends with him. Once, Puyi became acquainted with a person on a bus, immediately hitting it off and exchanging addresses with the man. Later, Puyi dropped in on him, when he passed by his house. After returning home Puyi told me that the comrade was a man of industry and ingenuity, who enjoyed cultivating flowers and doing scientific experiments. His home was neat and beautiful. Puyi praised him: "The ordinary friend of mine has special qualities. It's hard for me to learn to do them. Now I'm aware that labourers are very intelligent people."

A scholar who researched folklore recognized Puyi in the street and immediately consulted Puyi about some questions he had on the protocols and etiquette practiced in the Forbidden City and in the Prince's Mansion. Using his own experiences, Puyi answered all of them clearly. The scholar later used those worthy firsthand materials as

Pujie and Sagaro visiting Puyi and I at our home, 1964

The Last Emperor of China My Husband Puyi

the basis for his book entitled *The Old Anecdotes of Beijing*", which became popular because of its academic and research value.

In the summer of 1964, a strange old man came to call on us at our home. He introduced himself as a dispatcher at a nearby research institute. He wanted badly to read *The First Half of My Life*, but couldn't find a copy of it anywhere. So he chose to come to our home and stated that he was sorry to inconvenience us. But unfortunately, the several copies of the book we possessed had all been lent out to Puyi's colleagues. With apologies, Puyi pledged to send a copy to the old man when one of them was returned to him. A few days later, Puyi personally sent a copy to the old man, who was touched tremendously, telling the story to everybody he met. He exclaimed, "The emperor treated me, a dispatcher, so sincerely! I would never have dreamt it, would never have dreamt it!"

Roaming in a grove of bamboo in Hangzhou with Pujie and his wife,1964

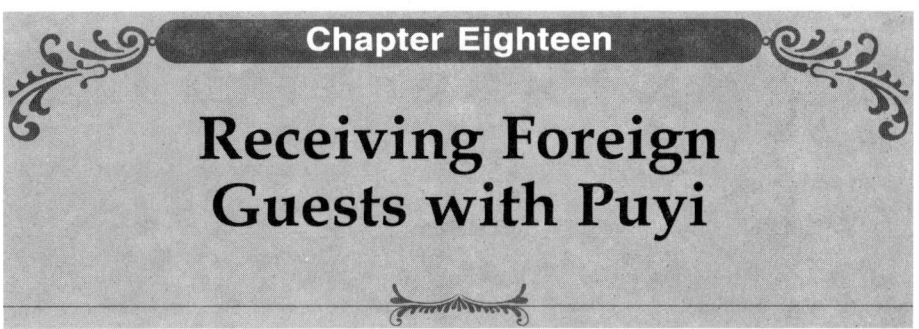

Chapter Eighteen

Receiving Foreign Guests with Puyi

Whenever foreigners visited China during the 1960s, all of them hoped to catch a glimpse of the last Chinese Emperor living in the new Socialist China. They didn't believe that a feudal emperor, with absolute power, could be changed into an ordinary citizen. Since Puyi was released and returned to Beijing, the government had arranged for him to receive many foreign guests. Espe-

Puyi meeting with a Ukrainian writer in 1960

cially during the years from 1963 to 1965, he received two to three groups of them per week and sometimes even several groups in a day. He recorded the visits in his diary. On most occasions, Puyi was taken to a hotel or the CPPCC HQ to meet them, and very often I was invited to go with him. A few of them preferred to come to our home, with me being present.

Foreign friends liked to raise questions about Puyi's life after he was released from prison, particularly his family life since our marriage in 1962. Once we met an English correspondent, who first asked questions about our family life.

"I want to know what kind of person your wife's father was. Would you mind telling me his profession?" quizzed the correspondent.

"He was a bank clerk," Puyi answered. The English correspondent instantly appeared to be very amazed:

"A former emperor married the daughter of an ordinary clerk. It's inconceivable in our country! Inconceivable!"

The Last Emperor of China **My Husband Puyi**

Puyi meeting with Edgar Snow, a world famous American journalist, 1960

"Now I'm a citizen," Puyi said. He didn't think it was amazing.

"Doesn't your wife work every day?" asked the Englishman.

"Yes, she works in a hospital, as a nurse."

"Very interesting, I think that only now you are living like a real family."

Puyi appreciated his evaluation. The English correspondent excitedly talked about the life of the English aristocracy. He mentioned how the Duke of Windsor abdicated his throne to marry a divorced American lady. It had stirred the world in the 1930s and Puyi himself also remembered it. But he didn't think that his marriage with me, after he became a citizen, was related to the Duke of Windsor's marriage. He said: "I can understand the Duke of Windsor's desire to marry the lady he really loved. He wanted a harmonious and happy home life, not just a family for show. It wasn't because I gave up my throne that I am now fortunate and have a warm and happy home life, it is because I became a citizen."

On May 22nd 1963, Puyi received Mr. Abe, from Hokkaido, Japan. He was a congressman elected by the Japanese Free and Democratic Party. He asked Puyi the same question from another angle.

"As an Emperor of China, you were served by many people before. Now it's different, don't you think it's inconvenient?"

Puyi answered him: "Not in the least. From birth, I 'lived in a bubble'. Unfortunately, I never learned how to take care of myself like a real person. I was 'like a flower growing in a large greenhouse', protected from the wind and rain, and my irregular life made me vulnerable. So it was the servitude of others that destroyed me."

Puyi went on: "After returning from Russia, for the first time in my life, I lived life in a group and learned to do morning exercises. Slowly, I became stronger. When I married last year, my friends suggested that we needed a housekeeper, but both my wife and I opposed the idea, even though housework was not something we looked forward to. We decided to do it ourselves. Now we enjoy a happy home life, and I have a much better mood than in the times when I was the puppet emperor in Changchun. I think that this is because I am an ordinary citizen now, without my previous worries."

Puyi told Abe that he was in fact controlled by others when he was emperor and had no freedom. Although he was born and grew up in Beijing, he had no any idea what the city of Beijing looked like. Particularly after becoming "Emperor Kangde" in 1932, he was controlled completely by the Japanese Imperialists and even had no right to see his father, siblings or relatives. Only in the second half of his life, when he was an ordinary citizen, had he become really free and happy.

Mr. Abe was moved considerably by Puyi's sincere words. To Puyi, a former "Son of Heaven", he laid bare his true feelings like this: "I was shocked by what you said. I must admit I was still feudal. Originally I was uneasy when I talked with you, for you were the former Emperor while I am an ordinary citizen. But I gradually found that you really treated me well in the status of a citizen. I recovered from the anxiety. Thank you very much!"

In just a few years, Puyi received several hundred foreign guests. His life and work in Socialist China influenced people all over the world. As far as I know, many of them were touched by his talks. A Japanese friend published an article with the title "A Miracle". It was about his own feelings while visiting Puyi.

A correspondent from Ghana once said that it was much easier for westerners to understand Puyi than Lei Feng (a model soldier of that time).

A French correspondent said to Puyi after their talk, "Now you have obtained your true identity. The work you

Puyi receiving Japanese reporters, October 11th, 1964

have done has made a great contribution to your country, and your book has influenced the world."

The book by Puyi, mentioned by this French correspondent, was *The First Half of my Life*. A correspondent from Hong Kong commented on the book by saying, "The story is a miracle and the book is a miracle too."

Many foreign friends adamantly requested the Chinese government to translate the book into their own languages. A friend from Chile expressed the hope to translate it into Spanish. Many readers of the book wrote to Puyi from various places of China and other countries. The CPPCC HQ had to appoint an official to help Puyi deal with the volume of letters. Four months later, he wrote a report about his work to his superior. It said, "Since Puyi started working at the CPPCC HQ, he has received many letters, and after the book was published the number increased tremendously.

Puyi meeting with a correspondent (left) from Hong kong

Of those from home, some consulted Puyi concerning Qing Dynasty antiques, or invited him to speak about his experiences in public. Some wanted to get Puyi's calligraphy, some hoped Puyi would send them the book, others asked Puyi to find jobs for them and some even hoped to serve Puyi at his side. The letters from abroad mostly wanted to get Puyi's signature on a photo. One letter requested Puyi to give his reason for amending the account about himself in the Book of *Who's Who?*"

A correspondent from Pakistan suggested to Puyi: "You are the first person in the world to change from emperor to citizen. You should travel to every country, telling all the modern emperors and kings that it's not good to be an emperor." Puyi had no opportunity to go abroad then. But later, his book spread as if it had wings, over mountains, seas and boundaries, in fact all over of the world!

Chapter Nineteen

The Publishing of the "Earth Shattering" Book

Before the Spring Festival of 1964, after learning that Puyi's monthly salary was only a hundred yuan while attending an educational forum, Chairman Mao Zedong stated that it was his intention to donate money from his own income, being part of the "contribution" from the books he had published himself. Mao wanted to improve Puyi's living standards. At the same time, Puyi was about to receive a substantial amount of money from the publication of his own book *The First Half of My Life*, which was published in March 1964.

Puyi amending his memoir in his office, 1962

Whilst dating me Puyi had never stopped revising the manuscript of *The First Half of My Life*. Clearly, he was very interested in doing this. He told me that he hoped to be a useful person to the country and the people by writing a memoir, which he felt was within his scope and ability. Sometimes, he took me with him when he went to the Masses Publishing House to seek advice on writing his book.

After we were married, Puyi spent a lot of time revising his work. In the evenings he was often hunched over his desk working until midnight. I couldn't sleep with the light on, and I would say to him that he had better go to sleep earlier and that going to sleeping too late would hurt his health. Hearing this he would smilingly coax me to go to sleep alone to let him get on with it.

From daily conversations, I gradually started to understand why he wrote his memoir and how he did it. As early as 1957, the authorities of the Fushun War Criminal Prison (FWCP) suggested to the prisoners there that they each write down their own history. Puyi, through the several years of being re-educated, had already realized that in the first half of his life, he really had committed crimes against his country and people. He was determined to write down his experiences in the first half of the century, especially the process of changing from emperor to citizen. He personally made the title of it *The First Half of My Life*.

Puyi's decision pleased the authorities of the FWCP. To help Puyi focus on the major events, they appointed Pujie to record his narration and Mr. Ruan Zhenduo, the former Foreign Minister of the Manchukuo, to collect suitable material for him. Simultaneously, they sent their officials to the Liaoning Provincial Library to consult the information about the period from the late Qing Dynasty to the Manchukuo for Puyi and they also provided him with useful material, written by the former Ministers of the Manchukuo.

From the second half of 1957 to the end of 1958, Puyi carefully wrote his memoir using almost 500,000 characters. It was structured chronologically from the origins of his family to the emotional visits organized by the FWCP in 1957. These included visits to factories, mines, schools and agricultural collective farms in northeast China. But at that time, he never imagined that he would publish it publically. He had hoped to leave behind records of his personal experiences to later generations. So, he wrote it with true emotion and criticizing himself openly and honestly, showing his sincerity by confessing his previous evil ways.

On December 14th 1959, in the Great Hall of the People, Premier Zhou Enlai gladly received Puyi and the other members of the first group of the war criminals who had just been granted special amnesty by the government. When he inquired of Puyi about his reflections on the "remoulding", Puyi reported to him that he had written a memoir including his ten years of remoulding. Premier Zhou immediately asked Puyi whether or not he had the memoir manuscript with him and requested that Puyi revise it thoroughly and give the revised edition to him to read, as early as possible.

Puyi was very grateful for Premier Zhou's concern for him. He told

Puyi writing his memoir at Fushun War Criminal Prison

Premier Zhou Enlai receiving Puyi and Zaitao at CPPCC HQ

Premier Zhou that he alone knew that ten sets of the manuscript had been mimeographed by fellow war criminals in Fushun Prison and that they were still stored there. Very quickly, Puyi wrote to Mr. Jin Yuan, the Governor of the FWCP, telling him the good news that he and other released war criminals had been received by Premier Zhou and according to Premier Zhou's instructions, he would start to revise his memoir manuscript, written while he was in Fushun Prison. In order to do this, Puyi stressed that he would need Mr. Jin's help in editing his book.

In reality, Puyi didn't know that the mimeographed manuscript of his memoirs had already passed through the thick security walls of the FWCP and were now with the Ministry of Public Security, the United Front Work Department of the Central Committee of the CPC and the CPPCC HQ. Before long, Mr. Xu Bing, the Deputy Director of the UFW Department of the Central Committee of the CPC, ordered that the manuscript be divided into three volumes and then for 400 copies of the unfinished version to be printed professionally.

These were issued to all the members of the Central Committee of the CPC. At the same time, Mr. Qi Yanming, the Deputy Secretary General of the State Council, approved the suggestion of the State Public Security and the CPPCC HQ, to instruct the Masses Publishing House to print 7,000 copies of the manuscript, in two volumes of A4 sized pages with grey covers. They were confined to release within the governmental, law and historical circles, in order to solicit constructive criticism from the officials and academics.

Mao Zedong, Zhou Enlai, Peng Zhen and other top leaders of the CPC gladly read the printed manuscript. These were the first memoirs written by a Chinese emperor. They all gave their honest opinions to Puyi and urged him to keep working on his book.

On January 26th 1960, while receiving Puyi and his relatives, Premier Zhou praised Puyi's courage to "declare war" against the feudal society and to expose his constant attempt to restore the Qing Dynasty, thus creating the miracle of changing emperor to a citizen. But he also said, "I think there is too much self-criticism in it. Let past be past." Premier Zhou requested Puyi to revise it again to improve it. From what Premier Zhou said, Puyi already understood the need to revise it.

Soon after this meeting with Premier Zhou, Puyi received his memoir manuscript in three volumes under the title of *The First Half of My Life*. Its front cover had "unfinalised" written on the right upper corner of it. He read the original version and, in confusion, wrote to Mr. Jin Yuan again in February 1960 for further clarification:

Front cover of the English translation of *The First Half of My Life*

I have a matter to discuss with you. Recently the UFW Department sent me a set of my printed memoirs, **The First Half of My Life**. *But I found that it didn't include my later addition to it. Do you think that it needs this addition? If so, would you mind adding my later addition to it? Or otherwise just send it to me and I will do it myself. Please write to me when you have time, telling me your opinion, so that this matter can be dealt with.*

Of course, Puyi himself was still unsatisfied with the revised memoir manuscript. He had not only hoped to add the late addition to it, but wanted to revise it further according to Premier Zhou's instructions and to also include his experiences from 1957 to the time when he and others received special amnesty, at the end of 1959.

The task to improve the manuscript was given to the Masses Publishing House, which belonged to the Ministry of Public Security (MPS). A major official of the CPPCC personally took Puyi to see Mr. Yao Gen, its Editor-in-Chief. Several days later, Mr. Ling Yun, Deputy Minister of the MPC and in charge of all the war criminal prisons in

China, treated Puyi to a banquet at the famous Quanjude Peking Duck Restaurant with Mr. Yao Gen and Mr. Li Wenda, Director of Literature and Art also being present. They decided that Mr. Li Wenda would help him improve his manuscript.

Later on, Mr. Li Wenda told others that in fact he had then been very depressed because he had just been discharged from the department in charge of confidential work and transferred to the Masses Publishing House for political reasons. Fortunately, because he was a veteran Communist Party member and had been a correspondent of the New 4th Army during the "The War of Japanese Aggression" and had already published some influential literary works and thus was considered well versed in literature. Therefore, he was chosen by Mr. Yao Gen to do the task.

At the end of April 1960, it was arranged that Mr. Li Wenda to live at the Xiangshan Hotel, near the Beijing Botanical Garden, to begin helping Puyi revise his memoir manuscript. For two and a half months, every morning, Puyi still worked in the Botanical Gardens. After lunch, he would go to the Xiangshan Hotel to revise his memoir manuscript with the help of Mr. Li Wenda. First, they reduced the self-criticizing sections, then re-organised some sentences, and added new information about his life, from 1957 until the special amnesty. Also included was the account of Puyi being received and entertained by Premier Zhou Enlai. Finally, they improved the rhetoric of the whole memoir manuscript.

But both of them were still unsatisfied when they read through the revised memoir manuscript of about 200,000 characters. After exchanging their views about its contents and sorting its chapters they believed that the major events needed further investigation and confirmation and that the process of Puyi's ideological change should be written clearly into the book. Therefore they put forward a proposal to the authorities of the MPS, to visit northeast China, where Puyi had lived from 1932-1945, to do "hands on research" by meeting with people who had experienced what happened and to view relevant historical archives. They wanted to use the most accurate historical facts that they could find. They were promptly granted permission concerning their suggestion.

Mr. Li Wenda and another official arrived in Fushun in August 1960, and travelled to the War Criminal Prison. Here they met with many former high-ranking "Manchukuo" officials and talked with governors, prison officials, administrative staff, doctors, nurses and even cooks, to find out about Puyi's re-education there. They reviewed documents written by Puyi during various periods of incarceration there, which demonstrated clear changes in Puyi's ideology. Afterwards, they went to Changchun and Harbin to visit Madam Li Yuqin, Puyi's fourth wife. At the same time in Beijing, Puyi "racked his brains" to recall passed events. Luckily, Puyi always kept the habit of

The Last Emperor of China My Husband Puyi

Li Yuqin, one of the insiders of the first half of Puyi's life, providing reliable information concerning the writing of Puyi's memoir, 1960

keeping a diary.

Even during "the Manchukuo" period, while being watched by Japanese spies, he had never stopped writing it. But, unfortunately, before the collapse of "the Manchukuo", Puyi had ordered his entourage to burn all of his diaries, written between 1932 and 1945, because in them, he had written many complaints about his Japanese boss. Puyi feared that the Japanese would not forgive him if they discovered it. At the same time, Puyi burnt his photos and documentary films about his official activities and daily life, which had been stored in the basement of his office. "I did this not out of fear of the Japanese, but in order to eliminate the traces of my crimes," he said later. But he never expected that he would need them twenty years later, when he wrote his memoirs. Fortunately, Puyi had a good memory. Even Premier Zhou once lauded him, stating that Puyi had a wide learning and a sharp mind. To confirm some historical events, Puyi went to visit the "insiders", such as his nephews, younger brothers, brothers-in-law, his former English translator, former Eunuch-in-Chief, as well as several other living eunuchs, in order to get useful material and clues. Librarians of the Beijing Botanical Garden recalled that Puyi was meticulous concerning the writing of memoirs, which included consulting all of the historical books available in the library.

To assist Puyi's revision of his memoir manuscript, the Ming and Qing Sections of the Central Archives broke its rule, and for the first time, opened up some of its original archives, which were from the late Qing Dynasty to Puyi's "Little Court" (from 1911-1932) including his life in Tianjin. Among them were the letters and memorials of the famous survivors of the bygone Qing Dynasty, such as Mr. Chen Baoshen, Mr. Zheng Xiaoxu, Mr. Zhang Xun, Mr. Luo Zhenyu, Mr. Kang Youwei and Mr. Reginald Johnston, to name but a few. The records about Puyi's communications with the Republic Government, Puyi's compositions and diaries written in his younger years, the notes written in Chinese and English by himself, Wanrong, Wenxiu and his siblings (which they all sent to each other when they played games while living in the Forbid-

Yixuan (1840-1891), the first generation Prince Chun (Puyi's grandfather) with his wife, who was the younger sister of Empress Dowager Cixi

den City), Puyi's unpublished cartoons, calligraphy and painting works and even his exercise-books used for practicing calligraphy—all truly showed his life of boyhood and youth.

Puyi looked up quite a lot of Chinese and foreign newspapers, magazines and pictorials, and even English, Japanese and Chinese books about his life which had been published all over the world. For the first time he read the diary of Regent Zaifeng (1884-1951), his real father, which was preserved by Mr. Puren, his fourth younger brother.

Accompanied by Mr. Shi Shuqing, a renowned historian and expert on cultural relics, Puyi went to the Chinese Historical Museum to read the diary of Mr. Zheng Xiaoxu, a famous scholar and one of Puyi's tutors. As an insider of those historical records, Puyi perused them, only using the real sections, as he wanted to present his readers with an accurate and realistic memoir.

In *the First half of my Life*, there is a whole chapter about Mr. Reginald Johnston, a Scottish gentleman who later went on to become Lord Johnston, who influenced Puyi greatly. In February 1919, Puyi was only 14 years old when Mr. Johnston was

The Last Emperor of China My Husband Puyi

Zaifeng (1884-1951), the second generation Prince Chun, Puyi's father, and his wife, Youlan, who was Puyi's birth mother invited to the Forbidden City, to teach him English. Five years later, when Puyi moved to Tianjin, he appointed Mr. Johnston to manage the Summer Palace. Afterwards, by the orders of the British Government, Mr. Johnston stayed in China, first to handle the matters relating to the "Boxer Uprising" then to take up the post of the Commissioner of the British-leased territory of Weihaiwei, from 1927-1930. He visited Puyi in Tianjin many times and later even went to Changchun, to see Puyi. While in China, he always kept in close contact with Puyi.

Puyi's father, Regent Zaifeng

After returning to Britain, Mr. Johnston wrote a book entitled *Twilight in the Forbidden City*, telling of his unforgettable times in China. But later Puyi wondered if some comments in Mr. Johnston's book were completely accurate. Puyi wanted to write into his book realistic accounts of some of the events. In Puyi's notebook he quoted a lot of Lord Johnston's original texts, then clarified them point by point, stressing that he wanted to depict the history correctly because it was his duty as an "insider of the events" and as a "Commissioner of the Historical Account of Past Events".

In the third chapter of *The First Half of My Life*, Puyi wrote about the internal conflict in his "Little Court" concerning his decision to study abroad. To retain the "Articles of Favourable Treatment" (see Preface) and their own positions, all of the princes and ministers had opposed Puyi's plan to study abroad. But Puyi was anxious to go because he was already aware of, and concerned about, the possibility of the abolition, at some stage, of the "the Articles of Favourable Treatment" by the Republic Government. To safeguard himself and open a new road to "restore the Great Qing Dynasty", Puyi, with guidance from a close friend and a relative's cooperation, secretly got in touch with a foreign ambassador. They drew up a plan to escape from the Forbidden City. However, Prince Chun (Puyi's father) and other ministers and princes discovered the plan, and prevented him from leaving.

The Last Emperor of China My Husband Puyi

After Puyi was transferred to the CPPCC HQ in the spring of 1961, every morning he went to the Masses Publishing House and in a small room, he revised his book with Mr. Li Wenda. In June 1962, the revised memoir manuscript was printed, in three volumes, using a large font of characters, the Chinese writing form. They were sent to relevant branches of the government for soliciting opinions, and four months later, the further revised memoir manuscript, also using a large font of characters, was printed again for another solicitation of opinions.

In November of 1962, in a seminar about his memoir manuscript, Puyi listened attentively to all the comments about his work from some of the most distinguished scholars and writers in China, such as Mr. Jian Bozan, Mr. Shao Xunzheng, Mr. He Ganzhi, Mr. Hou Wailu, Mr. Li Kan, Mr. Liu Danian, etc. Later, Mr. Lao She presented his opinions concerning the memoir manuscript and personally approved it.

The First Half of My Life was finally published in December 1962. It quickly stirred attention at home and abroad. Puyi knew that his success was the result of Premier Zhou's encouragement and the support of people from all circles of life. He was eternally grateful to those distinguished scholars, experts and many unknown people for their sincere help. Therefore, he magnanimously shared his contribution fee with them.

Puyi meeting with the Japanese Emperor Hirohito during his first visit to Japan in 1935

The First Half of My Life was a very unique book. It showed a former emperor's personal life experience, and featured his "ideological remoulding", which changed him from an emperor to a citizen. Other people helped Puyi collect materials for his writing, but none of them had the ability to write the process of how he underwent his re-education as realistically as he. I was impressed to see how eagerly he pushed ahead to write the book and I'd like to let the reading pubic know this.

Chapter Twenty
The Tour to Southeast China

From March 10th to April 29th 1964, as members of a tour group organized by the CPPCC HQ (The CPPCC Tour Group), Puyi and I journeyed to six provinces which were Jiangsu, Zhejiang, Anhui, Jiangxi, Hunan and Hubei, plus the city of Shanghai. They are all located in the middle to lower reaches and delta areas of the Yangtze River, and they are also the most economically and culturally developed parts of China. During the

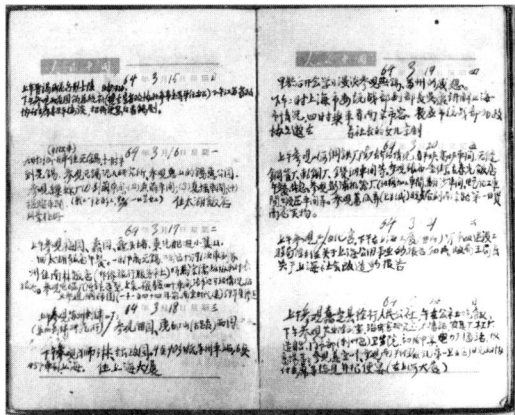

Puyi's diary showing his tour to southeast China between March and April, 1964

period of fifty days, we visited twenty-three factories, four people's communes, a university, an astronomical observatory, a hydro-electric power station, the Jinggang Mountain (which had once been a revolutionary base), the Shaoshan Mountain (Chairman Mao's hometown), and a lot of other scenic spots and historical sites.

It was Premier Zhou Enlai, who had personally arranged this tour. On November 10th 1963, Premier Zhou entertained the four groups of released war crimes prisoners (WCP) and their wives. After the banquet, he gladly announced that the following year, when spring had arrived and the flowers were in bloom, the CPPCC HQ would send all of them on tours to visit both the southeastern and northwestern areas of China, so as to observe the progress made in these regions since 1949.

At the beginning of March 1964, Mr. Zhang Zhiyi the Secretary General of the CPPCC, invited Puyi and other released WCPs to a meal at the CPPCC HQ. At that time, he formally announced that the CPPCC Tour Group would be led by Mr. Chen Cisheng and Mr. Lian Yinong, two high-ranking officials of the CPPCC and would be reported on by several reporters from some State newspaper offices and news agencies. Be-

The Last Emperor of China My Husband Puyi

At Plum Blossom Hill, Nanjing

cause its members consisted of former Emperor Puyi, Prince Pujie, Generals and Chancellors, the group was nicknamed "The Emperor, Prince, General and Chancellor Tour Group".

On March 10th, at 9:30 am the CPPCC HQ sent a bus to pick us up from our homes. Although I had a small cold, I was excited. Puyi felt terrific, gesticulating with hands and feet like a little boy. He told me that it would be his first opportunity to visit southern China. We entrusted Madam Yunying, Puyi's third younger sister and her husband to take care of our home. They said goodbye to us as we happily boarded the bus to arrive in plenty of time at the Beijing Railway Station.

Puyi and I, Mr. Song Xilian, honeymooning with his new wife, shared a room in a soft-berth carriage. We spent our first day on the train chatting happily, while appreciating the pretty landscape outside the window. The next morning, when the bright and beautiful rays of the sun were shining in the windows, we realized that outside, the vast wintry northern plains with the remaining ice and snow had almost completely been replaced overnight, by the enchanting spring scenery of southern China.

We arrived at Nanjing, one of the six ancient capitals of China (and which had been the Republican capital under the Nationalists between 1911 and 1949). As honoured guests of the local People's Political Consultative Conference (PPCC), we were sent to stay at the luxurious Fuchang Hotel. The following days, we visited Dr. Sun Yat-sen's Mausoleum. We also toured around the Linggu Temple, Plum Blossom Hill, Xuanwu Lake, the Purple-Gold Mountain Astronomical Observatory and the Fuzi Temple (Temple of Confucius).

At a small pavilion in front of the Plum Blossom Hill, Puyi heard that Wang Jingwei, the notorious traitor and collaborator with Japanese Imperialists had been buried there. He immediately asked those around, "Where is the tomb? Why was it destroyed later? What kind of funeral relics did it have?" We were informed that Wang had been buried there secretly by his family in November 1944 and that later, in 1946, Chiang Kai-shek had the tomb dynamited. But because it was not reported officially, Puyi had no idea about it. Surprised, he kept asking questions about it. Afterwards Puyi got the nickname "Meishiwen", meaning questioner of all things.

Seeing that I hadn't recovered from my cold, sometimes Puyi would advise me to stay at the hotel to rest. One day he didn't find me in our room after he returned. He became anxious and ran out to tell Mr. Zhou Zhenqiang that I was lost. Mr. Zhou immediately accompanied him, going to look for me in several streets. They eventually found me in a shop. Puyi grabbed hold of my hand when he saw me. I told them that I had been bored at the hotel, so went out to have a look around. On our way back to our hotel, Puyi never loosened his grip on my hand. It seemed as if he never wanted to let me go.

In the State-run Nanjing Chemical Industry Company, employing more than ten-thousand people, we were shown its worker's living quarters, one of its Primary Schools and a Kindergarten (for the staff's children). In the kindergarten, Puyi, who always loved kids, was fascinated by the vivacious and innocent children. He bent down to praise their wonderful song and dance show, asking them, "How old are you?" "Would you mind telling me your name?" When we all walked away, he was still reluctant to part from the children.

I remembered hearing from my father about the famous "Fuzi

At Chiang Kai-shek's office, in the Nationalist Party Presidential Palace, in Nanjing

The Last Emperor of China My Husband Puyi

At Zijinshan astronomical observatory in Nanjing

Temple (Temple of Confucius)". He had said that it had been a place filled with prostitutes, sing-song girls, gamblers and hooligans. Out of curiosity Puyi and I went to have a look. But in the meantime, it had more recently become a "Holy Place" to commemorate Confucius. The street outside its gate was lined with shops, selling souvenirs and local delicacies. We bought some souvenirs for our relatives and friends, as well as a big bag of rice dumplings (some with sweet and some with meat stuffing). Puyi smiled, "It's too much for the two of us to eat!" I knew it too, but I enjoyed the abundance.

Along the pebble path we reached the bank of the nearby Qinhuai River. Leaning on a balustrade, we chatted with some local people who lived on the wooden boats with fleabane shelters. On our way back to our hotel, Puyi couldn't help chanting, in low voice, the popular poem *Moored on River Qinhuai* by Mr. Du Mu, once one of the most distinguished poets of the Tang Dynasty (618-907).

At the former Nationalist Party Presidential Palace

Cold water veiled in mist and shores in dim moonlight,
I moored on River Qinhuai near wine shops at night,
Where songsters knowing not the grief of conquered land,
Still sing the songs composed by a captive ruler's hand.

At the Humble Administrator's Garden, Suzhou

He said to himself in a voice I could hear, "I'm sure that the Fuzi Temple and the Qinhuai River will never end up like the song."

In the morning of our last day in Nanjing, we paid a visit to Yuhuatai Revolutionary Martyrs' Cemetery* and were deeply grieved from that experience. Puyi and some members of our group stood in silent tribute in front of the tall memorial, which had been erected for the revolutionary martyrs, who were killed there. The memorial was surrounded by wreaths. They also took photos there as souvenirs. During that afternoon, we went to visit the Western Flower Garden and the former Nationalist Party Presidential Palace. Contrary to Puyi's expectations, Chiang Kai-shek's office was not huge. It

At Yuhuatai Revolutionary Martyr's Cemetery in Nanjing

---

* Yuhuatai Revolutionary Martyrs' Cemetery is a place where many communists were killed by the Nationalist Party Government between 1927 and 1949.

The Last Emperor of China My Husband Puyi

was at the end of his residence, with a Reception Room outside, which was only about seven square metres in size. Puyi was surprised: "Chiang Kai-shek's office was so small!" he expressed. We had a photo taken together in the reception room, with me sitting on the single sofa and Puyi sitting on the armrest.

Our second stop was Wuxi, a charming tourist city. Its Taihu Lake is one of the most beautiful lakes in China. In Wuxi, we excitedly visited the Plum Hill, Liyuan Garden, Turtle Head Island Park, and finally, visited a small island in the center of the picturesque Taihu Lake. Our guide explained

With Mr. Du Yuming and his wife at the Pagoda of Six Harmonies, Hangzhou

about the grotesque rockeries situated by the lake: "The rockeries in the Taihu Lake are slender and elegantly riddled with holes, rich in curves and lines on the surface. Being porous in substance, water passes up or down, distributing the moisture evenly." Puyi

At Huxin Park, West Lake, in Hangzhou

wrote down in his notebook some of the things that the guide had said and also observed and measured the rockeries, to see whether or not they were just like what the guide had described. As it suddenly dawned on him, he commented that there was no wonder many emperors sent masons to quarry the grotesque rockeries in Taihu Lake. It was in order to make artificial-miniature hills in the gardens of their own Royal Palaces. "The rockeries in the Taihu Lake are really fantastic!"

We were also taken to visit the Huishan Clay Figurine Workshop. I was attracted by the colourful, beautifully-shaped, clay figurines. It was not only good artistic work, but they were also used as a popular toy in China. Puyi happily bought several lovely clay models for me, as souvenirs.

Next, we travelled to Suzhou by the Grand Canal. With its great fame resting on its availability of silk and landscaped gardens, Suzhou is called "a paradise on earth", situated near the mouth of the Yangtze River. While touring the Humble Administrator's Garden, Lingering Garden, Lion Grove and Tiger Hill, Puyi praised their fascinating beauty profusely.

Embroidery is a kind of traditional folk art with quite a long history in China and the embroidered articles made in Suzhou are considered to be the best. In the Suzhou Embroidery Research Institute, we were shown the complicated process of how to embroider. Puyi especially loved the two-sided embroidery, as both sides were com-

At Wuxi Huishan Clay Figurine Workshop

At the Hydroelectric Power Station on the Xin'an River

pletely identical! Puyi was crazy about it and wanted to touch it with his hand, but was told that he couldn't touch it, otherwise the surface would become damaged. Reluctantly, Puyi smiled and pulled back his hand. Ms. Jin, the Director, had come to welcome us. As early as the 1940s, she had already been a distinguished embroiderer and in the 1950s, she had been invited to head the Embroidery Research Institute. She had offered to pass on her superb skills to her students, and had also been elected as the local People's Congress Representative. By Puyi's request, she patiently explained the principles of embroidery. Our guide commented that Comrade Jin had been invited many times to other countries, in order to demonstrate her excellent embroidery skills at exhibitions. Many foreign ladies admired her and often asked to touch her nimble hands. Puyi was so moved that he couldn't help touching and stroking Ms. Jin's hands. This made her embarrassed, but Puyi hadn't realized that she would feel that way.

During the several days in Shanghai, we were scheduled to see the Huangpu River, on iron and steel plant, a chemical factory, a printing and dyeing mill, a plastic product factory, a ball-bearing factory, a People's Commune, a worker's club, the Youth Palace, etc. Puyi especially appreciated the remarkable transformation of Fangua Lane, previously a notorious slum, but which had more recently been changed into a respectable working class residential area.

In Shanghai, Puyi and I didn't forget to tour the national popular "Yong'an", "Xinxin",

"Daxin" and "Xianshi" department stores, which are concentrated on the Nanjing Road, China's largest shopping centre at that time. Puyi always went to the children's sections! He loved buying toys such as toy pistols, masks, etc. "You need a pair of leather shoes!" I reminded him. "I like toys!" he replied. Since I knew he loved children's games, I didn't comment any further!

Puyi was always ecstatic on our tour. Sometimes he would get carried away and would even laugh at himself. Once in the dining hall of the Shanghai Mansion, we were served a dish of delicious fish. It suited Puyi's taste and he gladly devoured it as if there was nobody else present. But suddenly a piece of fish bone got caught in his throat. Our doctor had a hard time trying to remove it. Puyi humourously comforted those who worried about him by saying: "It's a pleasure when the stuck fish bone finally comes out!" I knew that for him to say those words, that it must have already been removed.

I still missed the Jing'ansi Road (now the Nanjingxi Road), the place where I had lived in my childhood. One day, when others went to enjoy an acrobatic show, Puyi and I went there, wandering along the entire road. I told Puyi of my early life on that road. He listened to me attentively, saying: "How nice it would be if your parents were still alive! I'm sure they would be very glad to see us."

At "Three Pools Mirroring the Moon", West Lake, Hangzhou

The Last Emperor of China — My Husband Puyi

I went to find my former neighbours there, but all of them had already moved away. It was nearly midnight, when we finally returned to our hotel by motortricycle.

From Shanghai we went to Hangzhou, my hometown. It was about 10 o'clock in the evening, when we got to the Hangzhou Hotel, alongside the West Lake. The tranquil and pretty night scenery of the West Lake made me recall my childhood in Hangzhou. My last impression of Hangzhou was in 1933, when my father had taken me for a return visit there. I could still remember the worn walls alongside the West Lake, which had since been removed. Puyi was excited too: "Who could expect so many changes? I could never have come to your hometown if there had been no changes!"

With Mr. Li Jue and his wife at "Viewing Fish at Flower Harbor", West Lake, Hangzhou

Next morning, before breakfast, Puyi and Mr. Lian Yinong and some other members of our group decided that we should visit the Yue Fei* Temple, to the side of the West Lake. Puyi had wanted to visit it for a long time. In the afternoon, on the West Lake, we boarded small boats, paddled by boatmen. Puyi and I, Mr. Du Yuming and his wife, Pujie and his wife and a reporter sat in the same boat. We were joyously chatting and laughing while enjoying the enchanted landscape of the world famous West Lake. Someone read loudly, with expression, a popular poem written by Su Shi, a great poet of the Song Dynasty, about the West Lake:

Drinking on the West Lake
Drizzling after Sunshine
The Sun plays on the waters, the scene is brilliant,
The drizzling mist of the mountains is also a grand sight.
Comparing West Lake to 'West Beauty,'
(Hangzhou being the 'Home of beautiful women')

---

* Yue Fei was a national hero during the Song Dynasty (960-1279), admired by everybody in China.

Both are charming, in light make-up as well as in bright make-up.

That afternoon, we toured the West Lake, Su Causeway, Bai Causeway, Solitary Hill, Three Pools Mirroring the Moon, Fish Wander at Flower Crook, Baoshu Pagoda, etc. At each place Puyi, with great interest, would ask me, a native of Hangzhou, to tell him its history. We also visited the tomb of Madam Qiu Jin (1877-1907), "China's Distinguished Lady Revolutionary". She had been beheaded by the Qing Government, after the Insurrection in which she led to overthrow the Qing Dynasty had failed.

Puyi was filled with deep respect for her: "Qiu Jin was a great 'Lady Revolutionary', who was killed by the Qing Government, three years before I came to the throne," he said. Not far away is the tomb of Su Xiaoxiao. Although a well-known prostitute, she was however, also a talented woman.

After dinner that day, we invited Mr. Song Xilian and his wife, to tour the flourishing downtown area. Hangzhou was a clean city, with several very active business districts, where the shops opened until midnight, selling delicious local products such as small walnuts, sesame slices and Longjing Tea.

On the third day in Hangzhou, Puyi went with the group to see the Hydroelectric Power Station on the Xin'an River, but I stayed at the hotel for I was too tired. The next

In the tea garden, Meijiawu Production Brigade, Hangzhou

The Last Emperor of China My Husband Puyi

At West Lake, Hangzhou in 1964

day we went via the West Lake to the Meijiawu Production Brigade, the West Lake People's Commune, and the place where the world-famous "Longjing Tea" was grown. The enthusiastic farmers picked the best tea leaves from their tea gardens to make tea for us. It tasted great and looked nice, thus earning the reputation it enjoyed. Mr. Lu Zhenhao, the Director of the Commune, briefed us about the Commune. He also talked about the changes in his own family. Before the Liberation in 1949, his father, an honest farmer, had his own

One of Puyi's diaries

farmland repossessed by a powerful landlord because he owed him money on a high-interest loan, so he finally died of depression. Not long after that, his mother was beaten by a tyrant and died too. Suffering greatly, little Lu Zhenhao had to take his younger brothers and sisters, roaming about everywhere, as beggars. Hearing this, Puyi shed sympathetic tears. When Mr. Lu finished his introduction, Puyi took out his notebook, asking Mr. Lu to leave his signature. Then we were taken to see tea picking in action. In the tea garden, I had a photo taken with Mr. Lu's wife. Finally, we went to see some farmers' homes where we found that most of the families had radios, sewing-machines and attractive furniture.

A picture taken in front of the laughing Buddha in Lingyin Temple in Hangzhou

While in Hangzhou, we also had a brief visit to the Lingyin Temple, Jade Spring Hill, Yellow Dragon Cave and Jinci Temple. In the Yellow Dragon Cave, marked by zigzagging paths, Puyi and I played "hide and seek".

On April 2nd, we left for Huangshan Mountain in Anhui Province. Mr. Lian Yinong, our tour leader, was kind enough to invite me to travel in his car, preventing me from being jolted in the coach. We reached the Huangshan Mountain Hotel that night.

Huangshan Mountain, with 72 steep peaks, is considered to be the most beautiful mountain in China. It displays green pines, grotesque rockeries, clouds vast like a sea and hot springs, which are called "The Four Treasures of Huangshan". I had no energy to climb the steep slopes so only wanted to stay at the hotel. Puyi, deserving a taste of the charming landscapes of Mt. Huangshan, was brave enough to do some climbing and take some photos there. After returning, only having had a short rest, Puyi changed into swimming trunks and relaxed in the Hot Spring's Bathing Pool.

On our last day at the Huangshan Mountain, two Deputy Chairmen from Anhui Province's Department of the People's Political Consultative Conference (PPCC) came by plane to treat all the members of our group to a banquet, so that we could enjoy the famous local "Hui flavour" food. Before

At Huangshan Mountain

The Last Emperor of China My Husband Puyi

Under Wuhan Yangtze River Bridge, April, 1964

With a local farmer, at Mt. Jinggangshan

the banquet, they received Puyi and me and other commissioners with their wives, to convey their warm welcome to us.

After visiting Huangshan Mountain, we returned to Hangzhou, and then went on to Nanchang, the capital of Jiangxi Province. At the "August 1st Uprising" Headquarters, Puyi was interested in the conference room, where Zhou Enlai, Ye Ting, He Long, Zhu De, Liu Bocheng and others had discussed the strategic matters concerning the Uprising, as well as viewing the relevant photos, documents and other exhibits concerned with the uprising. We were also taken to see General He Long's Memorial Hall.

On April 10th, along with other members of our group, Puyi went on the coach trip to see the Jinggang Mountain, which was a famous Red Revolutionary Shrine. How he wished that I could have gone along with him! Because I couldn't stand the jolting of the coach, which made me travel sick, I needed to stay at the hotel. They took two days to get there, passing by the Ji'an City on the way, before finally getting to Jinggang Mountain. Five days later, when Puyi returned to the hotel and saw me, he said regretfully, "You shouldn't have missed such a valuable opportunity. It's quite a lovely trip to Jinggang Mountain."

Although it was only April, it was very hot in Nanchang. A saturating rain had made the weather cooler briefly, but the temperature quickly heated up again. In the evening, when Puyi saw that I couldn't go to sleep because of the muggy weather, he fanned me until he was sure that I had fallen asleep. He would even fan me again when he was aware that I was turning over. While touring we were always together and when we had meals, he liked to take some of the delicious food from the middle of the table and place it onto my plate, as though I couldn't get it myself! The others of our group often joked with me: "Madam Li, how lucky you are! We are all envious of you having such a caring husband!"

At Shaoshanchong, Chairman Mao's home village in Hunan Province, Puyi was touched concerning the information about Chairman Mao's early life. In the bedroom, when he saw the carved old-style wooden bed that Chairman Mao was born on, out of respect to Mao, he stretched out his hand to stroke it. The guide reminded him that the bed was an exhibit and therefore it shouldn't be touched. But he repeatedly requested to touch it. The guide was moved by his sincerity, allowing only him to touch it. But, surprisingly, he suddenly changed his mind. He said he didn't like to be considered special, doing things that others couldn't do.

In Changsha, the capital of Hunan Province, Puyi, together with the others, finished a very delicious meat dish. But very soon, when he heard that it was the well-known "Hunan Dog Meat", Puyi felt regret. He tried his best to throw it up, but failed. He told me that, even though many say that dog meat was the most delicious kind of

Puyi and I next to the pond in Shaoshanchong, Chairman Mao's hometown. Mao swam in this pond many times during his childhood.

The Last Emperor of China My Husband Puyi

Puyi visiting Wuhan Iron and Steel Company

meat, he still had never eaten it. That day he was unhappy, complaining concerning why I hadn't told him the truth about it beforehand. In fact, I myself also didn't even know that it was dog meat.

Our last stop in southern China was Wuhan. In his diary, Puyi wrote: "I was so excited when I visited the Yangtze River Bridge and the Wuhan Iron and Steel Company, both designed and built by our people. I'm really proud to be Chinese."

At noon, on April 28th, our touring group boarded the train back to Beijing. The fifty day tour was a most rewarding one for Puyi. In his reflection on this tour, he had written the following: "This tour gave me a valuable opportunity to see the great achievements by the Socialist Construction in our Motherland. The 'New Society' filled my eyes with the sunshine and happiness of the people. Once more, I was touched tremendously by the prosperity and love of our Motherland and the incomparable superiority of the Socialist System."

With Mr. Du Yuming at a People's Commune in Hubei Province

Puyi and I with Zhou Zhenqiang and his wife at Nanchang Labor University

The Last Emperor of China **My Husband Puyi**

At Changsha Martyr's Park

Chapter Twenty One
Tour to Northwest China

At Shaanxi Provincial Museum of History, August, 1964

We returned to Beijing on April 29th. The next day, as arranged, Puyi and I joined a grand reception in the Great Hall of the People, organised by the twelve largest National Organizations in order to celebrate the "May 1st Labour Day". When Premier Zhou saw Puyi and I, he immediately invited us to the head table, where Chairman Liu Shaoqi and some other state leaders and senior foreign guests sat. Premier Zhou first enthusiastically introduced Puyi to the Speaker of the Burundian National Parliament. "This is Mr. Puyi, the Chinese 'Last Emperor'." Then he pointed to me, "This is Mrs. Puyi." The Burundi guest politely remarked, "It's a great honour to see 'Your Majesty' Puyi and your wife!" Puyi and I graciously and enthusiastically

The Last Emperor of China My Husband Puyi

proposed toasts to His Excellency and Premier Zhou.

Puyi and Chairman Liu Shaoqi had long before become familiar with one another, so Puyi took the opportunity to introduce us. Standing by Chairman Liu, Puyi said to me, "This is Chairman Liu!" Then he turned towards me saying, "This is my wife!" Chairman Liu kindly asked me my name, where I worked and if we had any difficulties in our life. As I answered his questions he nodded his head congenially. His voice and caring expression left me an unforgettable impression.

During this Labour Day Holiday, the Chinese News Agencies shot many scenes for its documentary film *The Last Emperor, Puyi*.

Our visit to northwest China lasted from the 5th to the 28th August 1964. The four cities we visited, namely Xi'an, Yan'an*, Luoyang and Zhengzhou, are all located in the middle reaches of the Yellow River, being the "Cradle of Chinese civilization". During the twenty-four days, we visited four museums, two people's communes, nine factories and many scenic spots and historical sites.

From the train station in Xi'an, we were taken to the People's Mansion, a Russian-style hotel in the inner city area. After checking into our room, we were led to the dining hall, to taste "Yangrou Paomo", the most famous local delicacy, which consists of a big bowl of stewed mutton, shredded wheat bread, bean-starch noodles and vegetables. Its delicious smell enormously stimulated Puyi's appetite. He slurped it down despite how hot it seemed.

After the meal, our group went to tour the Shaanxi Provincial History Museum. But I decided to stay at the hotel because I had felt faint in the sweltering heat. At noon, the coach returned to the People's Mansion, but without Puyi. In the afternoon, I returned to the museum but finally found Puyi at another place in the city, the "Forest of Stone Stele**". He was sitting in a corner, attentively copying the calligraphy from a huge slab of stone. He in-

At Zaoyuan, Yan'an, where Chairman Mao once lived. Puyi was asking a local farmer to autograph his diary as a momento.

---

* The Communist Party's wartime government seat, led by Mao Zedong from 1937-1948

** This is a beautiful area, situated adjacent to the City Wall which has over 3,000 stone tablets displaying ancient Chinese calligraphy and paintings. It is the largest collection of stone tablets anywhere in China. It got its name because the numerous upright tablets resemble a forest.

Puyi, Pujie with his Japanese wife in Yan'an

formed me that when he was a boy, Mr. Chen Baoshen, his tutor, had told him about Xi'an's "stone library" and that the most well-known Chinese calligraphy works are housed there. Today he was very excited to see them with his own eyes and therefore had lost track of the time.

On August 9th, our group went to Yan'an. Puyi was disappointed that I couldn't go with him but I couldn't stand the long jolting coach ride. After his return from Yan'an, he eloquently briefed me on his visit, airing his impressions on this "Shrine of the Chinese Revolution". I felt as if I had been there with him.

In Yan'an Hotel, it was originally arranged for Puyi to stay in a flat with bathroom, but he preferred to stay in a cave-house (an extremely basic home carved out of soil in a hillside, usually comprising of one or two rooms) like the others. Our tour leader immediately chose a better cave-house and let him move in. Puyi told me: "I didn't expect that living in a cave-house would be so comfortable. It's cool in the summer and warm in the winter." Puyi had often appreciated the Peking Opera, so he knew of a popular one called "The Cold Cave". He recommended that the name be changed, but Mr. Du Jianshi, a former National Party General and a fan of Peking Opera, didn't agree with him. Therefore they had a heated, but friendly argument.

When visiting Yan'an Pagoda on the tower-hill, Puyi saw a very old board on the lintel of its front door with a superstitious inscription on it. He asked the guide why such a feudal object was not removed when Chairman Mao and Communist Party's

At Fenghuo People's Commune

Headquarters were there (1937-1948). The guide replied that the Yan'an Pagoda was an historical site, being protected by the government; therefore it could not be touched without permission. The guide also informed Puyi that there were still two practicing Buddhist Temples in Yan'an and that everyday people went there to worship. The government, by then, had implemented the policy of "Free Practice of Religion".

Puyi told me that his Yan'an tour had made him further understand the Chinese Revolution and that he admired from his innermost being, Mao's great boldness of vision as a strategist. In the War of Japanese Aggression, when Japanese fighters bombed the Phoenix Hill (the place where Mao lived), Mao had not been frightened, withdrawing from there unhurriedly.

Puyi thought that he had ingratiated himself, and tried to bring himself into favour with General Muto Nobuyoshi, the Commander-in-Chief of the Japanese Kuantung Army, by suggesting to him that Japan should set up a good relationship with Russia to consolidate its rearguard if they planned to push forward to the south, and particularly that more fighters should be available to ensure air domination. By doing this, Puyi considered that he had committed a crime.

In Xi'an (previously Chang'an), the city where the earliest Chinese people lived and the capital during eleven ancient dynasties, we toured happily around the 1,300-year-old "Big Wild Goose Pagoda" in the Ci'en Buddhist Temple area. We also went to visit the Liaison Office of the 8th Route Army and the Fenghuo People's Commune.

We especially enjoyed our tour to the Lishan

Puyi's reflections of his tour in northwest China, organised by the CPPCC. He said the tour enhanced his revolutionary education.

Mountain, in Lintong County, about 30 kilometers away from Xi'an. At the foot of the picturesque Lishan Mountain is the reconstruction of the Huaqing Palace, the Winter Palace of the Tang Dynasty (618-907) Emperors. Puyi explained to me: "Each Autumn Emperor Xuanzong, the seventh emperor of the Tang Dynasty, would come to stay here with Lady Yang, his favourite concubine and one of the "Four Favourite Beauties" of ancient China. They wouldn't return to Xi'an until the following spring. The tributes from China's dependencies and all parts of the country were sent here in a steady stream. One of the delicacies that arrived was the litchi fruit, which Lady Yang loved eating. So, Emperor Xuanzong ordered local officials to deliver them to the Huaqing Palace from southern China on non-stop military steeds. Many steeds died of exhaustion on the non-stop three day gallop. Mr. Du Mu, a well-known poet of the Tang Dynasty wrote a satirical poem under the title of *Passing by the Huaqing Palace*:

> *Viewed from afar, the hill's paved with brocades in piles,*
> *The palace doors on hilltops opened one by one.*
> *A steed that raised red dust won the fair concubine's smile,*
> *But so many steeds that were bringing litchi fruit,*
> *Died on the gallop.*

Puyi sank into meditation. As a former emperor, he had personal knowledge of an Emperor's life. Puyi and I went to see the Crabapple Pool. Its bath tub was made of white marble, in the shape of a crabapple. Puyi said: "This is the place where Lady Yang took baths. Some people said she bathed in milk. I don't think so, bathing in a hot spring is more comfortable than bathing in milk." Chinese believe that hot springs can make the skin smooth and cure skin disease and arthritis. Puyi and I took this opportunity to have hot spring baths, in the male and female bathing houses respectively. Later, I heard that Puyi had slipped and almost fell while getting into the hot springs bath. He then complained that the hot spring was too slippery. A member of our group who was bathing together with Puyi in the same tub, laughed: "You should know that hot springs are slippery." One thousand years ago, Bai Juyi, in his poem *The Everlasting Regret* wrote: "She bathed in the glassy water of the warm fountain pool, which nourished and smoothed her creamy skin when the spring was cool."

After bathing, Puyi got out of the bathing tub with great care and put on his clothes. But he was astonished: "Why have I become fatter, after bathing in the hot spring? No wonder people said that Lady Yang was plump, maybe it's because she bathed in a hot spring every day." After a short while Puyi realized that he had put on somebody else's clothes, which were smaller than his, making him feel fat. Changing back to his own clothes, Puyi muttered to himself: "I had longed to smell again the lingering fragrance left by Lady Yang, but instead, I almost broke a bone in the slippery bath tub!"

The Hot Spring bath had given Puyi a better understanding of the notable poem, *Everlasting Regret*. He spoke out several other popular lines of it:

On the seventh day of the seventh moon when no-one was near,
At night in the Eternal Hall he whispered in her ear
On high, we'd be two lovebirds flying wing to wing,
On earth, two trees with branches twined from spring to spring.

Puyi pointed towards the reconstruction of the Huaqing Palace built on its original site, saying: "The Eternal Hall in the poem must be somewhere inside. It was said that at midnight on July 7th, in the seventh year (748) of the Tianbao Reign, Emperor Xuanzong and Lady Yang sat in the garden and faced the sky, vowing to be a couple forever. But Emperor Xuanzong wasn't able to keep his word.

Later, when the insurgent troops led by An Lushan prepared to attack Xi'an, Emperor Xuanzong and Lady Yang had to flee ignominiously to Sichuan Province. On their way, while passing through the village of Maweipo, not far from Xi'an, Emperor Xuanzong's own officials and generals (who already hated bitterly Lady Yang) mutinied, telling him to kill her, or lose the throne. To save his throne, Emperor Xuanzong would have to carry out the orders himself. But Lady Yang, in order to save her husband from being deprived of his throne kowtowed to him, and then hung herself from a tree by the road. Different from ordinary people, for various reasons, emperors seldom enjoyed real love."

Hearing of this dramatic story, I wanted to see the remains of the "Long Life Hall", but nobody could tell me its exact location.

On December 12th 1936, Chiang Kai-shek was captured by two of his own generals at the Huaqing Palace. He was forced to end the civil war with the Communists and set up an Anti-Japanese United Front,

Puyi learning to drive a tractor at Luoyang Tractor Factory

176

with all of the political forces in China at that time. The event is referred to as "The Xi'an Incident". Puyi and I went to see the one-storeyed traditional Chinese house that Chiang Kai-shek had stayed in when he was at the Huaqing Spring. Still obvious, in the glass windows of the lounge and bedroom, were the bullet holes from the gunshots.

On August 22nd, we arrived in Luoyang in Henan Province, the capital city during nine ancient dynasties. In the 1950s, the Central Government built more than ten large factories there. We were taken to see three of them, the ball-bearing factory, a mining machinery factory and a tractor factory. In the tractor factory, there was a line of tractors drove by us, Puyi couldn't help pulling me on to a tractor. He asked the driver to teach him how to drive a tractor and he finally was able to drive it for several metres,

With Sagahiro at Longmen Grottoes, Luoyang

winning an ovation. He was very excited, "If I stayed here longer, I'm sure I could learn to drive one in the fields." Immediately, a supervisor of the factory said to Puyi: "We welcome you come to work in our factory!" Puyi got off the tractor happily saying, "I'll come here again when I have the opportunity."

In Luoyang, we also went to tour the Longmen Grottoes, White Horse Temple and Luoyang Historical Museum. In front of the world-famous Longmen Grottoes, Puyi was very sad, sighing repeatedly, when he saw some precious stone Buddhas which had been carved, in succession, since the Beiwei Dynasty (386-534). But now they had no heads, arms or legs. He explained to me that they had been weathered or damaged in wars and that he had hated himself for secretly taking quite a lot of the national treasures out from the Forbidden City in the 1920s, thus losing most of them in Changchun, at the end of the War of Japanese Aggression.

Zhengzhou, the capital of Henan Province and the largest hub of the Chinese railway system, was our last stop in this tour. We made a visit to the Zhengzhou Textile Machinery Factory, the Henan Museum of History and the "February 7th Workers'

Appreciating the Longmen Grottoes, Luoyang

Strike Memorial Tower".

Zhengzhou was a young city and Puyi was impressed with its layout. Later, in his reflections of this tour he wrote the following:

Like Luoyang, most of 'Zhengzhou proper' has been changed into a completely new city, with tall and handsome buildings and a convenient network of roads suitable for a variety of traffic. It's a symbol of our successful Socialist Construction and it indicates a bright future for our Motherland.

The pleasant tour to eastern and northwest China made deep impressions on Puyi and I. "The tour gave us an even deeper respect for our Motherland, so that now we love it even more deeply," Puyi remarked.

At Zhengzhou, August 26th, 1964

Chapter Twenty Two

Being Attacked by Cancer

During our three-month tour, I envied how Puyi was able to sleep and eat well and easily climb and walk, while I had to miss seeing many sights due to my poor health and stamina. But we never then suspected that Puyi already had cancer.

I remember clearly, when we returned to Beijing from Zhengzhou, that a leader of the CPPCC came to meet us at the Beijing Railway Station. He told us that we should rest a few days after the long tour. But the following morning, Puyi told me that he would go to the Botanical Garden. "I haven't been to that 'home' for a long time. I will do some physical work and come back in three days." I thought that he would need to rest, but he looked so energetic, so I didn't say anything to stop him. Unexpectedly, he returned home the next day. I was surprised when he said that it seemed strange that he had blood

In March 1965, Puyi was diagnosed with kidney cancer.

stained urine again.

Actually, it was as early as in May 1962, when we had been married for only two weeks, that Puyi first discovered that his urine was blood-stained. We never suspected that it was the omen of kidney cancer and that the evil disease had already started inside his body. Now I grieve when I think of it. Due to our oversight we lost the valuable opportunity of having it diagnosed and, therefore, his condition being treated earlier.

Although Puyi went to see the doctor after his first haematuria experience, he had not been properly diagnosed. The doctor only prescribed Vitamin K to stop the bleeding. Puyi preferred Chinese medicine, so he had been to see Dr. Zhang Rongzeng, his good friend, who worked at the Navy Hospital. He prescribed three doses of Chinese medical herbs for Puyi according to "a warm bladder" diagnosis. It had worked quickly and stopped the bleeding. Over the next two years, Puyi often caught colds and ran high fevers, but he always quickly recovered following medication. The cancer cells in his body were never discovered. Then he was in seemingly good health and always full of vigour. From July 1964, Puyi was often worried about blood-stained urine, but he never had any pain and had never been feverish.

At the beginning of September 1964, Puyi passed blood-stained urine again. I panicked and accompanied him to have an immediate medical check at the hospital. He was diagnosed with prostatitis, only being injected with Vitamin K again to stop bleeding. No urine cultures were taken for further checking. In the following two months, Puyi's haematuria became more serious and he had to be hospitalised.

Not long after that, Premier Zhou Enlai was fortuitously notified of Puyi's condition. One day, in the afternoon at about 5 o'clock, a "Red Flag" brand car stopped outside the gate of our house. From it an official in a Mao jacket got out and entered into our courtyard. He politely gave me an invitation, telling me that Premier Zhou was inviting Puyi and I, along with some honourable foreign guests, to an important banquet. Previously, Premier Zhou had always arranged for his invitation to be sent to Puyi, through the CPPCC. But that day, because of his sudden decision and concern, a car was sent to our home directly. I told the official, with regret, that Puyi was hospitalised with haematuria."

"Which hospital?" he asked.

"The People's Hospital", I replied.

"How many days already?" he questioned.

"About ten days," I said.

"How about his condition now?" he asked in concern.

"He still has blood-stained urine." I answered, with hesitation.

The "Red Flag" brand car then left at full speed. That evening Premier Zhou Enlai personally phoned the authority of the CPPCC HQ, to order them to carefully attend to Puyi, even keeping "round the clock" care of him. Only then did the authorities of the CPPCC realize the gravity of the situation and followed Premier Zhou's instructions.

The next day, an entire consultation was held for Puyi, headed by Dr. Wu Jieping, the most famous Chinese urological expert and joined by several noted surgical and tumour experts. He was given a cystoscopy, a prostate investigation, a semen examination and renography, but nothing unusual was discovered. But Dr. Wu Jieping was sure that Puyi definitely had a problem. So while taking measures to stop the bleeding, he continued his study of Puyi's case. Twenty days later, Puyi's bleeding had stopped and he left the hospital to join a session of the CPPCC.

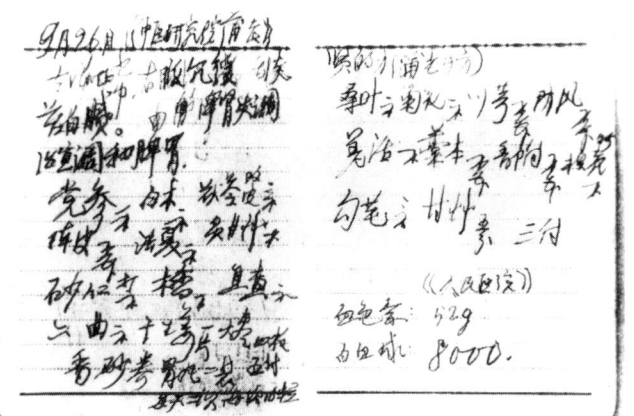
Puyi liked to copy out the doctor's medical prescriptions.

On February 5th 1965, Puyi had once again been hospitalised at the People's Hospital, because of more serious haematuria. In another cystoscopy, on March 6th, two tumours, one the size of a bean and another a little bit bigger, were finally discovered inside Puyi's bladder, and they were labelled pernicious. The diagnosis on the medical record was "posterior bladder tumour enlarged prostate gland". When Puyi's diagnosis and serious condition were reported to Premier Zhou, he instructed that Puyi be transferred to the Intensive Care Ward in the United Hospital so that high ranking doctors could attend to him. Several distinguished urological, surgical and tumour experts were appointed to be responsible for Puyi's care. Although they took various measures to elaborately treat Puyi's disease, Puyi had already been misdiagnosed for three years, thus losing the best opportunity for early stage cure and care.

Since our marriage, Puyi had been hospitalised in the People's Hospital and the United Hospital six times altogether. I knew that he liked to be with others and enjoyed chatting and joking with them, but was restless and even feared being alone, so I used to go to his ward almost every day, sitting at the end of his bed. I tried to think of subjects to chat with him about and did my best to console him.

But unfortunately, I myself often got ill. In 1965, while Puyi was still in hospital, I was diagnosed as having uterine fibroids. Before the final diagnosis of my health problem, Puyi was so worried about me, that he couldn't eat or sleep well for several days, often weeping. When I asked him why cried, he told me that he feared that maybe I had cancer and then he would cry again. I would joke with him, "If I get cancer, then you'd better marry again." He replied, "You cannot die! I shall never marry again if you really do die...." I smiled, "I'm not diagnosed yet, you needn't cry." On the way to learn of my final diagnosis, he was nervous and said nothing. But he immediately became glad and laughed when he was told that my womb fibroid was benign. After we returned home, he was still laughing and singing.

Towards the end of August 1965, in order to treat my gynaecological problem, Puyi entrusted Dr. Zhong Huilan, his friend and a member of the Standing Committee of the CPPCC and the President of Beijing Friendship Hospital, to introduce a gynaecological specialist to treat me. Dr. Zhong very quickly found Dr. Lin Qiaozhi, the best gynaecologist in China. She cured my medical complaint in half a year. She then suggested that I should have an operation to remove my benign fibroid. By Puyi's request, the President of the United Hospital recommended Professor Song, an excellent surgeon and specialist, to do my operation. When I was hospitalised for recuperation following the operation, Puyi came to see me every day. At that time, Puyi had just had his left kidney removed but problems in his right kidney were soon discovered when he continued to have blood in his urine. He was too weak to walk to my ward, so he called a taxi (although he had been given the privilege to call a car from the CPPCC HQ whenever he needed, but he never liked to use the courtesy car for private matters), in order to visit me and to encourage me before and after my operation.

Chapter Twenty Three

"Tricky" Situation that Happened in Puyi's Ward

In June 1965, Puyi had an operation in the United Hospital to remove his left kidney. After that, when he was still in hospital convalescing, an old maid, named Miss Wang, often went there to visit him. In his diary of June 14th, he recorded what happened that day when she was there:

At 2 o'clock in the afternoon, I was disgusted that Miss Wang came when I was having my sleep. Although Miss Yao, my nurse, told her that I was sleeping, she still entered my ward. My nurse came in again to have a look but seeing that I was sleeping, she left. I heard somebody in my ward and asked who it was. Miss Wang then took this opportunity to come in and asked me about my case. I told her that the doctor said I needed a good rest and that it was not good to receive so many visitors, so that she wouldn't come to visit me again. But she told me that her mother worried about me and would come to see me. I repeated what I had told her previously. But she sat there, with no intention of leaving. Only after I told her that I must have a sleep every afternoon, did she go away. How annoying!

The diary clearly showed that Puyi was fed up with Miss Wang. The "old maid", a Manchu lady, wore an embroidered Manchu robe and decorated herself with shining pearls and jadeite head-dresses.

Not long after Puyi returned to Beijing from Fushun, a relative of Wanrong called Dagege ("Da" means elder. "gege" is the name for a Manchu aristocratic girl.), enthusiastically invited Puyi to dine at her home. While enjoying the very delicious food cooked by Dagege who had excellent culinary skills, Puyi talked cheerfully and joked freely, not at all like the stately emperor in many people's minds. But Puyi hadn't expected that one of his jokes with Miss Wang, Dagege's daughter, would bother her. The daughter misunderstood the situation and thought that Puyi "fancied" her.

Miss Wang, was nearly 50 years old that year. Born into an aristocratic family and pampered from birth, she behaved in an affected manner and didn't want to go to work, although she had no reason not to do so. And because she was too "nit-picky" about choosing her husband, she never did find a satisfactory one, finally becoming an "old maid", nicknamed "Miss Wang".

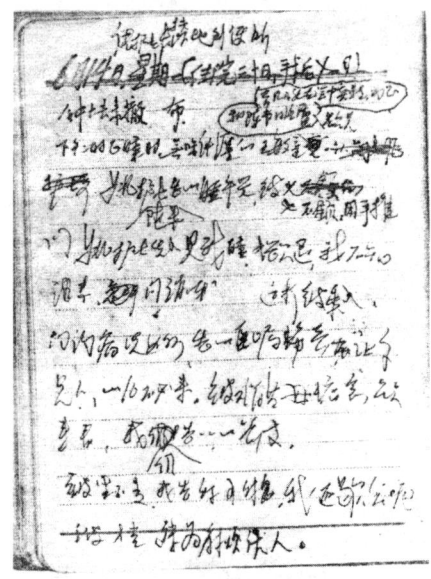

Puyi's diary on June 14th, 1965

Afterwards, she shared her secret desire for Puyi with a relative, who told Puyi that she was willing to date him. Puyi flatly refused her, but Miss Wang was still deeply in love with Puyi and pursued him for a long time. She couldn't help crying when she found that Puyi was dating a nurse. I heard that she "bawled her eyes out" on the day when Puyi and I held our wedding ceremony.

Even so, she never dropped the idea. When I had my operation to remove the fibroid from my uterus, she was filled with hope, believing it to be cancerous, so she thought that one day she could marry Puyi. Puyi was very furious and said: "She is hallucinating, I shall never marry her!" After I had had a successful operation and recovered very well, Miss Wang's hope was shattered again.

While Puyi was in hospital, on each visitor day, she would arrive early and take both of the visitor tokens. According to hospital regulations, each patient had only two visitor tokens and each visitor was allowed to take one each time, but Miss Wang always took both of them, so that nobody else could enter Puyi's ward! Her visit always made Puyi upset.

In December 1965, Puyi was hospitalized again and once more, Miss Wang went to see him in his ward. One day, while Puyi and I chatted happily, she entered Puyi's ward. But she angrily retreated from the ward when she saw me and stood outside. At once, I came out and invited her into the ward to treat her with tea, fruit and sweets, but she deliberately ignored me. Puyi was furious. He later grumbled to others: "She was so rude to my wife. Why is she so jealous of her?" Puyi let a relative pass his words on to Miss Wang, stating that he didn't want her to come again. In Puyi's diary, written on December 20th, was a paragraph about the matter:

Shuxian came to see me in the afternoon. The daughter of "Dagege" came too. Shuxian invited her to come in, but was snubbed by the daughter. I summoned the Charge Nurse, who told her that I needed a quiet rest and that she must go.

One time, Puyi woke from a dream and saw Miss Wang sitting at his bedside. He flared up immediately and shouted at her, demanding her to leave. It just so happened that at the same moment, Madam Saga Hiro, Pujie's wife and Puyi's sister-in-law had entered the ward. She mistook Puyi's anger and believed it was aimed at her. When later she learned the real reason, she shook her head to others, saying: "Over many years, I have never seen him as furious as that before!"

Later, I bantered with Puyi: "Puyi! Why don't you like her? She was born into a celebrated Manchu family with several generations of very high-ranking officials. Aren't your families alike?"

"She doesn't love me, instead she is fascinated with the Emperor Puyi. Today's Puyi is not able to match such a noble lady."

What Puyi said explained perfectly the reason why he refused her and I myself was very gratified by his loyalty to our love.

Before meeting me, Puyi had been introduced to another eligible lady named Qian. Many times he had invited her to join the weekend party at the auditorium of the CPPCC HQ. This young woman, in her thirties, was very pretty and her graceful dancing infatuated many people. At the beginning, she liked Puyi and Puyi had a high opinion of her. But, when a leader of the CPPCC found out, he warned Puyi: "As far as I know, she leads a dissolute and licentious lifestyle. You'd better be discreet with her." Very soon, Puyi ended their friendship. Later Miss Qian phoned Puyi many times, wanting to see him, but was politely refused by Puyi. She couldn't understand why Puyi liked me and not her. When she heard that Puyi and I had become married, she said angrily: "Aren't I as good as her?" Even after that, she still phoned Puyi several times, forcing Puyi to tell his colleagues in the same office: "If she phones me again, tell her that I'm away."

Before this, Mr. Jin, a high-ranking official of CPC, had invited Puyi to a meal. Present there was a female committee member of Shanghai People's Political Consultative Conference. Her flushed face left an impression on Puyi. After the meal, Mr. Jin suggested to them, "You may like to take a walk outside." But both of them didn't move, remaining seated there.

That's not all. Another leader of the CPPCC also recommended a lady friend to Puyi. He told the matchmaker that they weren't suitable for each other. A colleague tried to encourage him by saying: "The lady can speak several foreign languages fluently. She would be able to work as your interpreter when you receive foreign guests." Puyi pondered deeply over the matter, but still thought that she was not suitable for him. Puyi was very grateful to his leaders for their concern, but he had his own beliefs concerning his marriage.

Chapter Twenty Four

Friendship with Our Neighbour

The Chinese believe that "A far off relative is not as helpful as a nearby neighbour". In June 1963, when we moved to 22, Dongguanyinsi Lane, it was arranged that Mr. Dai, an electrician working in the CPPCC HQ, would move into a small house in our courtyard, too. His house was located near to the "scarlet gate". This was because, considering Puyi's age and my worsening health, the leaders of the CPPCC had asked Mr. Dai to "keep an eye out for us" and to assist us on needful occasions.

Mr. Dai, a reliable comrade, started to work in the CPPCC HQ, when it was established in 1949. On October 1st 1949, when the Grand Founding Ceremony of the People's Republic of China was held in Tiananmen Square, it was Mr. Dai, an ordinary electrician, who had been in charge of the electricity switchboard which supplied the electricity for the Tian'anmen Gate Tower, the "Gate of Heavenly Peace". This is where all of the state leaders stood when watching and inspecting any dress parades.

By the time he moved in, Mr. Dai's three elder children had married and lived independently outside. Only he and his wife, plus their two younger daughters lived in our courtyard. For approximately two years, our two families were harmonious neighbours. When hearing our guests knock on the gate, Mr. Dai, or one of his family members, always went to open it quickly. Whenever the CPPCC HQ held weekend parties or our hospital issued film tickets, Puyi and I always reserved extras for Mr. Dai's daughters. Our two families shared a big kitchen, so that when I cooked a good meal, I always sent them some and Mrs. Dai would do the same for us.

In the summer of 1963, an exceptionally violent rainstorm destroyed many houses in Beijing. Mr. Dai's old house was damaged too, causing leaking everywhere. When he heard the news, Puyi went immediately to see Mr. Dai and his family. He invited Dai's family to live in our sitting-room, temporarily. Mr. Dai knew we often had foreign guests visiting us and therefore declined the offer. Then Puyi personally urged the CPPCC HQ's Department of Housing to repair Dai's seriously damaged house, as soon as possible, being afraid that it might collapse and injure them. Their house was restored quickly.

In summer, Puyi and I often enjoying the cool air in our courtyard

Friendship with Our Neighbour

It was recorded in Puyi's diary on August 10th 1963: "Rainy Day, Dai Wenshan's rooms leaked."

I praised him by teasing him, saying: "Well done! Now you can truly care about others!" Puyi replied: "Before others always took care of me but I never thought of others."

When the leaders of the CPPCC learned of Puyi's concern for the Dai Family they commended him at the next Political Study Session of the Commissioners.

All of his commissioner colleagues happily praised him for doing such a good deed. Puyi said modestly that he was learning to care about others and he admired the virtues of the model Chinese citizens. So, he requested more reminders of his need to care about others instead of being commended for it. Then he could continue to grow as a caring person. Puyi said that this way could really help him to help others.

Puyi's diary on August 10th 1963; "Rainy Day, Dai Wenshan's rooms leaked."

Mrs. Dai always came to help me when I needed it. Puyi's diary written on September 11th 1963 recorded: "Today, Shuxian asked Mrs. Dai to make rice porridge for us."

During those days, Puyi became ill with a very high-fever and was often confined to bed. Everyday his colleagues and relatives came to see him. Because I was fully occupied in attending patients and entertaining guests, Mrs. Dai voluntarily cooked meals for us.

But in the summer of 1965, our housekeeper gossiped to Mrs. Dai and created a schism between our two families. At one point, Mrs. Dai and I even stopped speaking to each together. In spite of Puyi's disapproval I complained to Mr. Dai and one of Puyi's direct leaders. Puyi criticized me that it was not good to fuss about such a trifling matter.

To solve the problem, I thought it would be best to move. I knew that Puyi wouldn't agree, so I went to find another of Puyi's direct leaders. My reason was two-fold, firstly, to avoid the problem with Mrs. Dai and secondly to move to a place with a heating system. Puyi and I couldn't afford to fire several stoves for all of its rooms every day in the winter. We wanted to move into the apartments on Hepingli area, where most of Puyi's commissioner colleagues lived. Actually, Puyi himself preferred to live in a heated apartment, but he understood the kindness of the CPPCC leaders. He explained to me that we were privileged to live in such a big house with so many rooms and a spacious courtyard. Because we had so many foreign guests visiting us at home, it was very practical. So he stressed that we must be considerate in the overall situation and that we should never trouble our leaders any more with such petty matters. For this reason Puyi went to see Mr. Shen Dechun, "It's my fault for failing to keep on good terms with our neighbour. I hope that the leaders will encourage my wife to patch up the problem."

In order to get rid of the bad situation between Mrs. Dai and me, Puyi mediated between our two sides several times and Mrs. Dai was finally touched. One day, Mrs. Dai sent us a plate of self-made fried dough twist to show her desire for reconciliation and Puyi gladly received it. Nevertheless I was still angry with her and sent it back to her without any reason, making Mrs. Dai "lose face". Puyi wrote down the matter in his diary, which showed that although he was furious with me, he could still tolerate my bad behavior. This happened nearly forty years ago, but I still feel sorry whenever I think about it.

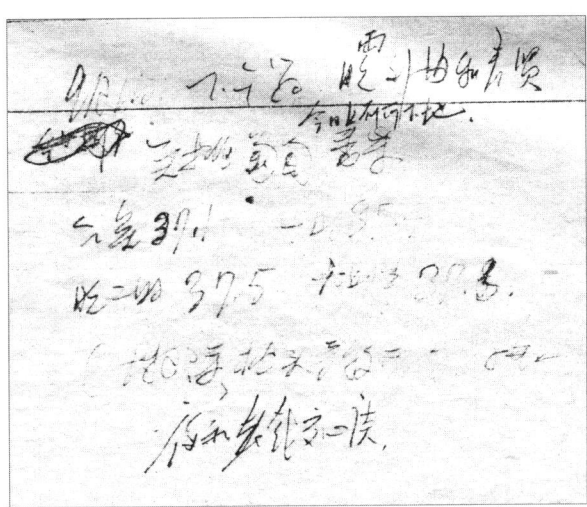

Puyi's diary showing his hearty coversations with Mr. Dai

On August 25th 1965, I was admitted to the United Hospital to have an operation and Puyi lived alone during my hospital stay. Mr. Wan, Puyi's fifth brother-in-law offered to stay with him, but Puyi preferred to take this opportunity to mend the situation with Mrs. Dai. He invited Mr. Dai to stay at our home. In his diaries of those days, there were continuous records:

August 25th
Today Mr. Dai stayed at our home.
August 28th
Evening—conversed with Dai Wenshan.
September 1st
Midnight—conversed heartily with Dai.
September 4th

Evening—had dinner together with Dai.

Several hearty conversations finally solved the problem.

By September 11th, I had recovered completely and was able to leave the hospital. That day, Puyi invited Mrs. Dai to pick me up at the hospital. I was touched by her thoughtfulness, in spite of the rift that had come between us. Our trivial quarrel "vanished into thin air". We became friendly neighbours again.

In his diary of October 1st, Puyi wrote:

Evening—enjoyed the fire-works display at Tiananmen Square, with Miss Dai Shuying (Dai's daughter).

The next diary recorded:

Evening—Mr. Wan and fifth younger sister came and we had dinner together. We invited Dai to join us.

Chapter Twenty Five

Performing the Rights of a Citizen

In the early spring of 1966, it was still very cold. Puyi's health had declined after his recent operation. He was fully aware that he had an incurable disease, but when he heard that the neighbourhood committee would hold a meeting to elect the representatives for the People's Congress, he was enthusiastic to join it. Because he was too weak to work, I actually thought it best that he shouldn't attend the meeting. I tried to persuade him:

"You are seriously ill. It's not good for you to sit there for a long time. I will go on your behalf." I begged.

"No! I will go myself," he stressed.

On March 6th, Puyi and I went to a voters' meeting at the home of Mr. Li Zhong, the Director of our Neighbourhood Committee. At first, Mr. Li Zhong made a speech about the responsibilities of a Peoples' Representative. He urged that they must express the peoples' desires and handle State Affairs at different levels of the People's Congress. Director Li stressed that before casting a vote, voters should think long and hard about who had foresight, intelligence, ability, and most importantly, who had already contributed well to socialist development. He said that those who served as People's Representative now yet who have been proven incompetent should be replaced. Next, he talked about how to nominate the candidates. He explained that the method we use currently was the combination of individual and group nominations and that all of the voters could

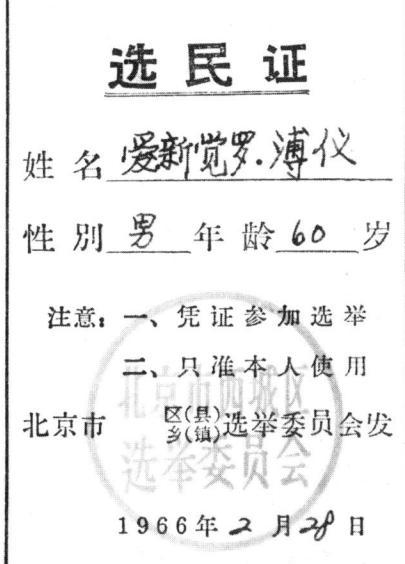

Puyi's voter's certificate, February 28th, 1966

nominate candidates and fully express their views.

At this stage, all of the preliminary candidates had been jointly nominated by the Xicheng District Committee of the CPC, the Xicheng District Committee of the Communist Youth League (CYL), the Trade Union, the Women's Federation and the CPPCC of the Xicheng District. These would not be confirmed before seeking approval from the voters of the whole district.

Finally, Director Li introduced the seven "preliminary candidates" nominated officially for election, three of them being women. There was a deputy director and general engineer of a rolling mill, a technician from an instrument plant, an experienced primary school teacher, a kindergarten nurse, a veteran steel plant worker, an extra-curricular teacher and a concerned and helpful citizen who always helped others. Director Li welcomed voters to air their comments on the candidates.

Puyi stood up to express his satisfaction concerning the choice of the seven preliminary candidates: "All of them are first-rate in their trades and professions and have already made spectacular achievements. I'm sure that they are able to consider the will of the people and precisely mirror their desires and demands." As a solemn citizen, Puyi commented on the seven candidates in a sonorous voice. All of the voters present were moved by his speech, but none of them realized that he was incurably ill.

On March 31st, while once again hospitalized in the United Hospital for a further medical checkup, Puyi found out that the vote was to be held at 9am on April 3rd. His doctor had warned him again and again to reduce his activities, so as to maintain his strength. I told Puyi, "You may fill out the ballot in the hospital, or alternatively, it is permitted for me to put it into the ballot box for you." But Puyi didn't agree. He asked me to help him to leave the hospital for a while and to walk to the Polling Station at a Primary School, within our electoral area. When we walked in to cast our vote, all the staff greeted Puyi enthusiastically. They were glad that the former emperor was once again performing his civic duty.

Once, when Premier Zhou Enlai invited Puyi, along with other chief guests, to a function, he introduced Puyi to the guests by saying, "This is the Emperor Xuantong of the Qing Dynasty." Puyi replied loudly, "Now, I'm a citizen of the People's Republic of China!" In front of everybody, Premier Zhou praised his wonderful answer! After that, Puyi had always introduced himself to foreign guests in this way.

Puyi was so adamant about voting for the People's Congress, because he valued his citizenship. In his *The First Half of My Life*, he narrated his excitement when he received his voter's certification for the first time on November 26th 1960: "I'm sure that it is more valuable than all my treasures." If Puyi hated giving up his title as emperor in the first half of his life, it was certainly his citizenship that he prized most in the second

A wax model of Puyi's voting

half of his life.

When Puyi joined the election for the second time in April 1963, he was already the Commissioner of the Historical Accounts of Past Events, but he loved his identity of citizen much more.

Before the formal election, Puyi joyfully took part in the preliminary meeting many times. He especially went to visit Mr. Wang Yandong, one of the candidates and felt very satisfied with him after their conversation. Mr. Wang was a geography teacher and had a great reputation amongst his students. He came from northeast China, and had been educated at Jianguo University in Changchun, while Puyi was its Honorable President. So, they had much in common, drawing them closer together.

On April 13th 1963, a day before the vote, as soon as I returned home from my work, Puyi told me excitedly: "Tomorrow, I'm going to vote!" Puyi was ecstatic to exercise his right as a citizen. That night he hardly slept, often flipping on the light to smoke a cigarette or to check the clock, which disturbed me every time, and therefore I didn't get much sleep either!

"I understand your excitement, but why don't you sleep?" I asked him.

"Shuxian, tomorrow I'm going to vote as a citizen for the second time. It's a milestone for me!"

In the early morning, at about four o'clock, Puyi had already gotten up, put on his blue Mao jacket, and then combed his shiny hair in front of the mirror. I joked with him,

"Are you going on a date?" He smiled, at the same time urging me to hurry, saying: "You'd better get up soon. We want to be the first ones at the CPPCC HQ!"

After voting, hand in hand, Puyi led me to the canteen in the Cultural Club. He happily said to me: "I'm going to treat you to a special meal there. Today is a great day. I hope you will enjoy it!"

He ordered many delicious dishes and ate more than usual. While we were eating, many of our acquaintances came to greet us, wondering why we had come so far to have lunch there. Puyi explained happily: "Today is a day of great rejoicing, so we are celebrating!"

After lunch, we played billiards in the recreation room, until 6 pm, enjoying ourselves to the utmost. I'm sure that Puyi would never have spent such a long time to eat and play there, if he had not been genuinely happy. He had, at the time, been quite busy amending *The First Half of My Life*, often working on it well into the night.

Three years later, Puyi cast his last vote.

Chapter Twenty Six

"Hurricane" Blew Suddenly

Granted a special amnesty at the end of 1959, Puyi began to live comfortably after having been assigned a satisfactory job. He had been able to publish his own book and also received special acceptance as a member of the CPPCC. What touched him most of all was the personal care from the top leaders of the CPC and State. This action motivated him to progress so much that, in the middle of the 1960s, the ailing "Last Emperor" even wanted to join the Communist Party of China.

On January 11th 1966, Puyi, who was then a patient at the United Hospital, met with Madam Liao Mengxing*, the elder sister of Mr. Liao Chengzhi. After the conversation with Madam Liao, Puyi excitedly wrote about it in his diary under the title of "I shall remember forever Sister Liao's most earnest expectation of me":

> During the afternoon conversation with Madam Liao Mengxing, she encouraged me to exert myself to make constant progress. She said that it would be a miracle if I could officially join the Communist Party of China. Although I have progressed in my "remoulding", I'm determined to continue to progress even further.

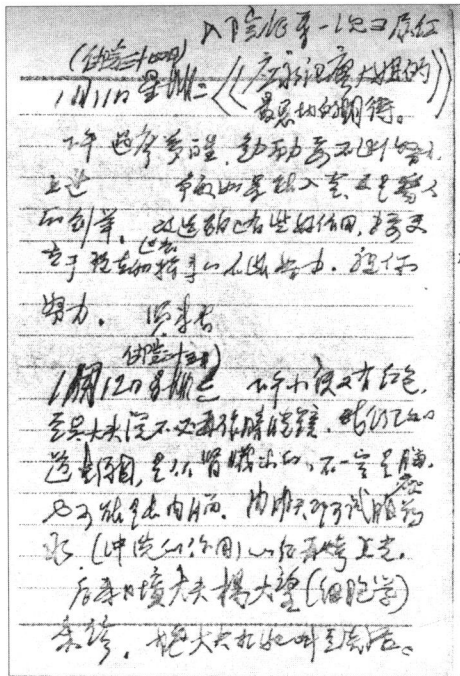

In his diary of January 11th, 1966, Puyi recorded his impressive conversation with Madam Liao Mengxing.

---

* Both she and her brother were high-ranking state officials. Their father was Mr. Liao Zhongkai, an outstanding democratic revolutionary and one of the founders of the Chinese Nationalist Party. After helping Dr. Sun Yat-sen in 1911 to overthrow the corrupt and incompetent Qing Dynasty and to set up the Republic of China, their father was murdered in 1925 by Nationalist Party Rightists.

Ten days after that, when Mr. Shen Zui (former National Party General and one of the top spies in the National Party Government's Secret Service) went to visit Puyi at the hospital, with his new bride, Madam Du Xuejie, Puyi and he had a heart-to-heart talk in the ward. Puyi demonstrated his real feelings, after having been re-educated. It was written in detail in his diary:

Today is the forty-third day since I was hospitalized. At about 10 am, Mr. Shen Zui and his wife came to see me. He told me that Mr. Shen Dechun, our direct leader, had already reported about my illness to our beloved Premier Zhou Enlai and Mr. Peng Zhen, the Mayor of the Beijing Municipal Government. They immediately instructed to request the best doctors in the country to give me urgent treatment. Upon hearing this, I failed to keep myself from weeping. It was the Communist Party of China, who had saved my life so many times. I'll devote all of my remaining days to wholeheartedly serve the Communist Party of China and the Chinese People. Mr. Shen Zui also told me that on the eve of this Spring Festival, all of the Commissioners of the Historical Accounts of Past Events were invited to attend the Grand Spring Festival Reception, held by the State Council. Previously, only the members of the Outstanding Committee of the CPPCC and the top leaders of the democratic parties had enjoyed the privilege of joining in the event. While appreciating the brilliant theatrical performance, Mayor Peng Zhen reminded Mr. Shen Dechun that he should not let the aging commissioners attend too many political study sessions, for they needed to have more time to relax. Mr. Shen Dechun conveyed Peng's concern to the commissioners. He said to them: "you should never allow yourselves to work too hard, otherwise we would get blamed for it if you got too tired and became ill.

Mr. Shen Zui and I couldn't find suitable words to express our heartfelt gratitude to the Communist Party, who had awakened our desires, changed the way we think and cared about us. Mr. Shen Zui mentioned that when Mr. Zhou Enlai received him, he was quite ashamed to inform the Premier, that several times he had been ordered by Chiang Kai-shek, to murder him. But Premier Zhou Enlai smiled that it was all over and now they were friends.

That day, Mr. Shen Zui told Puyi that he had once written an article regarding his assignment to murder Mr. Li Zongren (Chiang Kai-shek's long-time political opponent and acting President of China after Chiang's flight to Taiwan in 1949. Li lived in America following the Communist victory, but returned to mainland China in 1965, passing away four years later.) Before withdrawing from mainland China, Chiang had commanded Shen to hide machine guns inside Mr. Li's planes, so as to shoot him when he was boarding the planes. Fortunately, Mr. Li had never boarded

Puyi went to welcome Li Zongren when he returned to Beijing, July 20th, 1965.

any of them, thus escaping death.

After reading the article in "the Compilation of Historical Accounts of Past Events", Mr. Li Zongren invited Mr. Shen Zui and his wife to his home. While talking about old times over dinner, Mr. Li told Mr. Shen that he never thought that Chiang would go so far as to attempt to murder him.

Mr. Shen Zui was very excited, saying: "It's a miracle that former political opponents can now associate with each other and work together. This could only happen in the new China, under the leadership of the CPC." What he said made me think of my joyful meeting with Mr. Xiong Bingkun and also Mr. Lu Zhonglin (It was Mr. Lu who in 1924, by orders of General Feng Yuxiang, led the troops to drive Puyi out of the Forbidden City). We were opponents more than thirty years before, but now, after having been remoulded and nurtured by the Communist

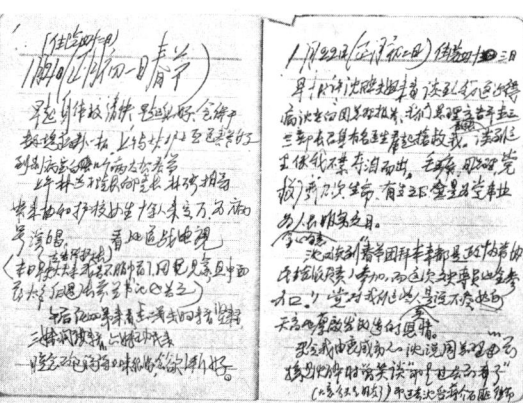

Puyi's diaries

Party of China, we are now Commissioners of the Historical Accounts of Past Events and able to serve the Chinese people together.

To Mr. Shen Zui, I voiced my admiration of the CPC, stating that, "The Communist Party of China is truly a great party. Earlier, when the Communist Party members had been captured by the Nationalist Party authorities, they were immediately killed. But now, you, a former major spy of Nationalist Party and I, a former lackey of Japanese Imperialism, whose sins could not even be expiated by death, have been remoulded and given good employment. We have both since remarried and rebuilt our home lives. How happy you and your wife are; so are Shuxian and I! Because of illness, Mr. Wang Yaowu has been unable to work for nearly four years, but is still being paid his full salary. What shall we do in our remaining time, so that we can repay the CPC and the Chinese people?"

Apparently, like me, Mr. Shen Zui was also filled with gratitude to the Communist Party. Before parting, I encouraged him: "Comrade Shen Zui, exert yourself to make progress." Shen replied: "Let's make progress together!" For the first time, since we had known each other four years, we have been able to speak to each other so honestly and directly."

While Puyi was enjoying growing confidence in making great progress, the "gunpowder smell" of the class struggle was becoming more and more intense and the political climate in China was gradually changing. The popular historical drama entitled *The Dismissal of Hai Rui*, written by Mr. Wu Han, Deputy Mayor of Beijing and a distinguished historian was viciously criticized in all of the newspapers and magazines in China. Everybody had to express similar sentiments to the authorities at the political study sessions.

Hai Rui* was an honest and upright government official of the Ming Dynasty (1368-1644). Mr. Wu Han had accurately followed historical documentation, laying particular stress on Hai Rui's courage in confiscating land from powerful landlords and distributing it among the poor people. But later Hai Rui was accused of being totally devoted to the feudal emperor and his "righteousness" and "justice" actually served to make the peasants satisfied with feudal rule.

Originally, Puyi was puzzled as to why Hai Rui, such an honest official, had become a target of criticism. But he firmly believed that the position advocated by the CPC and the government must be correct and reasonable, therefore that he must try his best to agree with them. He was obsessed with the matter for some days. Finally, he persuaded

---

* Hai Rui had been famous for his sympathy with the poor and his enlightened sense of justice. He had even dared to criticize an emperor openly, when he considered it was necessary to do so.

himself that, in the feudal society, what the corrupt officials did often enrage the people, forcing them to rebel and thus "dug the graves" for the feudal emperors, while the upright officials intentionally confused the people and effectively sapped their will to resist the feudal ruling class and prolonged the reactionary rule of the feudal society. At the political study session, Puyi made a speech concerning Hai Rui. He concluded in fact that "the upright officials are worse than the corrupt officials".

In "Red May" 1966, the Cultural Revolution began. The original targets were three senior government officials: Mr. Deng Tuo, the Secretary in charge of culture and education of the Beijing Municipal Committee of the CPC; Mr. Wu Han, the Deputy Mayor of the Beijing Municipal Government and Mr. Liao Mosha, the Director of the Propaganda Department of the Municipal Committee of the CPC. They were harshly criticized, beaten and finally imprisoned.

After returning to Beijing, for almost seven years, Puyi had frequently contacted Mr. Liao. He knew that Mr. Liao was a scholar with great learning and always took him as one of his most cordial friends. Now it was very difficult for him to criticize Mr. Liao, but he was certain that he must say something during the political study session to indicate his position. So while "racking his brains" he suddenly remembered a sentence that Mr. Liao had once said to him: "With your own expertise, you are able to research the history of the Qing Dynasty. I'm sure that by doing this you can achieve what others can't achieve!" During his critique of Mr. Liao, Puyi said: "He encouraged me to be an expert in the study of the Qing Dynasty, but didn't encourage me to serve the people, which was an omission on his part." Puyi tried to find some harsh words, but with Mr. Liao's amiable image in his mind, he couldn't express them.

Near the beginning of June 1966, on the vast Chinese expanse of land and in the expansive Chinese sky, a "hurricane" suddenly blew, with riotous clouds seething violently.

The large wall posters, which had appeared originally in Peking University, quickly spread over the whole country. All of the leading officials, at various levels, had overnight become "the capitalist-sympathizers". In the CPPCC HQ, Mr. Shen Bochun, the Deputy Secretary General was the first leader to be viciously criticized. He was accused of using "the dregs of the Old Society" (the commissioners), writing "inflammatory articles" (referring to "the Historical Accounts of Past Events") and publishing them in *The Anthology of Historical Accounts of Past Events*, with the intention of overthrowing the "Red State power" (the Communist Regime). The People's Daily, the organ of the Central Committee of the CPC issued the notorious editorial, *Sweeping Away All the Ox Devils and Snake Demons* (class enemies) which immediately caused tremendous confusion and chaos in the whole country. Mr. Wang Shuceng, a former

Nationalist Party senior official, then one of Puyi's colleagues, was ferreted out by rebels, because he had written a pamphlet titled *The Story of the Swallowing of the Leek*, which was said to "use the past to disparage the present". Mr. Runqi, Puyi's third younger brother-in-law was verbally attacked because he was Mr. Liao's close friend and had kept the photos taken with him. The Cultural Revolution, a catastrophe of the most unparalleled savagery in human history began to touch every corner of Chinese society.

One day, in the morning, a small park near our home was filled with a sea of people. We heard that Mr. Liao Mosha would be denounced there. Puyi, very worried about Mr. Liao's welfare, wanted to see him. We hurried to squeeze into the crowd and finally found Mr. Liao, standing on the front of a truck with his hands securely tied behind his back. His name, written in black ink on a heavy board hung round his neck, had been crossed out in red ink. The "Red Guard" gripping his arms tightly, forced his head down roughly. While being tortured and insulted so cruelly, Mr. Liao's face flushed with anger and humiliation. He gasped for breath and beads of sweat, as big as peas, rolled down his cheeks and trickled down onto the cab of the truck. Puyi, being horrified at what he saw, watched Mr. Liao for a few seconds. At that moment, the truck began its journey to parade the streets. Puyi desperately squeezed out of the crowd and ran after it. We were separated from each other in the crowd so that we lost each other. I couldn't find Puyi so had to walk back home, ahead of him.

I was anxious when I arrived home and discovered that Puyi had not yet returned. About twenty minutes later, our neighbour, named Mr. Wang escorted him home. When I asked where he had been, he replied: "I was very disturbed and lost my way. I'm grateful to Mr. Wang for bringing me back."

After seeing Mr. Wang off, Puyi sat on the sofa, saying nothing but only sighing. At last, he shed tears sadly. I tried to comfort him, with some encouraging words about Mr. Liao, saying that he was a tolerant man and looked better than would have been expected.

After a long silence, he said to me: "Haven't those Communist Party veterans spilt their blood, sweat and tears for the revolutionary cause? But in old age, they are to be humiliated by having their hands tied up behind their backs, a heavy name board hung from their necks and shoved towards the ground into a bowing position. Why? Even though they have made a few mistakes, their contributions to the revolutionary cause are outstanding. They shouldn't be tortured so brutally!" He talked again and again, questioning, "What about the officials of the war criminals prison?" "Have Director Yu, Mr. Tian and Mr. Hu in the Botanical Garden been denounced?" He was anxious to go to the Botanical Garden to see them, but being seriously ill, he couldn't attempt to walk over there. He wanted me to go to have a look instead of him. But I told him that now the Cultural Revolution was spreading, without a letter of introduction, I wouldn't even be able to enter into the gate of the Botanical Garden. He sighed and didn't mention it further.

With a heavy heart, Puyi almost forgot that he had been notified to go to the CPPCC HQ that day to attend a political study session. When he arrived at his office, his sadness left an unforgettable impression on his colleagues. Later, Pujie recalled:

In that tumultuous time, Puyi was most bewildered. One day, when we were supposed to study and disauss the government documents concerning the criticism of "The Three Family Village" (an anthology of prose by Wu Han, which was censured to vilify the socialist system and oppose the CPC), Puyi was late. Upon entering our office, he gave way to tears, telling us, "On my way here, I saw Director Liao being paraded around the streets, while bound to a truck. He is an honorable man. I wanted to help him get untied and off the truck, but the truck moved too fast. I couldn't catch it, only running after it and shouting his name...." His voice choked with tears. All of us were touched by his sincerity and kindheartedness, but at the same time worried about his straight forwardness. Although Mr. Wang Yaowu, who had been presiding over the meeting, was puzzled and sad too, he had to encourage Puyi not to get aggravated, but to trust the CPC and his government. But Puyi still said that he was sure that Mr. Liao hadn't committed any crimes, because he knew that Mr. Liao was really a respectable gentleman.

Chapter Twenty Seven

The Puyi Who Dared to Speak Out the Truth

On June 16th 1966, at about 5 pm in the afternoon, Mr. Li Jinde, Deputy Secretary General of the CPPCC, came to the Commissioner's Office, to announce several decisions that had been made by the CPC Committee of the CPPCC HQ:

1. Because of the vehement claims from the revolutionary working staff of the CPPCC HQ, all of the commissioners had to join the Cultural Revolution.

2. The CPC Committee of the CPPCC HQ has decided to send an investigating group to the HAPE, so as to make a thorough investigation of these complaints. (The revolutionary working staff of the CPPCC HQ had already posted up many large wall-posters to show their complaints and harsh criticisms concerning the works of the Committee of the HAPE and its leader, Mr. Shen Bochun.)

3. All of the Commissioners should assist the investigating group with their work. They are encouraged both to confess their own political problems and also to expose the political problems of others.

Before this, when the commissioners had been summoned to study and discuss newspapers, magazines and documents about the Cultural Revolution, they were only asked to talk about their views and the reflection they had gained from studying it. To protect them, the leaders of the CPPCC hadn't even let them go to read the large wall-posters posted up by the working staff of the CPPCC HQ. It was a case of "praise the sea, but keep on land (just watching, but not participating)". But now, the leaders themselves were being attacked verbally, thus they had no power to protect the commissioners.

The next morning, Puyi and the other commissioners were led into a large meeting room, where many of the large wall-posters were hanging. One of posters questioned Mr. Wang Shuceng, a commissioner, as to who had instigated him to write and publish a pamphlet, which was considered an attempt to promote the overthrowing of the socialist system. The working staff of the CPPCC HQ accused Mr. Shen Bochun of committing many crimes and one of them was to shield Puyi. That afternoon, the commissioners had a meeting and all of them had to air their views about the contents of the wall-posters they had seen that morning. Puyi expressed that he welcomed the "revolutionary working staff" criticizing him, but the truth was that he himself was very fearful and depressed.

Very promptly, the commissioners' normal work was ordered to cease and all of the "Historical Accounts of Past Events" were sealed. Every day, all of them, even though some of them were ill or very old, had to join the political study session and also do some physical work. The rebels gave consideration to Puyi, Pujie, Du Yuming and Song Xilian, assigning them to do rather easier jobs. But Kang Ze, though he was suffering from an illness, was ordered to do heavy jobs, because he had once been a major Nationalist Party spy.

One day, Puyi and some of the commissioners, called "the monsters and demons" ("*Niu Gui She Shen*"), being those who were considered to be the dregs of the society, were ordered to change the dirt in fifteen rose pots. They eliminated the lumps from the new earth and sieved it first, then poured out the original earth from the rose pots. Before replacing the rose plants with new earth, manure had been placed underneath them. Finally the rose plants were replaced into the rose pots. Room was left at the top of each pot, for watering purposes. One of the commissioners later recalled this interesting labour in his memoirs:

Shen Zui was rather young and in good health, so he could do his job quickly. Seeing that aged Mr. Du Jianshi (a former Nationalist Party General) was doing his job slowly, the earnest "Emperor" went to help him. He carried the rose pots, with the already changed soil, and placed them down into the sunshine, while at the same time putting his nose to a rose to smell its sweet aroma. He wasn't aware that the flowers in new earth shouldn't be in the sun and that they must be kept in the shade and watered for one or two days first. Therefore, an hour later, all the roses and leaves had wilted and drooped. "Emperor" cried out in alarm: "The beautiful flowers are dying. I had said that their earth shouldn't be changed because they are just young plants.... They also have their lives. It's terrible! They are all dying!" I went to find a gardener. He said: "It doesn't matter. Just move them to the shade, please. They will slowly recover." The roses finally revived, only a few petals having dropped to the ground. "Emperor" picked them up with heavy heart: "It's a pity, I'd like to keep them in my pocket to smell their perfume." His love for flowers infected us, so we followed him, picking up the petals and putting some into our pockets too, enjoying their fragrance.

During the break, each of us took out our home-cooked lunches to eat. One person showed us his lunch which was "pungent bean curd in chili oil". Choudoufu is a kind of strong-smelling preserved bean curd, very popular in China). He amused us by saying, "We have appreciated the fragrance of the roses, now I'd like to give you something foul to smell." He opened his lunch-box and immediately a stench burst out to greet us. Puyi hated the smell, covering his nose with one hand and complaining: "We enjoyed a sweet smell just now, who created that foul smell? How annoying!" Some people say that "pungent bean curd" is a kind of delicious dish, which only China has. Someone said, "I love pungent bean curd. The famous experts and scholars who are criticized now are, in fact, like pungent bean curd, they smell awful, but taste delicious!" Hearing what we said, Puyi, with a steamed bun in his hand, went to where the pungent bean curd was. "May I taste a little bit?" he requested. He gripped a small piece of it, placing it into his mouth and biting just a little bit. "Wonderful!" The expression on his face had suddenly changed from intenseness to joy. While nodding his head, he praised the pungent bean curd, "How delicious!" He bowed to us, giving the thumbs up, "Thank you for letting me realise that I like the pungent bean curd."

Mr. Dong Yisan, a former Nationalist Party General and one of Puyi's colleagues, had to join in this labour effort too. He recorded it in his diary: "June 19th 1966, in the morning, cleaning and changing the dirt in the rose pots. In the afternoon, reading newspapers and changing the rose pot earth."

From June 1966, Puyi and his commissioner colleagues had to write some large wall-posters and hold several general meetings to criticize Mr. Shen Bochun, their respective direct leader. But in the depth of his heart, Puyi never lost his conscience. One day, in their office, Mr. Shen Zui told Puyi that he had seen that Mr. Shen Bochun and some other major leaders of the CPPCC bound and paraded along the streets by Red Guards. All of them had been insulted by being forced to hold a worn shoe in their mouth, and some others had been forced to hold a tuft of rice stem in their mouth. (In China, a "worn shoe" is used as slang for a prostitute or woman who sleeps around with many men and a rice stem suggests "opportunist".) They were also beaten up and abused by the Red Guards. Upon hearing this, Puyi immediately began wailing and kept stressing: "They are all honorable people. They have done their best to work for our country, why are their achievements insulted in such a savage way?" He defied the slogan, "Rebellion is Reasonable!" which was very popular in China at that time. Holding Shen Zui's hand in his, Puyi anxiously asked him, while weeping: "Mr. Shen, why do the Red Guards dare to commit such atrocities? Why has our orderly country been stirred up into such chaos? Who instigates the Red Guards to do so?" Mr. Shen Zui himself, like most of the Chinese at that time, was also puzzled. He was unable to answer Puyi's questions and at the same time, worried that Puyi would be in trouble if he said anything undesirable. Finally, he sighed, only encouraging Puyi to take good care of himself and to recuperate at home and not to think of those vexing things. But Puyi still complained loudly that he didn't understand why those atrocities were occurring.

Mr. Shen Zui recalled later:

For a long time, at our political study sessions, Puyi always made his speech according to the essence of the newspapers and documents that we were arranged to study, seldom airing his own view. This made us frustrated. We considered that he avoided expressing his own ideas and we criticized him several times for this. The top leaders of the CPPCC had explained to us that although Puyi had been an emperor at that time, he never personally handled any affairs. So, it was no wonder that he couldn't put forward his own opinions on many matters. They said that they didn't think that Puyi intentionally concealed his real views, or was a double-dealer, therefore shouldn't be criticized. We all actually knew that Puyi was always keen on studying politics and that his extracts from newspapers and magazines had filled many notebooks. But that day, Puyi boldly poured out his views. He didn't agree with the rebels "seizing power from the hands of the leaders" at various levels. He sympathized with the leaders who were criticized brutally, even shed tears for them, although he knew that by doing this he would possibly be putting on the "terrible hat" of opposing the Cultural Revolution, or even being labeled "active antirevolutionary". Many years have passed, but I'm still touched by his sincerity, justness and brave behavior, whenever I think of it. Before, we considered that we dared to air our own opinions, but the fact was that at critical moments, only Puyi dared to speak out the truth. While what we cared about was our own safety, we should apologize to Puyi for misunderstanding him. It is us, not Puyi, who should be blamed for the selfishness in protecting ourselves.

During the last ten days of July, the commissioners were again told that, once a month they must do physical labour at the Beijing Low-Voltage Electrical Equipment Factory. Puyi, with a blue Mao jacket, worked in the same group as "the 10th Panchen Erdeni Lama", one of the two major Tibetan Buddhist leaders, who wore a peaked cap. They assisted workers to drive in screws and fix elements. It was known that in 1964, Panchen had been denounced wrongly, and was dismissed from all of his posts. Premier Zhou Enlai worried for his safety, removing his whole family to reside in Beijing. Zhou arranged for him to meet with Puyi on November 24th 1965. His purpose was to let Panchen Lama gain enlightenment and to see his possible bright future from Puyi's experience. On that day, they had a long talk and had their lunch together. Eight months had passed since they had last meet, and the two acquaintances were glad to meet again to do physical labour together. Neither of them ever expected that this would be their last meeting.

During "Red August" (literally meaning "Revolutionary August", but actually, the August of 1966 was a bloody August! The notorious Red Guards carried out quite a lot of atrocities during "Red August", which shook the whole of China and also the world), in the CPPCC HQ grounds, some of the naughty teenage children of the working staff followed Mr. Du Yuming and Mr. Shen Zui, calling them "big bad eggs" and attacking them with balls of mud, which turned Shen's white shirt into a filthy one. Their direct leaders could then do nothing to help them.

Puyi's photo on his employee's ID Card

Mr. Shen Dechun kindly reminded the commissioners about the slogan "The son of a hero is always a great man but an anti-revolutionary father produces nothing but a bastard!" which was a very popular saying everywhere in China at that time, he warned them that their children could be connected with them, being despised or bullied, because of their special political status and that we should be careful concerning their safety. The commissioners were already aware of the gravity of the situation and worried that they would have nowhere to go. In those days, as the "Last Emperor of the Chinese feudal society", Puyi was always on tenterhooks, not knowing when disaster would come his way. At home, he frequently swept our courtyard and the road in front of our house and often went to dump rubbish. He discussed with me that hiring a housekeeper would be easily considered as exploiting others, so that we had better dismiss her. From then on, we had to do all of the housework ourselves. It was really very difficult for us because of our respective illnesses.

On the evening of August 8th, after listening to the communiqué, known as "The Sixteen Points", which was announced by the 11th Session of the Central Committee of the CPC, Puyi's distraught mood changed to excitement, but only for a time. When he and the other commissioners had a discussion about it at the CPPCC HQ, he made an enthusiastic speech: "The Cultural Revolution movement was bogged down into confusion in the preceding stage, but now, that the Central Committee of the CPC has announced 'The Sixteen Points', being the rules to direct the Cultural Revolution Movement, I hope that it will put an end to the present perplexing situation."

But their glorious desire was quickly smashed by the harsh realities. The confused situation deteriorated further after Mao Zedong received the millions of Red Guards at Tian'anmen Square, urging them to "incite revolution" throughout the whole country. Immediately, all of the country's systems and laws didn't exist anymore. The crazed Red Guards destroyed all the things which might be described as representing the "Four Olds" (old ideas, old culture, old customs and old habits). They converted many street names into revolutionary ones and the quaint shop boards, some were several hundred years old, became their objects, being smashed completely. All shops were ordered not to sell high-grade food, dresses, cosmetics, etc. Books were burned on the streets and artists, experts, writers and professors were cruelly persecuted, being insulted openly. The whole of Beijing City was filled with the smell of blood.

A general order compelling all of the democratic parties to disband immediately was posted on the streets. At the same time, in the CPPCC HQ, some large wallposters appeared demanding the reduction of the salaries of the commissioners and ordering them to do physical labour. Hearing that many homes of the capitalists (who had lived on fixed interests granted by the government) were raided by the Red Guards and that Mr. Liao Yaoxiang's wife and Mr. Wang Yaowu's wife had been abused by Red Guards, all of the commissioners were very well aware of the precarious situation they faced. As expected, on August 25th, all of the commissioners were summoned to their office in the CPPCC HQ. The rebels announced the decision to reduce the salaries of the commissioners by 30%, and some members of the CPPCC's salaries were even reduced by up to half. All of those former Nationalist Party Generals realised that they had no way to haggle, so they didn't say anything against it. But naive Puyi didn't realize this. He felt anxious that his reduced salary, plus my limited salary, was really not enough for our living expenses and medical fees, so he honourably requested that the rebels maintain his salary at 130 yuan per month. He was sure it was reasonable, but of course, he was refused.

The next day, in the grounds of the CPPCC HQ, all of the commissioners were forced to do hard physical labour, which included chopping wood for the canteen, sweeping the floor, doing weeding or clearing away the antiques that had been smashed by red guards. Seriously-ill Puyi, with several other commissioners, was told to chop

The Last Emperor of China My Husband Puyi

wood. A carpenter first cut the large logs into several sections with an electric saw, and then Puyi and his commissioner colleagues were told to carry them away to chop them into small pieces. For Puyi it was the first time in his life that he had been requested to do this. He was terribly scared by the deafening noise made by the electric saw, cowering back against the wall and stiffening his body in fear. The others could carry two or three sawn sections each time, but Puyi could only carry one and often leaned on the wall to gasp with fatigue. When chopping wood by axe, he felt pain all over, so would shake his hands to relieve the pain after each chop. Seeing this, the kindhearted carpenter offered to saw each ciruclar log section into quarters, which then made it much easier for Puyi to chop them again into smaller pieces by axe. Puyi bowed to the carpenter repeatedly and thanked him. Towards the end of August, three groups of Red Guards rushed into the homes of several commissioners, without any license, raiding their homes. Puyi and I were sure that the Red Guards would never let us off, but thankfully, at that time they never came.

Some people said that the reason our home was not raided at the beginning of the Cultural Revolution and that Puyi was not verbally attacked and beaten was because Puyi had enjoyed great popularity, therefore the people around him wanted to protect him. Although that was not the only reason, it was really the main one. Since we moved to live at 22 Dongguanyinsi Lane, Puyi had promptly developed a good relationship with all of our neighbours. All of the people living nearby, especially the elderly, as well as the children loved him and always gladly greeted him whenever they met him.

At the beginning of the Cultural Revolution, the Red Guards were only a student organization, but later many young people were encouraged to follow their example, setting up "Red Guard" organizations wherever they worked. On August 27th, some young working staff at the CPPCC HQ announced themselves to be "Red Guards". Just that afternoon, Mr. Shen Bochun was sent to transmit their orders to all of the commissioners. From

Puyi's desk in his office

that day on, all of the commissioners ceased going to work at the CPPCC HQ, instead choosing to study the *Selected Works of Mao Zedong* at home. Knowing that it was useless to say anything, Puyi and his colleagues had to pack a bag of "political study materials" and the documents about the Cultural Revolution and indignantly left their office. From that time on, they had no place to go to work.

Whilst at Fushun Prison, Puyi had always dreamed that sometime in the future, he would become a citizen and be able to work like ordinary people. Later he had been granted special amnesty and assigned a satisfactory job, realizing his dream. How happy he was when he could serve the people with his own

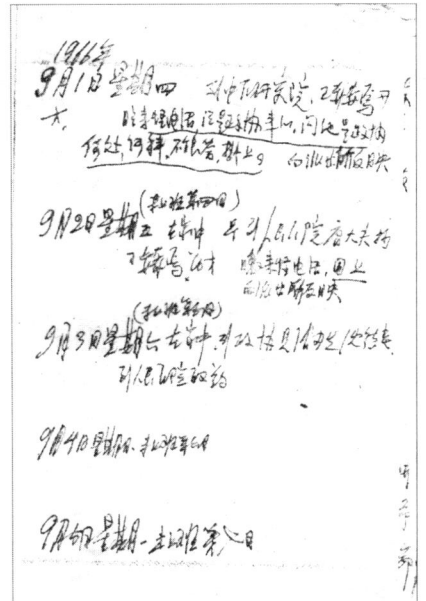

Puyi's diary in September, 1966

work. But now he was deprived of his precious right to go to work. His pain couldn't be described with words. The first sentence of his diary entry of August 28th 1966 was: "The first day of being unable to work…."

Following this, for a long time the first sentence of his diary always recorded his date of "not going to work". It showed his wordless denounce of the Cultural Revolution.

In the following few months, Puyi had to stay at home, recuperating. Besides the times going to visit his doctor, he enjoyed practicing calligraphy or reading the *Selected Works of Mao Zedong*. Sometimes, he went to the nearby streets to read the large wall-posters on the wooden frames there and would always tell me the sensitive news when he came back home. One day, he told me: "I read the large wall-poster viciously denouncing Comrade Liu Shaoqi. In my opinion, Comrade Shaoqui worked wholeheartedly for the Chinese people. It was he who signed our special amnesty."

He was also very sad after reading the large wall-poster which viciously denounced Mr. Xu Bing and Mr. An Ziwen, saying to me: "Those large wall-posters had no actual facts, only a series of 'fear-provoking untruths'. The Cultural Revolution's purpose is to purge all of the honest and respectable revolutionary veterans."

He was even furious when he heard that one of the leaders of the Masses Publishing House, who had helped Puyi with his amendment of *The First Half of My Life*, had been labeled "a spy". He shouted angrily at me, "I'll never believe it! We worked together for a long time. I know him. How can he be a spy?" Puyi sighed: "Our country will suffer further heavy losses if the Cultural Revolution continues!" I was deeply impressed by his painful and helpless expression as he said this.

In deep depression, Puyi's condition worsened day by day. Before, Puyi just like all of the commissioners, was privileged in the same way as the high-ranking government officials. He needed only to phone the CPPCC HQ, if he got ill. They would send a car to take him to hospital, but now the rule had been abolished by the rebels of the CPPCC HQ. I had to escort him myself when going to hospital, although I was also ill. Occasionally, when I couldn't go with him for any reason, he was often bullied or met some trouble on the way. Once at the People's Hospital, Puyi was seen by Madam Xin Fengxia, who was our friend and had also gone there to see a doctor. Later, she told me of Puyi's experience there:

Puyi was very honest and kindhearted. I saw him sitting in a line on a bench. He looked terrible, with his head drooping, while awaiting his turn to see the doctor. A nurse came to call his full name: "Aisin-Gioro Puyi!" He hurriedly stood up, but stared blankly. With his hands at his sides, he didn't know what he should do. The scene amused the nurse, who bent over with laughter. She pointed at him, "Go to hand over your registration receipt. There, go there...." Puyi went forward, walking like a straight stick. The nurse was still cruelly mocking him, "How funny! He still behaves the same as when he was in the Imperial Palace. With his hands at his sides, he looks like a menial...." Her unbridled laughter made the seriously-ill Puyi puzzled. When Puyi came back from the registration desk, his original seat on the bench had already been occupied by a young man. Daring not to say anything, he had to stand there, staring blankly. I pushed myself to one side, making room for him and waving to him to come and sit in my place, but he didn't feel good about coming. "That's not my seat," he said. I walked up to pull his arm to my seat. How burning it was! I realised that he must have a fever. I was anxious, telling him not to be stubborn, "Your seat has been taken by others. Sit here, please." With hesitation, he sat on the seat next to me. His body was also boiling. But several young men sitting on his bench still tried to maliciously tease him: "Brother, don't be silly! This is a hospital, not your home. Do you dislike me sitting on your seat? You may come here and I'll return it to you!" While saying this, the young man actually stood up, seeming as if he would give the seat back to Puyi, so he slowly walked up there and sat down on his original seat. But the two young men, on either side of him, intentionally pushed into him with their bodyweight. With his face alternately blushing and turning pale, he was clearly embarrassed. I went to plead with the young men for mercy for Puyi: "He is in pain, and has a high fever. Don't bully him anymore! Let him go to see the doctor first! How distressed he is!"

Later, I asked a doctor there about Puyi's condition and he answered that Puyi had already been hospitalized."

At that time, quite a lot of jokes about Puyi had circulated, but I knew that he was able to draw clear distinctions between the cardinal issues of right and wrong. Even lying in the sick bed in hospital, he still worried about our country's fate. When his colleagues went to see him, he always asked them about whom else among the leaders of the CPPCC and the UFWD had been viciously criticized recently and if any others had also been paraded along the streets by the Red Guards. By his request, whenever I went to the streets, I would often buy some tabloid newspapers edited and published by the Red Guards and other rebels for him. Some of those tabloids had contained the contents flattering Lin Biao, Mao's "Deputy Commander" or Jiang Qing, Mao's wife, the "Revolutionary Pioneer". The contents vilified the respected revolutionary veterans, labelling them as "opposing the CPC and Socialism". Puyi told me that he could analyse the current situation through reading the tabloids.

One day, when Mr. Shen Zui came to visit, Puyi asked him secretly: "A tabloid said that 'so and so' was a 'Nationalist Party spy'. You worked in the Nationalist Party Spy Agency for many years, do you remember him?" Shen Zui replied that he had neither seen him nor knew him before and he added: "I would have exposed his real identity to the government if I had known him then". Puyi again questioned him, whispering into his ear: "Many tabloids said that Lin Biao had always followed Chairman Mao and that Jiang Qing had made a great contribution to the Chinese Revolution. Why have we never heard this before?"

Later, Shen Zui recalled that he had been scared by Puyi's questions and had immediately cautioned him never to talk about that matter anymore. He stressed to Puyi that it would possibly create a fatal disaster, if he mentioned this again to others. Only after hearing this, did Puyi stop asking.

Chapter Twenty Eight

Our Venture in "Red August"

The torrents of the Cultural Revolution finally involved Puyi. We now know that this was because after being granted amnesty, Puyi had often had dealings with Premier Zhou Enlai, receiving his meticulous care and so cherished a deep affection for Premier Zhou. The extremely evil "Gang of Four" (the rebel heads) wanted to overthrow Premier Zhou. Because Puyi heartily esteemed and loved Premier Zhou, the "Gang of Four" also couldn't ignore Puyi.

In August and September 1966, we often received strange anonymous telephone calls at home, which aroused Puyi's vigilant concern. He told me worriedly that this meant somebody was already secretly scheming against us. Sure enough, we soon met with a series of unexpected troubles.

At the registration office of the United Hospital, the staff would inquire about each patient's family background first. Puyi was not able to lie, but he worried that the staff would be frightened if he replied that he had been "Emperor Xuantong". Feeling depressed, Puyi had no idea how to answer them, so he went to ask Mr. Dong Yisan, one of his colleagues and close friends. Mr. Dong didn't know how to answer them either. Finally, they decided to find their direct leaders, to gain instruction. On September 3rd, 1966, they found Mr. Shen Dechun and Mr. Zhang Renxian at the CPPCC HQ. But at that time those leaders were actually like "clay idols fording a river", hardly able to save themselves either. It was impossible for them to give Puyi any instruction as to what to do. The two leaders had to tell Puyi, "Right now, the whole CPPCC HQ is already paralyzed. You must go to get help from your local police substation or neighborhood committee, if you encounter difficulties."

At the beginning of September, when I went to buy our grain ration at the nearby designated grain shop, I was informed that we were not allowed to buy wheat flour and rice any more, but only corn flour. After this, I would go to buy wheat flour steamed bread with grain coupons every day. Puyi consoled me that in fact corn flour was more nutritious, so we might as well buy some to cook our meals. I bought several kilos of corn flour and cooked corn flour steamed buns for us. Puyi gladly praised it as deli-

A scene from the film *Fire Dragon*: Puyi and I in the Cultural Revolution

cious while eating it!

A gang of Red Guards were sent to the CPPCC HQ to post large wall-posters (*dazibao*—big-character written with the brush, prevalent during the Cultural Revolution, 1966-1976) on the wall which banned Puyi from continuing to enjoy a luxurious lifestyle. Then on September 10th Puyi got one hundred yuan, only half of his original salary at the Finance Section of the CPPCC HQ. According to commodity prices of the time, for most of the families, fifty yuan per person each month was quite enough. But both Puyi and I were suffering from several illnesses, so had to go to hospital almost everyday. Although we had free medical service, we had to pay for many costly tonics ourselves, such as white ginseng and American ginseng. Besides, we also had to pay expensive taxi fares when going to hospital. Puyi's two hundred yuan monthly salary had been barely enough for us, but now we were to receive only one hundred a month, how could we manage? But Puyi comforted me: "Don't worry about it. We can cut down on our expenses. I'm sure that the CPPCC will help us, if we really come across difficulties and need money."

Back then, what had made Puyi terribly upset was a letter that he had received on September 15th. That afternoon I was cooking dinner in the kitchen, when I suddenly heard Puyi scream in the living room. I hurried to see him. He was standing there staring, with an opened letter in his hand. I took it from his hand quickly and read it. It was written by one of Puyi's former pages in the Imperial Palace in Changchun, who was now a rebel. He ferociously criticized *The First Half of My Life* and the letter was filled with threats and words of intimidation. He apparently wanted to get even with Puyi. Standing by the telephone, with his hands trembling, Puyi was scared to death, as if losing his mind. I called to him anxiously, but he was muddled and couldn't answer me.

As soon as Puyi managed to "get his thoughts together" he wondered about reporting this to his leaders to get advice. He quickly phoned the CPPCC HQ, but couldn't get through. He then turned to the Masses Publishing House, but nobody answered it. That night he didn't eat or drink anything and had a hard time falling asleep. He even had nightmares. I did my best to soothe him, but he was still frightened and worried.

The next day, according to the unreasonable demands in the letter, Puyi turned over to the CPPCC HQ the whole of the writing fee for his book *The First Half of My Life*, which was several thousand yuan! He said that he wanted to "return it to the country".

But, the former page's fury could not be dispelled. He wrote seven more letters, to remind Puyi of the crimes against him. Puyi answered him with nine self-criticizing letters, however even this still failed to satisfy him. The matter continued to worry Puyi, until he passed away.

Among the Aisin-Gioro Royal Clan, the home of Mr. Puren, Puyi's fourth brother, was the first one to be raided by the Red Guards. Quite a lot of jewelry, antiques, calligraphy and painting works were taken away. Next, a gang of Red

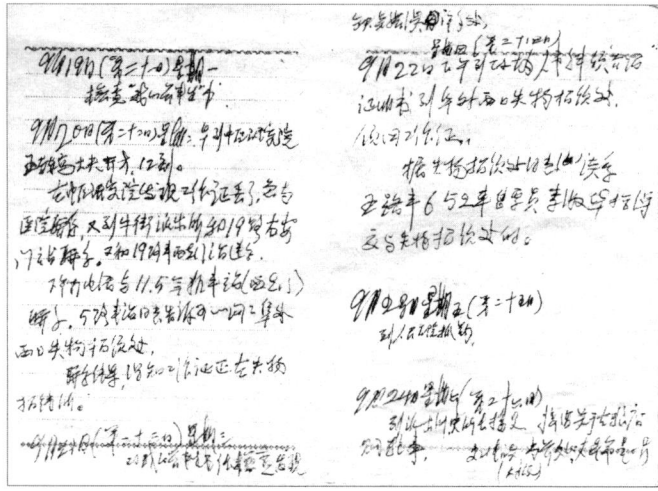
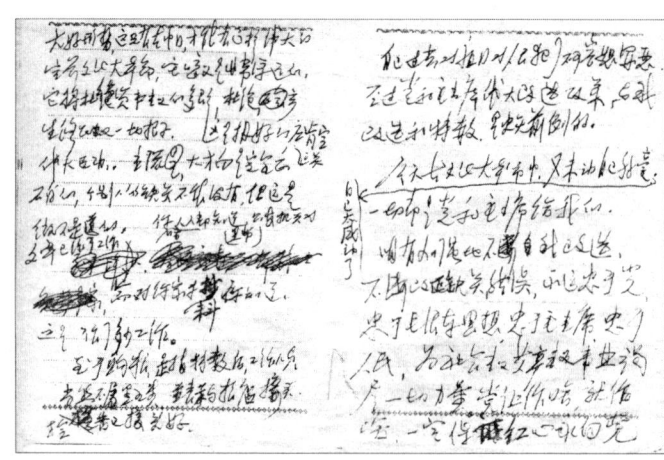

During the Cultural Revolution, Puyi severely self-criticized himself in his diaries.

Guards rushed into the home of Mr. Zaitao, Puyi's seventh uncle. In an attempt to prevent any atrocities, Madam Jin Xiaolan, Zaitao's second wife, committed suicide, by slitting her wrists. But the Red Guards still persisted in their raid.

Another group of young Red Guards from a middle school, headed by one of Puyi's nephews (Puyi's second sister's son), who had already announced his decision to split from his "feudal family", broke into Pujie's home. While shouting, "Down with the stooge (running dog) of Japanese Imperialists!" They rushed into the kitchen, smashing into small pieces the soybean and vinegar bottles which had Japanese trade marks on them. Madam Saga Hiro, Pujie's Japanese wife, shrank to the floor with fright, unable to move.

The homes of Madam Yunhe and Madam Yunxian, Puyi's second and fourth younger sisters, were also raided by Red Guards. Mr. Puxi, one of Puyi's distant cousins and a distinguished painter and calligrapher, had the most miserable experience. As early as in 1920s, Puyi had invited Mr. Puxi to visit and view the collection of paintings and calligraphic works stored in the Forbidden City. Later, when Puyi was staying in Tianjin and Changchun, Mr. Puxi would go there to give his congratulations on Puyi's birthday. Since Puyi's return to Beijing, he had still kept close contact with him. But after his home had been raided and having also been beaten by the Red Guards, Mr. Puxi took his daughter, left home and disappeared forever.

Chinese people often say: "Heaven never seals off all the exits." During the early period of Cultural Revolution, when the crazed Red Guards were beating, smashing and looting everywhere, Puyi and I always felt a "great force", which seemed to protect us. We were clear that it came from the great figure, Zhou Enlai, who was loved and respected heartily by both Chinese and other peoples of the world.

The Fusuijing Police Substation, the one in charge of the public security of our living section, was ordered to protect our home's security and they did their best to fulfill this duty. When Mr. Shi, its director, heard that the nearby grain shop had stopped the supply of our wheat flour and rice, he immediately went to its leader,

In 1966, Puyi still received the invitations to participate the reception party and celebration for the National Day.

asking him to review the decision, which meant that we didn't have to worry about our food problem anymore. And the CPPCC HQ also received an order from its higher authorities to resume Puyi's original salary. Fortunately, he received a reduced salary for one month only and was given two hundred yuan again the following month. We were pleased to have our daily life's needs guaranteed again.

As in previous years, on the eve of the 1966 National Day, Puyi gladly received an invitation for our National Day's reception and celebration party. Although he had already attended those kinds of national activities for many years, during the Cultural Revolution, it had a special meaning. For at that time, all people used to judge the political life and status of VIPs and celebrities, according to whether or not they could attend the National Day party and other CPC's protocol activities and their numerical positions on the name lists in newspapers. Being valued politically made Puyi feel gratified and actually meant he was given "an overcoat of political security".

One day, while chatting with Puyi, Mr. Shi, the Director of the Fusuijing Police Substation, revealed a secret to Puyi: "You are known to everybody. You don't know how much we have done to protect you from being verbally attacked by the Red Guards and your home from being raided by them!" What he said was true!

We were out when the group of Red Guards, who had already raided many homes of the Aisin-Gioro Royal Clan, first came to our home. After entering our courtyard, they had first looked around, and then announced that they had come to "smash the old and build the new". They didn't destroy the lock outside the door of our living room, but before leaving, they asked Mr. Dai, our neighbour, to pass on to us their demand that we demolish the pair of stone lions on the roof of our house. The next day, the group of the Red Guards came to our home again. They rudely questioned Puyi as to why he hadn't demolished the pair of stone lions on the roof yet. I informed them that Puyi was ill and that he couldn't climb onto the roof. The Red Guards then ordered us to have them demolished within two days! Soon afterwards, they went into our living room to check around, and then they came out to reprimand Puyi: "Why do you still enjoy such a luxurious life, still eating steamed rice and still sleeping on a soft bed? You can't use that furniture, move them away!" Hearing that the Red Guard had gone to our home, several working staff from our neighbourhood committee and Director Shi hurriedly came to save us from the dilemma. They had entered our courtyard when we were feeling bewildered, not knowing how to answer the Red Guards. They explained to the leading Red Guards:

"It has often been arranged that Mr. Puyi should receive foreign guests at their home. The furniture in his lounge was allocated by the Government for that reason."

"There are no foreign guests in China now. Take all of them away!" the Red Guards said firmly.

The Red Guards were going to rummage through chests and cupboards at our home, but were curbed immediately by Mr. Shi: "We have received instruction from higher authorities, not to allow anybody to raid Mr. Puyi's home. They may open their trunks for you to check."

I opened the bookcase in the living-room, the wardrobe and several wooden trunks in our bedroom for them to inspect. They found only *The Selected Works of Chairman Mao* and our daily clothes and daily necessities in them. Actually, before this we had already burnt most of Puyi's diaries, notebooks and calligraphy works and had stored in a safe place those worthy enough to be preserved. The Red Guards failed to obtain the objects they wanted. One of their leaders was surprised: "At Puren's home, there were so many valuable objects in the safe. Why are you so poor?" Finally, they had to withdraw from our home with disappointment.

After the Red Guards had left our home, to avoid making any more trouble for us, Puyi decided to move the furniture in our home away, for it was the furniture which at that time seemed to be drawing their attention. He still wanted to move it, even though the working staff of the Neighbourhood Committee and Mr. Shi advised him that he often received foreign guests at home, and so he needed it. The following day Puyi went to the CPPCC HQ to get two trucks. They returned with Puyi and the two second-hand wooden single beds but took away our sofa, soft bed and carpet to the CPPCC HQ, only leaving a wooden table and two chairs. Puyi didn't know that one of the two secondhand wooden single beds had an unstable frame, so during that night, Puyi's bed collapsed to the ground, waking him up. Promptly the following day, I went to buy a new wooden single bed for Puyi. Puyi had still not yet recovered from the fright and he phoned to the CPPCC HQ, requesting them to send people to demolish the pair of stone lions on the roof of our house, which was considered by the "Red Guards" to be one of the "Four Olds".

The policemen of the Fusuijing Police Substation were concerned about this matter, and so took more specific measures to protect Puyi. They told us to phone them immediately when the Red Guards turned up again.

On October 14th, just after dinner, a group of the Red Guards from other parts of country rushed into our tranquil courtyard. They were boarding in the classrooms at a nearby primary school. At that time, all education in the schools throughout China had been cancelled and while some of them were having their haircuts at a nearby barbershop, they heard that Puyi lived here. Those Red Guards said that they wanted to see, with their own eyes, Puyi, the famous "Little Emperor". Puyi had phoned the Fusuijing Police Substation immediately as he had been advised. Director Shi and Director Tang arrived at our home very promptly. They called the head of the Red Guards out of our lounge and questioned him:

"Who allowed you to come here? Do you have an introduction letter?"

"We heard that the 'Little Emperor' lives here. We wanted to have a look at him," the Red Guard said.

"According to the higher authority's instruction, you must have the special approval by the Central Government, if you want to see him. This is a major matter relating to our government's United Front Work Policy. You must go!" ordered Director Shi.

The Head of the Red Guards returned to our lounge and led the other Red Guards away from our home. After that day, still more groups of Red Guards came to our home from other parts of country. They claimed that they just wanted to see whether or not the "Little Emperor" was different from ordinary people. They would always look Puyi up and down and say: "Oh, I see, this is what the emperor looks like!" then they would go away. Once a naughty boy invented doggerel after seeing Puyi: "Hearing his great name for a long time, he is the famous Chinese Last Emperor, known throughout the world. But today I was disappointed when I saw him. He is just like me, wearing a pair of spectacles, too."

In those turbulent days, Puyi was lucky not to be persecuted by the Red Guards. But we had always felt heartbroken whenever we thought of the two precious missing photos: one was Chairman Mao with Puyi and the other one was of Chairman Mao, Puyi and five esteemed celebrities. Later, Mr. Shen Zui told me that Puyi was the only one among those who had received special amnesty, to be received by Mao and to have a photo taken with him. Puyi had displayed the two valuable photos in our bedroom. When the Cultural Revolution started, we worried that they would be taken away by the Red Guards if they rushed into our home. Puyi therefore thought it over and over again. Finally, he decided to send them to the CPPCC HQ to be kept there. But we never expected that in the Cultural Revolution even the CPPCC HQ would not be a safe place either and that we would lose them forever!

Chapter Twenty Nine

Bitter Taste of Revenge

Although Premier Zhou's forceful protection sheltered Puyi from the frontal attacks of the Red Guards, he was still being harassed by the intolerant letters mailed by the former page in Changchun. While scrutinizing *The First Half of My Life*, page by page, Puyi had given considerable critical thought, while attempting to find faults with himself. He sincerely felt regret that he had made the former page and the other pages suffer a lot while he was at the Imperial Palace in Changchun and he could recognise his anger in the sarcastic ridicule which filled his letters. Puyi didn't blame the former page for feeling the way he did, but tried his best to appease him, acknowledging that he had ill-treated him at times.

Even at this time, Puyi still had faith in his direct leaders who had taken good care of him for a long time. He would take the letters from the former page and his own letters to him, to the CPPCC HQ, showing them to his direct leaders, in the hope of getting their help. On October 24th 1966, Puyi went to the CPPCC HQ again. He talked with Mr. Shen Dechun and Mr. Zhang Renxian about how to draw more criticism about his book *The First Half of My Life*. That day, the two leaders encouraged Puyi: "It's good to believe in Socialism and the Communist Party and to rely on leaders for assistance." But Mr. Shen Dechun reminded him that he still needed to think hard for himself when he met with puzzling problems. During the civil strife of the Cultural Revolution, all of the honest leaders, at various levels, such as Mr. Shen were also concerned and perplexed by so many incomprehensible matters. They had already been deprived of their powers, so how could they help Puyi?

Puyi thought of the Masses Publishing House, which had edited and published *The First Half of My Life*. He contacted them several times to get their cooperation in "finding any possible errors" in the book. On December 2nd 1966, once again, Puyi phoned the Masses Publishing House, but he was told that the editor of the book was out. Puyi realised that they said this because they were afraid to be involved in this matter. He sincerely told the receiver, that with his own limited standards of understanding, he really couldn't make a satisfactory self-criticism which could please the former page, who was now a rebel. So, he hoped that the Masses Publishing House could help him to do this. The receiver stalled him further by saying, "I'll convey your words to our leaders." He received no further response after that.

Puyi had no idea about how to continue his criticism of the book. Vexation tortured him endlessly. I suggested to him that we might go to find our good friend Mr. Dong Yisan, who was living very close to our home. Mr. Dong was quite knowledgeable and always very kind to Puyi. "Maybe he can find more problems from the book," I said and we went to Mr. Dong's home together. Mr. Dong told Puyi his honest opinion of the matter. Finally, he said: "Mr. Pu! It seems that now you must face the difficulties and solve them on your own. Chairman Mao once said that by being earnest, one can resolve any difficulties. I'm sure you are able to deal with this problem. Never be afraid of threats—everybody knows that you have confessed all your past mistakes to the government and that you have already been remoulded to become an excellent citizen. Now, you have already received official acceptance as a model citizen, therefore don't be afraid of his threats! Be patient and be prepared to write to him on this matter over a period of time. I'm sure that while doing this you will slowly learn how to deal with him." Dong's words encouraged Puyi. From that time, Puyi showed Mr. Dong each of the letters from his former page and his replies to him, so as to get his opinion. Following Puyi's suggestion, Mr. Dong reread *The First Half of My Life*, helping Puyi to find any possible problems in it. Puyi was very grateful for Mr. Dong's valuable help. On the evening of December 12th, grasping Mr. Dong's hands and with warm tears in his eyes, Puyi said to Mr. Dong: "I'm like a person struggling in the water for survival. It's you who are kind enough to pull me out with your own hands."

In December 1966, Puyi wrote several long letters to the former page, to further criticism concerning his book *The First Half of My Life*. In his reply the former page had to acknowledge that Puyi had already realized his mistakes, but at the same time, he demanded that Puyi "confess who helped you write the replies to me...." Puyi was angry and anxious so much that his blood pressure rose abruptly. This alarmed and bewildered me and I didn't know how to console him.

The intense mental stimulation seriously impaired Puyi's health. His uraemia reoccurred and once again on December 23rd he was sent to the United Hospital. Not long after that, another letter of threat from the former page came to us. I didn't let Puyi know about it, so I wrote a reply to him myself instead. I informed him that Puyi was currently very ill in hospital, but that he would contact him when he recovered. Surprisingly, my reply offended this rebel. At the end of January 1967, he wrote a threatening letter to Puyi and I. It read:

Mr. Aisi-Gioro Puyi and Mrs. Li Shuxian

I received your letter. I want to know what kind of serious disease made you unable to write! None of your little tricks! I'm informing you that I'm planning to print leaflets to distribute in Beijing, to appeal to the revolutionary workers, peasants and soldiers to oppose you. I expect you to reply to me. I'll make you suffer if you fail to satisfy me. I'm ready to go to Beijing at any time.... Replying to me is up to you!

Now, I understood completely that the former page would never let Puyi "off the hook", until Puyi's heart stopped beating.

It was also in the January of 1967, that Puyi got another shock which he never expected. Madam Li Yuqin (Puyi's former concubine and fourth wife) and her sister-in-law came to find Puyi in Beijing. That day, Li Yuqin, wearing a Red Guard armband (though she was not entitled to one) and her sister-in-law, who was also masquerading as a Red Guard (although she was in her forties at least) appeared in the wards of the Peking United Hospital, where Puyi was hospitalized. She pushed open the door of Puyi's ward and entered, while I was helping Puyi to move about in his hospital bed. His body was very swollen. Suddenly seeing Li Yuqin, Puyi's face immediately turned pale. With difficulty, he removed his quilt and got out of his bed. He stretched out his hand to greet Li. I noticed that his hand was trembling.

But Li Yuqin didn't shake the trembling hand Puyi offered to her. She just angrily nagged at Puyi words she had already prepared: "You ruined my life. You know that I became your concubine by being cheated and after I married you, you made 21 prohibitive rules restricting my freedom. Now, I'm called the 'people's enemy'. This is simply because I used to be your concubine. You must write a letter of clarification, saying that I had nothing to do with the crimes you committed in the Manchukuo during those days. Then, maybe the Red Guards in Changchun will leave me alone."

"I committed a lot of crimes in the first half of my life," Puyi admitted, feel-

The letter of clarification for Li Yuqin. It was written down by Pujie because Puyi was too weak to write.

ing sorry for his wrongdoing and sincerely apologizing to her. At the same time, he mumbled that he was too sick to write anything. Li Yuqin didn't believe it. She continued, saying, "Everybody knows you wrote a book. You mentioned my name in it, making trouble for me. You owe me for that! How much money did you make on the book?" Puyi told her that the fee on the book was not much and that he had already given most of it back to the government. Li was still unsatisfied with what he said. "You must have made a lot of money on the book. I should get my share," she snapped.

After Li and her sister-in-law left, Puyi cried for a long time. He told me: "I don't know why I was so alarmed and nervous when I saw her." He further commented that Li Yuqin had changed from the lovely girl that she had been in the Imperial Palace in Changchun and the attentive young wife who had gone to visit Puyi at the Fushun Prison in 1950s. Later, Li Yuqin still went to see him whenever she came to Beijing, for they had decided to stay friends after they divorced in 1957 in Fushun.

As Puyi's former concubine, Li Yuqin had been despised for a long time by some of the people around her, and in the early 1950s, she couldn't find a job to support herself. Her elder brother, a former Chief of Police (he had been promoted to that position because he was Puyi's relative) at the beginning of 1950s, was classified as a "historical anti-revolutionary". For being former relatives of the "Manchukuo Emperor", all members of her native family had, to some degree, met troubles in their life and work after the liberation and suffered a lot in the Cultural Revolution too. So, it was a reasonable demand to ask Puyi to write a letter of clarification to help clear their names.

But, they should also have treated Puyi, a seriously-ill patient, with kindness and consideration. Witnessing how ruthlessly she had bullied Puyi, I was furious. Even nineteen years later, when I had the opportunity to see Li Yuqin again, I still couldn't help reprimanding her saying "Anyway, you and Puyi were a married couple before, how could you force Puyi to write a letter of clarification for you, when he was too weak to do that?" I put to her.

A few days later, when it was close to Spring Festival, Puyi was given a laboratory test. After that, I was told that Puyi was getting a little better and that I may take him back home to enjoy the Spring Festival. But I was afraid that, without heating, Puyi would easily catch a cold at our home and that his condition would worsen. Therefore, I arranged for him to be moved to the common ward of the People's Hospital which had heating.

Very quickly, Li Yuqin pursued us to the People's Hospital. She took some Red Guards in green Mao jackets and red armbands with her. They weren't aware of the real situation. Li interrogated Puyi fiercely: "Puyi, you must confess how you cheated me to marry you and how you promoted my elder brother to be the Chief of Police. We

During the period of the Cultural Revolution, Li Yuqin and her family were sent to live in remote countryside to be "reeducated" by local peasants.

were originally the children of a poor family, but now we are denounced as the relatives of the former Manchukuo Emperor. You must write a letter of clarification to explain that we have no connection with what you did at that time and you never gave me and my family members any privilege and special care." She was more ferocious this time, not allowing Puyi to say anything and seeming intent on overwhelming him. I was not there that evening, but fortunately, another patient in the common ward, a student of the Peking University, was enraged by their arrogance and thoughtlessness. The young man came over to right the wrongs. He shouted at Li, "You are not a real Red Guard!" He seemed to be able to see through her actions. "Your armband is just a disguise to make you think you can force your way in here to harass a dying man. You want him punished, so that people in Changchun will think that you are real revolutionary. I'll inform the Red Guard Headquarters in Beijing about who you really are, if you don't leave here immediately."

What the young man said worked. Li Yuqin and the other Red Guards left at once. The next day, Puyi told me about her having brought Red Guards to the ward. He said, "They said that I owe the People in northeast China 'blood debt' (Indicating that Puyi had helped the Japanese to carry out a lot of atrocities while in the Manchukuo). They wanted to take me back there to be punished. I was lucky to have the young man, Xiao Wang, to rescue me."

Wang Qingxiang and Li Yuqin in Changchun during the 1980s

However, Puyi still understood Li Yuqin. He explained to me several times: "She is right to ask me to write a letter of clarification for her, to free herself from her predicament. I'm going to write one for her, according to the facts." Because he was too sick to hold a pen to write anything, he called for his brother Pujie to record his dictated account, so as to write the letter of clarification which Li and her elder brother wanted.

Finally, following the request of Li Yuqin, the CPPCC HQ provided the train tickets for her and her sister-in-law to return to Changchun.

In this critical time, Premier Zhou Enlai openly praised *The First Half of My Life* and the documentary *The Chinese Last Emperor Puyi* when he realised that some people were viciously criticizing them. His speech was reported in many newspapers: "Puyi has been back from Russia for sixteen years. With a deep feeling of remorse, he has written a book about the first half of his life. We have successfully remolded the Chinese 'Last Emperor'. It's a world famous miracle." Mr. Wan Jiaxi, Puyi's fifth brother-in-law, pleased with the news, went to the hospital, to tell Puyi these glad tidings. I saw tears well up Puyi's eyes. He uttered excitedly, "I heard the Premier's voice. It was really the Premier's voice...."

It was our esteemed and beloved Premier Zhou, who never forgot to protect the "Chinese Last Emperor", now a citizen of The New China, saving him from being swallowed up by the Cultural Revolution.

Chapter Thirty

Being in Bondage to an Incurable Disease

Terrible illnesses continually ate away at Puyi's body. After his left kidney was removed in June 1965, only six months later, his right kidney was found to have a suspicious shadow again. And not long after that, he needed to have surgery to have his appendix removed because of the unbearable pain he had experienced. After the operation, Puyi fell into a stupor for several days, black and purple froth being frequently vomited from his mouth. It led to uraemia and Puyi's condition further deteriorated. He suffered greatly from dizziness, abdominal pain, nausea, coughing, constipation and especially diminished urinary output, so the doctor decided to insert a urinary catheter. The Chinese medicine that he took also helped. Eventually, he could urinate normally.

From January to April 1966, Puyi was hospitalized in the Peking United Hospital, to be treated for the shadow in his right kidney. The doctors there used radiotherapy and a mixture of Western and Chinese medicine, for Puyi had favoured using Chinese medicine to control his condition. But it was evident that the right kidney was still cancerous.

Puyi had some medical knowledge, had asked to be shown the reports after each laboratory test, and so therefore understood his condition clearly. Worrying that I couldn't cope, he had requested that the medical staff would not reveal any distressful news to me. As his wife, I certainly knew what kind of disease he had. I myself had begged the medical staff not to tell Puyi the true situation concerning his illness, so as to avoid adding to his worries. However one day, I accidentally came across his open diary which he had hidden under his pillow. Reading that he had already known his real condition, my emotional line of defence immediately collapsed and I burst into tears. Puyi quickly grabbed his diary out of my hands, blaming himself, "It's my fault, it's my fault!" he said, "I shouldn't have placed my diary there." He tried to console me by telling me not to worry, and that he would recover because the Chinese medicine would cure his disease.

After this, Puyi decided to take only Chinese medicine, while recuperating slowly at home. His condition was controlled for as long as half a year. But the threatening letter received in September 1966 had seriously affected Puyi's health, promptly raising his blood pressure. A month later, in a repeated laboratory urine test, cancer cells were discovered again and the doctor found that he also had severe anaemia.

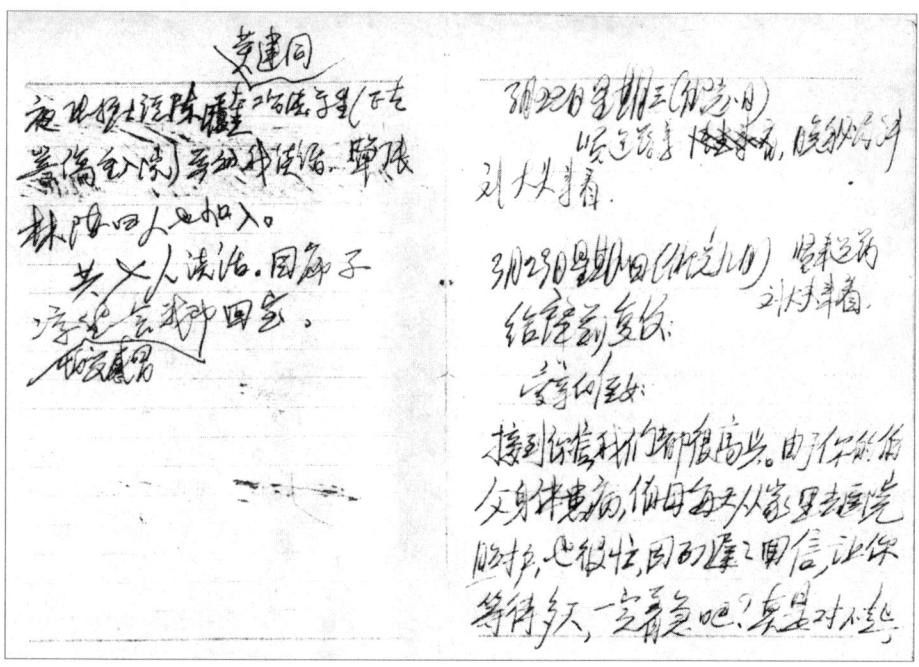

Puyi's diary written six months before his death. It shows his handwriting slowly deteriorating as his heath declined.

In those days, the Cultural Revolution was striding ahead and the whole of China had been cast into a state of utter confusion. How could poor Puyi get suitable treatment? On December 23rd 1966, Puyi once again was sent to the United Hospital, due to the resurgence of his uraemic condition. I was terribly frightened, having no idea how to deal with Puyi's condition. I really wasn't able to endure the cruel reality, so I couldn't resist the urge to visit Mr. Dong Yisan at his home, tearfully informing him and his wife of my dilemma.

The continuous infusion with added medication didn't work for several days. Puyi's condition worsened day by day. He requested to be treated by Dr. Pu, a distinguished Chinese doctor and also his close friend, who would give him Chinese medicine. But none of the doctors there took notice of this "Last Chinese Emperor" who had a terminal disease.

And what made me more indignant was that the factional strife among the medical staff in the United Hospital, had even involved Puyi. The "rebel faction" censured the "royalist faction", insisting that they shouldn't let "the previous feudal emperor" continue to stay in the special ward for high-ranking officials, so threatened to drive Puyi from that ward. One evening, the "order to leave" was finally issued by the rebels of the United Hospital. Dr. Wu informed me that the "Revolutionary Staff" of the hospital didn't agree that Puyi should continue to stay in the "high-ranking official ward" and that he must leave immediately. Hearing this, my heart felt as if it had been "fried in shallow oil".

I went wild with anxiety, jumping up and down. Puyi was so seriously ill, how could he possibly leave the hospital now? I dared not tell Puyi the news, so I begged Dr. Wu not to let Puyi know about it and that I would find a solution.

I promptly went to the CPPCC HQ, but it was then already about 8 pm, so most of the staff there had already gone home. I asked a familiar staff member the telephone number of Mr. Shen Dechun's home, but he informed me that the telephone at Mr. Shen's home had been demolished by the rebels. I left the CPPCC HQ tearfully and hurried to Pujie's home. I told Pujie what had happened to Puyi at the United Hospital and of his hope to be treated by Dr. Pu. Pujie immediately went to report this to Mr. Shen Dechun. Mr. Shen promptly reported it to the office of Premier Zhou Enlai. After having this reported to him by his secretary, Premier Zhou personally phoned the

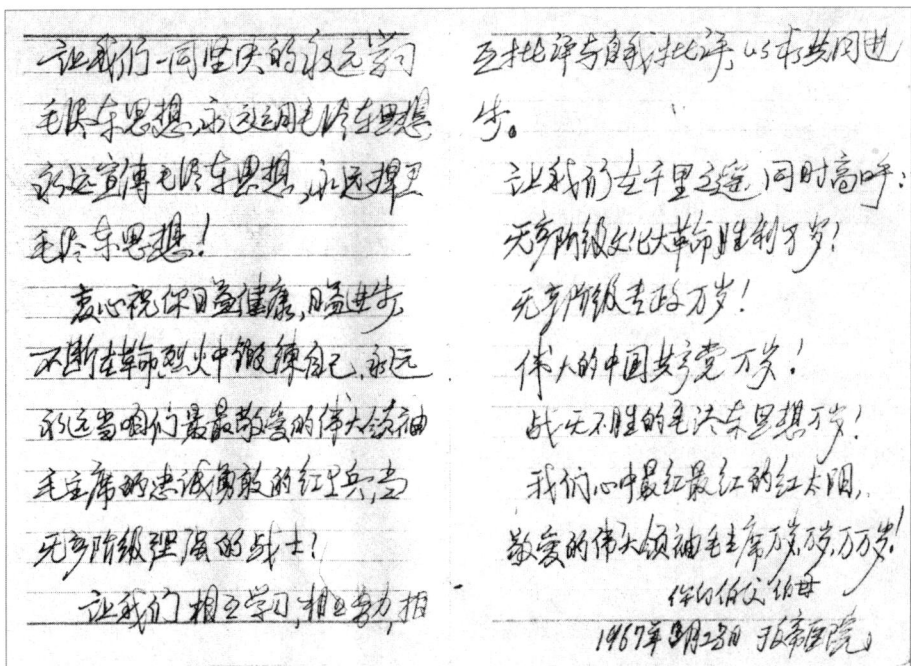

Puyi's diary written six months before his death. It shows his handwriting slowly deteriorating as his heath declined.

United Hospital, explicitly indicating to them that Puyi should continue to stay in the "high-ranking official ward" and that the United Hospital must continue to give him intensive treatment and nursing. Premier Zhou himself also informed Dr. Pu that Puyi wished him to treat his illness. Premier Zhou also asked Dr. Pu to convey his best wishes to Puyi. Thus, the two matters were resolved smoothly. After being treated by Dr. Pu, Puyi's uraemia improved and his condition was controlled again.

In the five and a half of years of our life together, Puyi was hospitalized nine times altogether. In the last half year of his life, he couldn't take care of himself. In the day time, I often held him by the arm, walking to the hospital because I couldn't find a car to send him there. Every evening, I would wash his feet and give him a massage. I needed to assist him when he needed to go to the toilet. Puyi preferred to use Chinese medicine, often taking a concoction of Chinese medical herbs. I worried that the hospital pharmacy wouldn't prepare them correctly, so I would always take the medical herbs back home to simmer them slowly myself for Puyi. Very often, in order to make up a correct dose of the prescription, I would have to go to search in many Chinese pharmacies dotted around the city, for one or two types of herb. Puyi once said to me tearfully: "Without your love and warmth to me, I couldn't have lived until today." I feel gratified that I had tried my best to take care of Puyi.

But there is one matter which, whenever I think of it, makes me deeply regretful. I can still remember clearly that day in January 1967, when Dr. Ni, my former colleague in the Jingshan Clinic, advised me that cancer cells had been found in Puyi's right kidney. As it was now his only remaining kidney, it couldn't be removed. But, he advised me, that in order to save Puyi's life, it could be replaced by a human donor or an artificial one. What he said was like lighting a candle in the darkness, giving me hope. Yes, I had two healthy kidneys, therefore I should dedicate one of them to Puyi! I decided to donate one of mine and went to discuss it with Puyi, but immediately he became angry, asking me whose idea it was? Seeing that he was so disturbed, I tried to comfort him by informing him that Dr. Ni had suggested giving Puyi a new kidney to save his life. Puyi retorted: "Why did he suggest doing this? This would be causing me to kill you! Without you, what could I live for?" Due to his uneasy reaction and expression (seeming as though we were going to have further surgery to remove my kidney to donate to him), I quickly "changed my tune", saying: "I'm only discussing it with you. This is only a suggestion!" Puyi replied to me firmly, "I won't allow you to mention this anymore." In his diary that day, Puyi wrote:

Xian is very kind to offer one of her kidneys to me, but I firmly opposed it. I'm sure that after taking Chinese medicine my condition will be controlled, even improved!

I don't think that I need to replace my kidney with one of Xian's.

    I very much regret that I failed to persuade Puyi at that time. If Puyi had taken Dr. Ni's suggestion, maybe his life could have been finally saved. Then, how happy we would have been! A few days after this, the United Hospital, which had been renamed, "Opposing Imperialism Hospital", was chosen to have the "glorious political task" of treating the wounded Chinese students who had been studying abroad, but had been severely beaten by the police there because they had wanted to "oppose revisionism" (the Russian government) in Moscow and Iraq. Therefore, all of the patients in the high-ranking official wards, which of course included Puyi, had to leave their wards. Puyi was sent to the common ward of the People's Hospital, but shortly afterwards, Puyi was told that he must leave there too, so he had to return home.

    As a result, a few days later, his uraemia had a further relapse. On March 1st, he was sent back to the People's Hospital again, but received only ordinary observation and treatment. On March 15th, Puyi was transferred back to the "Opposing Imperialism Hospital". But this leading Chinese hospital's quality of treatment and their medical staff's sense of responsibility to their patients were quite different from before.

    However, towards the end of April 1967, Puyi's illness had improved somewhat. During the bright and beautiful lights of springtime, he gladly left the hospital and returned home.

Chapter Thirty One

Puyi's Last Summer

Due to Premier Zhou's personal concern and instructions, Puyi was pampered and given privileges by the hospital. Puyi spent most of the time lying in his sickbed, but his misfortunes in the previous few months had already deeply hurt and affected him physically.

In March 1967, Miss Zhao Li, one of Puyi's nieces and a Red Guard, had come to Beijing to be inspected by Chairman Mao, along with hundreds of thousands of other Red Guards from all parts of China. One day she came to the People's Hospital to see her uncle, Puyi, but unfortunately Puyi was not in the ward, so Zhao Li left a note behind for Puyi, before leaving the ward. When he returned to the ward, Puyi saw the note. Immediately, he started to worry about whether or not Zhao Li had participated in the beating, smashing and looting, together with other Red Guards. He hoped that Zhao Li had kept a cool head, never doing the things she shouldn't do. On March 23rd, Puyi wrote a letter of more than one-thousand words, to Zhao Li, on behalf of both of us, which was motivated by his longing and concern for this niece. In the letter Puyi reminded her to never neglect her studies and encouraged her to continue the study of her curriculum privately (from 1966 to 1968, all schooling in China was stopped), and at the same time, imbue herself with communist ideals, so in the future she would be able to serve the people wholeheartedly. Finally, Puyi urged her not to worry about him, expressing that he would receive excellent treatment by the doctors and nurses, so that he could recover as early as possible.

On April 1st, the Red Flag Magazine and the People's Daily Newspaper, the organs of the Central Committee of the CPC, simultaneously published a long article under the title, "Patriotism or National Betrayal?" Its author, Qi Benyu, was one of the most popular rebels of that time and the so-called "Theoretician of the Cultural Revolution." The article opposed the famous "Wuxu Reform*" of 1898, launched by Emperor Guangxu

---

* "Wuxu Reform" had promoted the spread of scientific knowledge and Peoples' rights in China. It stood for reforming the Chinese feudal system and culture, hoping to rescue the nation from its crisis, to develop capitalism and set up a constitutional monarchial system in China. But Emperor Guangxu actually had no real power; so the reform was soon strangled by the conservatives, who were headed by Empress Dowager, Cixi.

In the last spring of his life, Puyi was standing under a tree in bloom in his courtyard, 1967.

(who was Puyi's adopted father and uncle) and some distinguished Chinese scholars.

Qi Benyu sharply denounced the "Wuxu Reform", saying that it would result in China becoming controlled by western imperialists. The publishing of the article aroused Puyi's attention and deep thought. Shortly afterwards the film *The Inside Story of the Qing Imperial Palace* (*Qing Gong Mi Shi*), which described and promoted the "Wuxu Reform" was shown all over the country, but was denounced vigorously.

During the following months, from April to June, many students, teachers, officials and workers came to visit Puyi in hospital or in our home. Some of them asked Puyi questions about the film and his previous daily life in the Forbidden City, wanting to find "fuel" to attack the film, but Puyi soon realized that some of them had actually just come "to see him with their own eyes", or ask for some of his calligraphy.

On April 20th 1967, while visiting Puyi, two teachers from the Beijing International Relations College invited Puyi to write calligraphy for them, using a writing brush, *Xuan* paper (Chinese painting and calligraphy paper) and some Chinese ink that they had brought themselves, but they were flatly refused by Puyi! Writing calligraphy had been one of Puyi's pleasures and before the Cultural Revolution, Puyi always gladly did it for all of his visitors from home and abroad whenever they expressed their hopes to get his calligraphy. He never let any of them be disappointed. But he refused to write calligraphy for anybody in this period, not because he considered his calligraphy valuable, but because he didn't know how much longer he might live. He didn't want

The Last Emperor of China My Husband Puyi

anybody to be in trouble for collecting his calligraphy.

Puyi thought he should be prudent in such a political climate, although at that time he still didn't realise that some people had already secretly schemed against him. They viciously criticized the documentary *The Chinese Last Emperor Puyi* as being a continuation of another film *The Inside Story of the Qing Imperial Palace*. Leaflets and large wall-posters denouncing the films had already been distributed or appeared on the huge advertising boards in the downtown and Tian'anmen Square areas of Beijing. On July 8th, an honest worker called Ren Yongda, at great risk, found our home to tell Puyi about some of the contents of the leaflets and large wall-posters relating to Puyi.

In the deep moonlight of that night, Mr. Ren Yongda hurried to our home again, to give Puyi the copies of some large wall-posters he had copied during the day. After Mr. Ren left, Puyi anxiously lit a cigarette, sat on a sofa and read through them. Realizing that he would suffer from the stress of giving considerable thought to this, I was worried about him and took the copy to read myself. Its contents produced by "the Red Flag Corps", a "Red Guards" Organization, condemned the documentary *The Chinese Last Emperor Puyi*, stating that it was more reactionary and traitorous than the film *The Inside Story of the Qing Imperial Palace*. Clearly, its target was seemingly aimed at Mr. Liao Chengzhi and Mr. Fang Fang (both of them worked under Zhou Enlai and were his reliable assistants), but actually, it was a "poison arrow" shot at Premier Zhou Enlai. At that time, Puyi was already used to abusive words aimed at him, but what he worried about was that somebody had started to attack Premier Zhou Enlai. Through the long re-education period, Puyi had already turned into a qualified citizen, with honesty and uprightness, and he was aware that he should care about others. He knew that our country's interests and our nation's future were most important.

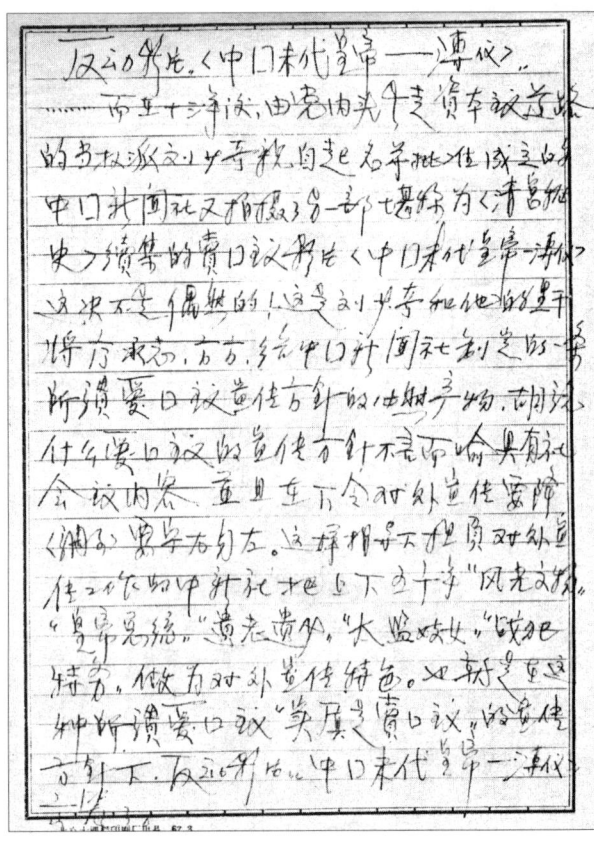

The copy of the large wall-poster seen by Ren Yongda. The poster criticized The Chinese Last Emperor-Puyi as a "reactionary film".

In the diary for that day, Puyi poured the heaviness of his heart out:

Our tours to east and northwest China were suggested by Premier Zhou and he announced this good news to us personally. I had hated myself for committing so many crimes to our nation and people. I knew that even death would not be a sufficient punishment for my crimes. In the history of mankind, only Chairman Mao and the Communist Party of China had the ability and boldness of vision to change a feudal emperor into a citizen.

In accordance with the special amnesty suggested by Chairman Mao, to release the war criminals who had been genuinely remolded, I was released on December 4th 1959. I was then very excited to see a bright future in front of me. I have always remembered that it was Chairman Mao and the Communist Party of China, who gave me my second life, therefore I was determined to remold myself continually, and never let Chairman Mao and the Communist Party of China down. But sometimes, I was complacent with the progress in my ideological remolding. Now I realize that I still have a long way to go in my ideological remolding.

Before, I didn't consider the documentary "The Chinese Last Emperor" was a poisonous weed. (During the Cultural Revolution, all of the criticized literary and artistic works were called "poisonous weeds".) I admired it for demonstrating my work and daily life after I became citizen. It publicized that the Communist Party of China led by Chairman Mao had obtained brilliant achievement in reforming the world, reforming mankind and remoulding criminals.

Some large wall-posters criticized that the documentary shouldn't have shot more scenes about my visits and daily life than about my political study sessions and doing physical labour. Some even said that the documentary actually beautified me, a former criminal. Maybe what they said is somewhat reasonable, but I'm sure the purpose of shooting the documentary is to eulogise the CPC's great policy of reformation.

In the political atmosphere of that time it was impossible for Puyi, a former war criminal, to directly refute the vicious attack to the documentary. He skillfully aired his view by using this method. In those days, he was not afraid of being tied up with the matter, what he hoped was letting the public understand and support the CPC's wise policy of remolding war criminals.

However, with the special government protection, neither the leaflets nor the large wall-posters could harm Puyi directly. However, his distress was slowly increased, by the daily bloody fights among the rebels themselves, which was happening in many parts of the country. In the summer of 1967, inside the CPPCC HQ, several of the rebel groups were fighting each other to "ferret out traitors", denounce the Capitalist "roaders" and to seize power. (Capitalist "roaders" and "traitors" were those who had some different views from Mao.)

Puyi's honest leaders such as Mr. Ping Jiesan, Mr. Zhang Zhiyi, Mr. Shi Yong, were cruelly persecuted. Puyi was overcome with sorrow when he heard that the respectable Mr. Xu Bing, Director of the United Front Work Department of the Central Committee of the CPC, had committed suicide, after having been cruelly treated for such a long time. Occasionally, there were still some rebels that came to disturb the seriously-ill Puyi with some questions, wanting to gain "great discoveries" from him.

Therefore the last few months in Puyi's life were spent in constant anxiety. However, what comforted Puyi greatly in those days, was that around him, all of his colleagues, neighbors, acquaintances and friends sympathized with him, trying their best to take care of and protect him. One day in the summertime of 1967, a depressed Puyi went out for a stroll alone. But he lost his way near Xizhimen. Black clouds suddenly gathered overhead and rain came pouring down, while he was pacing up and down there. Hungry and thirsty, Puyi felt in his pockets for money, but he didn't have any. He had no alternative, but to walk into a nearby house for help. He worried about how the people in the house would treat him, when they found out who he was. But the reality was quite different from what he expected.

The hosts of the house, a middle aged couple and an old man, were ecstatic when they were told that the chance comer in front of them was Puyi, "The Little Emperor", now a citizen. They entertained him very enthusiastically, with tea and cigarettes and at the same time, quickly cooked a meal for him before finally taking him back home. Later, Puyi hated himself for being so moved, that he forgot to ask the names of the good souls. He realized this when he later told Mr. Dong Yisan about his adventure.

Chapter Thirty Two

I Watched Puyi Passing Away

In the last two months of his life, Puyi had a feeble appetite and felt much weaker than before. He couldn't help gasping for breath when he walked. But with my help, he still struggled on, going to hospitals almost everyday, sometimes to the United Hospital for a check-up, sometimes to the People's Hospital for a drip and sometimes to the Hospital of Traditional Chinese Medicine to see Dr. Pu for a new prescription. Without the usual administration, the whole of the CPPCC HQ was in chaos, so that Puyi couldn't get a car from there to take him to hospital like before. On the occasions when I failed to find a tricycle-taxi, I had to support him by holding one of his arms, while walking towards the hospital.

In those difficult days, I worked for Puyi as a real "house-nurse". Everyday, I would simmer a dose of medical herbs for him, give him several injections and also help him take western medicine. Puyi's anaemia became more serious around this time. To improve his nutritional intake, I bought a lot of baby chickens and raised them in our courtyard. After a few days, I stewed one of them, letting Puyi eat its delicious meat and drink the nutritious chicken soup. In 1967, "chicken-blood therapy" had been very popular throughout China. With no intention of leaving things to chance, I gave Puyi an injection of chicken blood, but of course it didn't work and Puyi's condition continually worsened. At the beginning of September he started suffering from congestion in his lungs and breathed heavily all day long. He couldn't lie down while sleeping. I had to put two or three pillows underneath his head. Even with those, it was still hard for him to fall asleep. I knew that this was a symptom of cardiac failure.

I shall never forget the evening of September 30th 1967. Outside the window of our bedroom, the bright moonlight was sparking like water on the courtyard and the falling leaves from the trees were wafting quietly to the ground in the autumn wind. The intermittent sound of firecrackers celebrating the National Day came from far away, breaking the terrible silence in the room.

Puyi, lying in his sickbed, was aware apparently that he was not far from his last moment of life. Grasping my hand, he pulled me to sit on the edge of his sickbed. He stared at me intently, with tears in his eyes. I knew what he was hoping to say to me, but I still didn't want him to say it. I wiped his eyes gently with my handkerchief. For a long time, both of us couldn't utter a word. Since June of 1966, in our country all I had heard was hubbub, all I had seen was confusion. Today I finally had quietness, but what a desolate quietness it was! At last, Puyi felt the need to pour out the words, which he had kept in his heart for a long time:

I'm going to leave this world. For such a long time I haven't wanted to say this to you, because I was afraid of hurting you. I know that what I have is an incurable disease. To console you, I have said to you that modern science and technology could cure my illness but I knew that I couldn't recover at all. In my life, I was both emperor and citizen. I have been very fortunate to have you to take good care of me in my later years, otherwise I would have suffered a lot more. Now, I'm calmly coming to the end of my life and I'm glad to have you with me to the very end. But what made me feel guilty was, firstly that I owe a great deal to the Communist Party of China. They spent ten years with a considerable amount of effort, to change a thorough-going feudal ruler into a qualified citizen. This is one of the miracles in the history of mankind. Only the Communist Party of China had the ability and boldness of vision to do this for me. I'm sorry that my contribution to the Communist Party of China has been so little, and that I shall have no further opportunity to do more work for the them. Secondly, I'm very, very sorry for you. We have been married only five years, but I'm leaving you alone. I'm much older than you and I hate myself that I can leave neither money nor property, nor any other valuable items for you. You are in very poor health and now we are in the midst of the Cultural Revolution, so after I go, who can you rely on? Who will take care of you? What concerns me the most is you!

What Puyi said made me feel very sad. I knew he had to say those words to me, but I forced myself to bear the tremendous pain in my heart and to hold back my tears. I consoled him: "Don't think that way anymore. Be patient and have good recuperation! When you get better, we can go to tour the Summer Palace and the Beihai Park together again...." How I hoped this would come true! I hated to believe that what Puyi had said just now would be his last words! But the terrible end was really coming to us.

On October 4th, in the morning, I took an extremely weak Puyi to the United Hospital for another medical check. While breathing heavily, he walked very slowly because his legs were terribly swollen. During that afternoon, some friends came to our home to see Puyi. He chatted with them excitedly, inviting them to have dinner with us. Our housekeeper, who was an excellent cook, gladly cooked several very delicious dishes for us. I was overjoyed to see Puyi, who had had no appetite for a long time, eating two small bowls of steamed rice, a portion from a number of dishes and he even drank a little bit of Chinese rice wine. At about 9 o'clock in the evening, Puyi happily said farewell the guests from our gate. But unexpectedly, only less than an hour later, Puyi's uraemia symptoms became evident again. Not being able to urinate, he felt very distressed, so that he couldn't go to sleep and was moaning in pain during the whole night. I frantically tried all the methods I knew to make him urinate, but he still couldn't go.

At 5 am the next morning, I was anxious to phone the CPPCC HQ to try to get a car for Puyi, but was told that, no-one had the authority to send a car for Puyi. I tried to call a taxi company repeatedly, but nobody ever answered. At last, I had to run into the street, to try my luck. Thank heavens, after searching several streets, I finally caught a taxi near the Huguosi Temple. It was already close to 7 am in the morning when I sent Puyi to the emergency ward of the People's Hospital. But I never expected that from then until 7 pm, that poor Puyi would have to lie in the cold and windy emergency ward for twelve hours, with nobody ever giving him any treatment. This was because the rebels among the medical staff in the hospital opposed accepting "a feudal emperor". They explained that the limited sickbeds there should be left for workers, peasants and soldiers. I was thrown into a panic, running here and there like "an ant on a hot tin roof", not knowing what I should do. Later, I hurried to the CPPCC HQ, but couldn't find any leaders there. Again, I went to Pujie's home for help and he quickly reported Puyi's condition to Mr. Shen Dechun. Mr. Shen immediately phoned the authorities of the People's hospital, reiterating to them Premier Zhou Enlai's instruction of "taking good care of Puyi". Eventually, the People's Hospital agreed to accept Puyi, but sent him to its medical ward, instead of the Urological Ward, where Puyi should have gone. The reason they gave was that the Urological Ward didn't have enough sickbeds for so many patients. In the medical ward of the People's Hospital, Puyi spent the last days of his life.

I couldn't take breath until 9 pm that evening, after Puyi was settled in the ward. I quickly returned home to get a little something to eat, then came back to Puyi's ward to look after him. Poor Puyi was still in pain, he was having difficulty breathing and he couldn't urinate at all. None of the medical staff came to catheterize Puyi, for they were afraid that they would be considered to be "sympathizing with a feudal emperor". I went to see Dr. Wang, who was in charge of Puyi's ward. He said that the medical department couldn't cure his uraemia. I told him that because of his inability to urinate, Puyi's abdomen was distended and was now as big as a pregnant woman's abdomen and that it was terribly painful for him. But he was quite impatient: "I have so many patients. It is not just your husband, do you realise this?!"

I then hurried to see Dr. Meng, the Director the Urological Department. He was familiar with Puyi's case and actually thought that he should have been the one to treat Puyi's uraemia in the first place. I told Dr. Meng that Puyi would "smother to death" with urinary retention. With all of the words I could muster, I threw myself onto my knees before him, begging him to save Puyi. He finally felt pity and went to Puyi's sickbed. But all he did was just to look at Puyi's large round abdomen, smile and walk away. From that night onwards, Dr. Meng didn't appear again.

It's distressing for me to look back and consider that in May 1962, when Puyi went to the People's Hospital to have a medical check-up because he had been passing blood-stained urine, that the careless Dr. Meng hadn't checked him thoroughly. Instead he only gave him some injections to stop the bleeding, according to the wrong diagnosis of prostatitis. It was not until three years later that a proper diagnosis was finally given. In 1965, in order to investigate Puyi's case further, Premier Zhou Enlai had instructed the CPPCC to invite the most distinguished Chinese urological, surgical and tumour doctors to give Puyi a group consultation. At last, Puyi was diagnosed as having kidney cancer, but the cancer cells had already spread. After the group consultation had finished, a dinner was held by the CPPCC to thank all the doctors who took a part at the group consultation. During the dinner, a leader of the CPPCC angrily criticized Dr. Meng who had diagnosed prostatitis, for his irretrievable mistake. I'm not sure whether this aroused Meng's anger, but it was true that the Urological Department of the People's Hospital later refused to take Puyi when he was terminally ill. Many people knew that Puyi had not been given proper care during his last days in the People's Hospital.

On October 6th, according to Puyi's wishes, I went to the Academy of Traditional Chinese Medicine at Guang'anmen Street, to invite Dr. Pu to see him. With a quite heavy heart, Dr. Pu felt Puyi's pulse and wrote a new prescription for him. Although it was obvious that "The Last Emperor's" time in this world was very short, Dr. Pu was still kind enough to do his best to comfort him.

After Dr. Pu left, with his trembling hand, Puyi made great efforts to write something in a small notebook. During that afternoon, when I was ready to return home to fetch something, Puyi handed me the notebook. On one page of it, there were a few almost illegible characters:

Little sister, I'm suffering from lack of vital energy. Be sure to bring me the "Ziheche" (a kind of Chinese medicine made from placental powder) when you come back. I'd like to take it tonight.

It is the most precious memento that Puyi left for me. I always read those characters, whenever I miss Puyi. He preferred calling me "little Sister"! How warm hearted it had always felt when he called me this!

Just like all of the happily married couples in the world, Puyi and I had a profound love between us. Since we married, I received the sincere care that only my parents had previously given me. The heavens shouldn't have been blind and taken my husband from me, my only relative on earth!

I had carefully attended to Puyi day and night, listening to his pitiful shouting, "Catheterize me, please! Catheterize me, please!" I paced about in an agitated state of mind, feeling as if a knife was piercing my heart. Mr. Zhang Chongxin, an intern at the People's Hospital later recalled:

Puyi's face was rather swollen-looking. He liked to chat with another patient in his ward, who was a "living Buddha" from Tibet. But with his limited Chinese, the "living Buddha" often couldn't correctly understand what Puyi said, so always answered him with strange words, which were difficult for Puyi to comprehend.

While Puyi was hospitalised at the People's Hospital, Madam Li Shuxian, his wife, attended him wholeheartedly. Puyi was very short-sighted, so it was still very hard for him to see, even with his thick lens glasses. I often saw Madam Li Shuxian reading letters or newspapers to him. His memory was terrible too, often forgetting to take with him what he would need, for example, a bowl when he went to collect his food for his meal.

Puyi's condition deteriorated day by day. He suffered greatly when he urinated. One day, seeing that Puyi was painfully moaning, while Madam Li Shuxian was sobbing sadly by his sickbed, I went to catheterize Puyi. He felt much better after his bladder was emptied, nodding at me to acknowledge his gratitude. Madam Li Shuxian also expressed

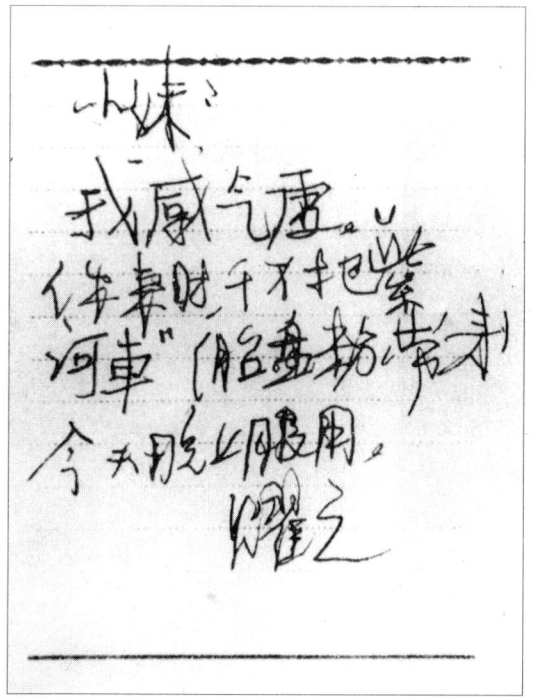

Puyi wrote this note to me eleven days before he passed away, October 6th, 1967.

The Last Emperor of China My Husband Puyi

her gratitude to me. Knowing that Puyi's life was coming to an end, I was very sad. I was sure that, Madam Li Shuxian, herself a nurse, was also quite aware of this.

I had to beg the nurses and doctors to catheterize Puyi, in spite of often being given a cold response and ironic remarks. After he urinated, he would always feel much better and could then go peacefully back to sleep. On October 8th, when Mr. Song Xilian and Mr. Yang Botao came to see him, Puyi was receiving oxygen therapy and being injected with amylaceum (a grape sugar mixture), for extra nutrition.

In the last few days of his life, Puyi's colleagues and friends came to hospital one after another to see him, although some of them had various troubles or problems of their own, for they used to be the senior officials and generals of the National Party. They felt very sad when they saw a dying Puyi, being indignant about his unfortunate experiences during the Cultural Revolution.

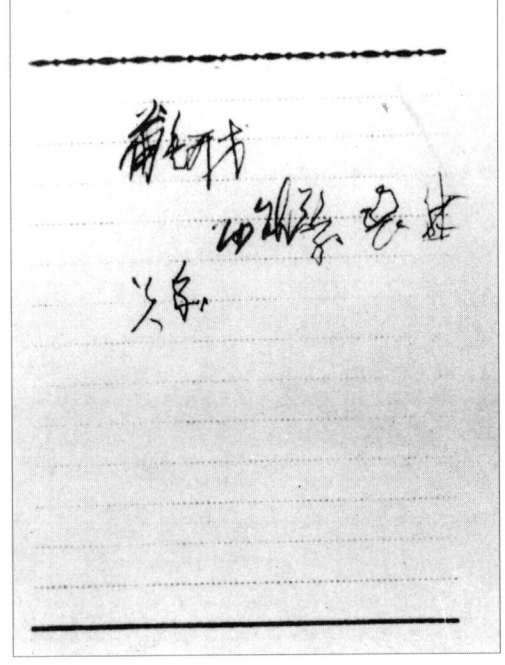

Puyi's last written words, five days before his death. They are illegible.

Later on in his recollections, Mr. Shen Zui wrote that he himself had been depicted as a notorious spy head who had cruelly killed a lot of Communist members in the popular novel *Red Rock*, because of that, the medical staff in the hospital had looked at him with obvious contempt and hatred. Once a nurse even roughly pushed him out of Puyi's ward while shouting, "Bad egg! Leave! Leave!" But he worried about poor Puyi, giving thought to what might happen to him. He would still go to the hospital and secretly slip into Puyi's ward to see him and after that, he would slip out again quickly and quietly. He recalled that at that time, Puyi's biggest problem was that he couldn't urinate normally, thus needed to have a urinary catheter inserted. But the nurses there often ignored him, unwilling to do it, for fear of being denounced as "sympathizing with the feudal emperor".

On October 12th 1967, Puyi wrote down his last ever diary entry. In it, he was going to copy out the new prescription that Dr. Pu had written for him that day. But after writing only seven unclear characters, he really didn't have enough energy to hold the pen and it slipped out of his hand. That morning, once again, I went to get Dr. Pu's new prescription for Puyi at the Academy of Traditional Chinese Medicine. Unfortunately, the pharmacy there had no white ginseng, one of the medical herbs in the prescription. I went to buy it in several of the Chinese pharmacies in the east of the city, but I couldn't find it. I had to search in the rest of the city, and eventually, I found some. I returned home quickly to simmer it for Puyi. Then I took the medicinal soup to the hospital, to feed Puyi with a spoon, so as to give him energy. Puyi had believed in Chinese medicine all his life, continuing to take it until he died. But, he passed away before taking the other two doses of his prescription. (Each Chinese herb prescription makes three doses from three separate simmering sessions. Puyi only had the opportunity to take one dose before he died.)

Also on that day, the dying Puyi was shifted into a tiny single ward. Besides a single bed, it didn't even have enough room for a chair. I had to place two small wooden stools at the door, sitting on them to doze a little during the night time. I was becoming exhausted, with considerable weight loss too.

On October 16th, at 10 o'clock in the evening, Puyi struggled to say in a feeble, but clear voice, to Mr. Li Yikuan, who had enthusiastically presided over our wedding ceremony and Mr. Fan Hanjie, a former National Party General, who had come to see him: "I shouldn't die, I'd like to do more work for my country!"

Not long after Mr. Li and Mr. Fan left, Puyi was gasping for breath with more and more difficulty. He seemed to be in a great deal of pain, but was still in his right mind. When the doctor on duty came to give him three injections (one of them being aminophylline), I took the opportunity to go to the washroom. As soon as I returned to the ward, I heard Puyi say: "He gave me aminophylline—I'm suffocating!" He began to gasp and show the whites of his eyes. I hurried over to look at his eyes more closely. His pupils were already dilated. His condition was serious! Ms. Wang Caiyun, one of our neighbours, who had come to see Puyi, instantly attempted to give him artificial resuscitation. I was alarmed and bewildered, calling a nurse to measure his blood pressure. It had dropped down below normal.

It was so dreadful in the small hours of the morning. A sense of desolation overwhelmed me. Puyi gazed at me with open eyes. He was still breathing, but mucus in his throat made him wheezy. Suddenly, I realized that maybe he was waiting for somebody. I ran to phone Pujie, who arrived at the ward very quickly. Whilst looking at his younger brother, Puyi took his final breath.

At this moment, all of the clocks in China pointed to 2:30 am, October 17th 1967.

Besides Pujie and me, Zong Guang, one of Puyi's nephews and Mrs. Wang Caiyun were also present. I couldn't help throwing myself onto Puyi's body, bursting into loud howling. Mrs. Wang, while sobbing herself, advised me not to be too upset. She said that I must hold myself together in order to make arrangements for Puyi's funeral.

For a long time, I had been occupied completely by looking after Puyi and had hated to accept that he would die, plus nobody had advised me concerning the funeral preparations. Only now, at this moment, I realized that I hadn't even got his shroud ready. We were told to remove Puyi's hospital gown, leaving him wearing his grey sweater, short pants and stockings. A nurse, without any feeling, walked over and we moved Puyi's body onto a wheeled stretcher. She ruthlessly covered Puyi's body with a sheet, and then she pushed the wheeled stretcher out of the ward. Pujie, Zong Guang, Mrs. Wang and I lost control, and cried loudly while escorting him to the mortuary.

Chapter Thirty Three
Puyi's Memorial Ceremony Was Held Thirteen Years Later

The grieving Pujie, Zong Guang and Mrs. Wang accompanied me as I returned home to prepare for Puyi's funeral. Thinking that I didn't have enough money to cover it, I was very upset and confused. I thought it over again and again, then as a last resort, I said to Pujie: "Second brother, tomorrow not only do I need to pay the 'Eight Treasure Mountain Cemetery' for Puyi's cremation, but I must buy a new pair of shoes, socks and an urn for him too. Recently we have spent quite a lot of money treating Puyi's medical condition, and now I really don't have enough money to do all of this. Would you mind paying some expenses first and then I will repay the entire amount owing to you, after the CPPCC HQ have reimbursed me."

At the end of 1970s, more than ten years after Puyi's death

Pujie agreed to assist me financially, concerning the expenses. He consoled me: "Sister-in-law, don't be too sad please, we shall take care of you in place of elder brother Puyi." That morning, Mrs. Wang and Mrs. Zhang, neighbours of ours, helped me at the hospital mortuary to put a shroud on Puyi. His face was still swollen and had not changed, looking as though he was asleep. He had already stiffened, so that the grey sweater he was wearing couldn't be removed. With the help of the two ladies, we first put on him a new black cotton-padded jacket and trousers, and then removed his socks, replacing them with the new ones sent by Pujie, as well as a new pair of cloth shoes which I had bought for him. Mrs. Zhang reminded me: "Did you prepare a new pillow, a cotton-padded mattress and a piece of cloth for covering Uncle Pu's face?" I hastened to buy those, then returned to spread the cotton-padded mattress underneath him and set the new pillow in place for him. Finally I put on his head the deep-blue woolen cap, which he had often worn.

With one of his eyes open and mouth too, Puyi seemed still worried about something. I carefully closed them while whispering to him: "Puyi! Be at ease, please. Don't worry about me...." Puyi had been fastidious about his appearance, especially in his youth. He had been noted for being noble and dignified. One of his habits had been to frequently comb his shining hair, whenever he was in a good mood. Now, with tears in my eyes, I combed his hair for the last time, letting him go with dignity! Gradually, the members of Aisin-Gioro Royal Clan came to the hospital mortuary. Again and again, they tried to persuade me to leave the mortuary. At last, I had to succumb to their concerned request. So, I stood up and looked at Puyi for the last time. Slowly, I pulled across the special white sheet to cover his body, before sobbing uncontrollably.

Premier Zhou Enlai had learned very quickly about Puyi's passing away. The following day he sent his representative to convey to me his condolences. According to Premier Zhou's instructions, the representative inquired in detail concerning Puyi's final moments. Finally he told us that Premier Zhou had said that Puyi's remains may be buried at the Revolutionary Cemetery or any other cemetery I chose. Alternatively, he could be cremated, then his ashes buried in one of those cemeteries. But we all knew that, at that time, being the high tide of the Cultural Revolution, it was impossible to bury him. We had to choose cremation. Pujie, Mr. Li Yikuan, some other friends and I escorted Puyi's body to the Eight Treasure Mountain (Babaoshan) Cemetery for cremation. We couldn't even hold a ceremony to pay our last respects to him. I would like to have bought an elaborate urn for his ashes, but there was only one kind there, which cost five yuan.

On October 21st, the principle members of the Aisin-Gioro Royal Clan came together to discuss how to deal with Puyi's ashes. First, aged Mr. Zaitao, Puyi's seventh uncle, suggested keeping them at the People's Ashes Hall, at the Eight Treasure Mountain Cemetery. Pujie immediately agreed, saying: "We should show our gratitude to Premier Zhou's kindness. Now, that the Cultural Revolution is underway, he will also be experiencing unmentionable concerns. So we shouldn't add any further difficulties for him to consider. Puyi's ashes can be preserved in the public cemetery."

I supported what they said: "Puyi had had a bright and cheerful disposition. He preferred to be with others. I'm sure that he would be glad to be kept there, being together with ordinary people." Therefore, we unanimously decided to house Puyi's ashes at the People's Ashes Hall of the Eight Treasure Mountain Cemetery. Therefore, on October 22nd, Pujie, one of our neighbours and I took Puyi's ashes there and we paid the 15-year fee for keeping Puyi's ashes in that location.

For six months, after Puyi's passing away, I was lost in extreme mental distress. I also felt physically weak, as I couldn't eat well, due to loss of appetite and was often unable to sleep properly. Thus I was getting weaker and weaker, becoming much thinner. I suffered greatly from missing Puyi, going almost daily to the Eight Treasure Mountain Cemetery to see his ashes. I would remove his urn from the niche, stroking it and wiping it with my handkerchief. Then I would feel better and return home. Later, I bought a monthly bus ticket. I was eager to take my lunch with me each time I went to the Ashes Hall. I would take out his urn in the morning and remain with it until about 4 pm, when the Ashes Hall closed. I would have my lunch while in the company of his ashes.

At our desolate home, I was often crying bitterly and many times I met Puyi in my dreams. He would earnestly console me, saying: "Don't cry, Shuxian, take good care of yourself. You'd better go to work, then you will feel better. I hope you live on bravely." Then I would tell him: "You are my only relative, without you my life has no interest and I'd like to go with you!" I burst into tears in my dream.

When I woke up I found I had blurred vision and my pillow had been wet with my tears. I not only had pain of soul, but also practical living difficulties, as Puyi had predicted. It was then in the midst of the Cultural Revolution, so who would be able to take care of me? Where could I get money for my living expenses? With five chronic diseases, I was in very poor health and often had to ask for leave from my work. As early as in July 1964, the authorities of Guanxiang Hospital, where I worked, advised me to stop work so that I could care for myself and convalesce at home. They promised that I could return to work there when I had recovered.

At the beginning of 1968, in order to earn a salary so as to support myself, I applied to the authorities (then called the Revolutionary Committee) of the Guanxiang Hospital to resume my work. But they said that I had not recovered, and therefore refused my application. I therefore persuaded myself to pluck up the courage to write a letter to Premier Zhou Enlai, informing him of my condition and difficulties, asking for a job. However, the letter didn't reach him, but was forwarded to the Guanxiang Hospital, arousing their dissatisfaction with me.

For several years, I had no income, living on the several thousand yuan that Puyi had left to me (the CPPCC returned the book fee back to Puyi after he had returned it due to his former page's threats, because they didn't know what to do with it), being the remainder of the contribution fee from his book *The First Half of My Life*. I could no longer afford the rent for our large and comfortable residence at 22, Donguanyinsi Lane, in the west of the city, so in 1969, I asked the CPPCC HQ for a much smaller place. They arranged for me to live in a small unit in Jianchang Lane, in the east of the city. The room had been changed previously from a bathroom, so it was dark and damp inside.

Without work, I had no free medical service and had to pay for my treatment myself. Later, I had to borrow money from others to pay for it. Again and again, I went to beg the authorities of the Guanxiang Hospital to allow me to resume my work. They informed me that I must go to the Public Health Bureau of the Chaoyang District, the superior organization of the Guanxiang Hospital, to get their consent first. I went there, but its leader stated that it was a petty matter and that the hospital should settle it. Like kicking a ball, they kept "kicking my petty matter" to and fro to each other. For about three years I had no idea how many kilometers I must have walked, but I still couldn't resume my job as a nurse.

Towards the end of June 1971, I was running out of money, so I mustered up the courage to once again write to Premier Zhou Enlai. In the letter, I explained to him how difficult my life had been, asking him to arrange a job for me.

Only a few days later, Premier Zhou sent Mr. Hou Chunhuai, a high-ranking official of the State Council, to visit me. After entering into our courtyard containing several houses, Mr. Hou presumed that I lived in the principal house, the best one, which had several big rooms which all faced to sun. But he was soon led to my small and shabby house. That day, I was out, so he didn't see me. He came again the next day. The first sentence he said to me was, "Who let you move here?" He inquired carefully concerning my life and health. I mentioned two needs: the first being to resume my work, so as to support myself, the second being to change to a better residence. Before leaving my home, Mr. Hou said to me: "I'm going to report your concerns to Premier Zhou. The CPPCC HQ will inform you of the results."

Not long after that, the CPPCC HQ sent an official to my home to tell me that, considering my very poor health, it was difficult to arrange any work for me. Therefore the CPPCC HQ would issue me a subsidy of sixty yuan each month and that they would soon find a residence with two sunny rooms for me. The official especially informed me that: "Premier Zhou personally arranged this for you. He has considered your needs in detail." I was moved to tears.

In the early morning of the following day, I went once again to the Ashes Hall of the Eight Treasure Mountain Cemetery. I took out Puyi's urn. While stroking it, I comforted Puyi's soul in Heaven: "Rest in peace, please, the matter you worried about greatly has been handled, by our esteemed and beloved Premier Zhou. You may put yourself at ease and sleep your long sleep." My tears fell on the urn.

Soon afterwards, I was told to move to one of the living quarters for the working staff of the CPPCC HQ at 20, Dongsibatiao Lane. It consisted of three courtyards, with eleven households, including mine. My unit had two rooms, a big one and a small one. I cherished a good relationship with the neighbours there, most of them sympathizing with me and often offering me their help, especially when I was ill and had to lie in bed. They bought my rationed grain, coal and necessities to me. I shall never forget one of them, Ms. Liu Yuxia, who, when I was ill, would come to clean my room and fire my stove for me each morning, before she went to work. Several times she escorted me to the hospital, letting me wait on the bench, while she queued up in a long line to register for me. Then she would support me by holding my arm, while on the way to see the doctor.

On January 8th 1976, "mountains cried and seas sobbed". Our whole nation was heartbroken with grief. Our esteemed and beloved Premier Zhou Enlai passed away. After I heard of the death announcement, I was too sad to eat and drink anything for three days. Over and over again, I looked at Premier Zhou's portrait and the photos of him receiving Puyi and I. I sobbed while wiping the photos and my heart bled. I went to the Eight Treasure Mountain Cemetery, to tell Puyi the bad news. While I was crying, it seemed that he was sadly sobbing there too....

In 1979, the Guanxiang Hospital, which hadn't allowed me to resume my work before, now tried to persuade me to resign from my work. They informed me that, although I couldn't retire (because I hadn't reached the legal retirement age), that according to the government's new policy, I could apply to resign because of my poor health and then receive 40% percent of the monthly salary of more than fifty yuan, which would amount to about twenty yuan each month, as my ill-health resignation fee. It would certainly be better than getting nothing from them, and more importantly, I could resume my free medical service, thus relieving me of the heavy burden of paying my own medical costs. I thought it over and finally decided to receive it. At that time, with an income of more than eighty yuan monthly (resignation fee twenty yuan plus the sixty yuan subsidy from the CPPCC HQ) it would be quite good, besides, I would also have my free medical service.

I shall engrave on my mind forever, that in my most difficult time, it was our esteemed and beloved Premier Zhou Enlai, who had given me a way out. After the smash-

The Last Emperor of China My Husband Puyi

ing of the diabolical "Gang of Four", and the end of the Cultural Revolution in 1976, the People's government had granted to me, as the widow of Puyi, a new life. I often received invitations to take part in state banquets, tea parties and wonderful performances.

On February 12th 1980, at nine o'clock in the morning, the CPPCC held a tea party to celebrate the Spring Festival, to show their loving care and concern to the kinsfolk of the late members of the CPPCC, as well as some famous public figures. I was among those who were invited. And before it started, I was pleased to be received by our State Leaders. What moved me most was that all of the state leaders present immediately stood up and shook hands with me, when I was introduced as "Madam Puyi". While the tea party was in progress, all of the guests around our table spoke their minds freely. Our happy time together attracted a lot of the reporters from TV stations and newspapers. Madam Kang Keqing, a respectable former female Red Army General and wife of Marshall Zhu De and Vice-Chairman of the CPPCC, made a speech which said:

.... *More than ever on festive occasions, we miss our dear relatives and friends who are far away. Now, our country has entered into a new historical era with great prospects of progress. While we are celebrating the first Spring Festival of the 1980s, we further remember our past loved ones.*

What she said made me think of my dear husband Puyi, and the most magnificent period in my life which he brought me.

Once again, I went to the Ashes Hall of the Eight Treasure Mountain Cemetery, to see Puyi. I stroked and wiped the familiar urn, telling him that I had already started a new life, along with all of the other Chinese. But at the same time, the load in my mind was becoming heavier and heavier, concerning the fifteen year time limit for housing Puyi's ashes, which was soon to expire. Where should I store them after this? Because I had often been to the Ashes Hall, the working staff there knew me. One person advised me: "A dead man can never come back to life. To keep his ashes is not the only way to give expression to your grief. You'd better find a suitable place to bury them, when the time limit is over." But I couldn't persuade myself to accept his suggestion. I couldn't forget the deep love that Puyi had given me. How could I leave his ashes alone at the cemetery?

As one Chinese proverb goes, "Heaven will always leave a door open".

At this time, I was pleasantly surprised to be informed that the authorities of the CPPCC would hold a memorial ceremony for Puyi, because he had made a considerable contribution to the country and to the Chinese people during the second half of his life. They also stated that his ashes would be placed at the revolutionary cemetery forever!

The heavy load was immediately taken off my mind.

At half past three on May 29th 1980, a grand memorial ceremony for Puyi, Wang Yaowu and Liao Yaoxiang, all three former members of the CPPCC, was held at the auditorium of the CPPCC HQ. I was moved to tears. I said to Puyi in my mind: "Puyi, you have been gone for thirteen years. If you still really do have a soul, you may rest in peace now...."

The Communist Party of China and the Central Government highly praised the work that Puyi had done for his country, during the second half of his life. The official Xinhua News Agency reported this memorial ceremony:

The CPC and the state leaders Deng Yingchao, Wu Lanfu, Peng Chong, Hu Zi'ang, Wang Kunlun, the CPPCC, the United Front Work Department, the Historical Account of Past Events of the CPPCC, each presented their wreathes. Ji Fang, Liu Lantao and Hu Yuzhi, three Vice-Chairmen of the CPPCC and some of their friends and colleagues, which included approximately three hundred people, took part in the ceremony.

The memorial ceremony was presided over by Wang Shoudao, Vice-Chairman of

After the Cultural Revolution finished, the Chinese government held a grand memorial ceremony for the late Puyi, Wang Yaowu and Liao Yaoxiang, three former memebers of CPPCC, May 29th, 1980.

The Last Emperor of China My Husband Puyi

At the memorial ceremony, Wang Shoudao, Deputy Chairman of CPPCC, shook hands with me, to extend his regards.

the CPPCC. Liu Ningyi, Vice-Director of the United Front Work Department of the Central Committee of the CPC, made the memorial speech. Then, the leaders and the comrades, in a long line, slowly filed in front of me and shook hands with me, to show their sincere care. It seemed that Puyi stood near me. With much satisfaction, he seemed to smile and nod his head at me and at all of the people there.

When the memorial ceremony was over, Pujie was holding Puyi's portrait in front of me and I was holding Puyi's urn to send it to the Revolutionary Cemetery of the Eight Treasure Mountain Cemetery, according to the decision of the Central Committee of the CPC. Puyi's urn was placed in its First Hall for Housing Urns, where the urns of deceased state and the CPC top leaders were housed, as well as those of many respectable revolutionary martyrs and celebrities.

On June 12th 1980, about two weeks later, the CPPCC HQ moved me to another home in the new living quarters for the working staff of the CPPCC HQ, located in the Tuanjiehu Residential Quarters. Although it was a small flat with only two rooms, it had a kitchen, heating, gas and an inside toilet. Actually I had longed for many years to live in this kind of flat, with convenient equipment and I would never have expected that I would realize my dream after Puyi had passed away.

Chapter Thirty Four
Publishing of My Memoir and the "Puyi Craze"

In 1984, after several years of hard work, 300,000 copies of my memoir, *Puyi and I* (compiled by Mr. Wang Qingxiang) were published. As expected, it was warmly welcomed by readers, causing a sensation throughout China. Many newspapers and magazines competed with one another in serializing

Li Shuxian was writing her memories of Puyi

Puyi and I and not long afterwards *The Selection of Puyi's Manuscripts*, *The Last Empress and Concubines* and several other books about Puyi were also published. Each of them achieved great impressions from the readers. A period of "Puyi Craze" occurred in China soon afterwards, arousing more and more people's interest and curiosity concerning the life of this mysterious "Little Emperor" (Chinese had liked calling Puyi "Little Emperor").

In April 1984, only two months after *Puyi and I* was published, Mr. Li Hanxiang, a world-famous Hong Kong Film Director, came to visit me at my home. He expressed to me his desire to produce a film about the second half of Puyi's life and he hoped to get my support and cooperation. I considered that Puyi's unusual experiences during his second life *were* a great success, changing him from a feudal emperor into a citizen and that it could not only educate modern Chinese, but also our descendants and foreigners. Moreover, I trusted Mr. Li Hanxiang, his film company and the China Central Television Station, who wanted to produce the film jointly. Being sure that they had the ability to present the world with a successful film about the second half of Puyi's life, I gladly

The members of Aisin-Gioro Royal Clan watching the documentary *The Chinese Last Emperor Puyi*. From left: I, Pujie and Saga Hiro

consented to his request.

Mr. Li Hanxiang told me that he wanted to name the film *Fire Dragon*. This was because, unlike all of the other Chinese Emperors, Puyi had no grand mausoleum, but had been cremated during the Cultural Revolution, a special era in the history of China, and indeed, the whole world. He was the only "dragon" in Chinese history who had been cremated, so we referred to him as *Fire Dragon*. (Chinese call their emperors "Dragon" and their empresses "Phoenix".)

Mr. Li Hanxiang concluded that Puyi was not only born in a time of hardship, but also died in a time of hardship. He considered that Puyi's marriage to a nurse and their happy life together in the 1960s showed people that he was actually a person with real human feeling. I appreciated his understanding of Puyi.

In June 1984, Mr. Li Hanxiang and I signed the contract to film *Fire Dragon* and six months later, the shooting of the film was commenced at 22, Dongguanyinsi Lane, the place where Puyi and I lived. I went to watch their work several times and I was very satisfied with the brilliant performances of both Mr. Liang Jiahui and Ms. Pan Hong, who were popular Chinese film stars. They were selected by Director Li Hanxiang, from many performers who auditioned to play the roles of Puyi and myself in this film. In order to act out our lives accurately, they inquired about many details of our daily lives.

Once at the United Hospital, when they were shooting the scene of Puyi attending to me, while I was hospitalized there in 1965, I felt as if Puyi was sitting beside me. I couldn't control my emotions and tears flowed down my cheeks.

On October 15th 1985, when the shooting of *Fire Dragon* was completed, Director Li Hanxiang held a large reception in Beijing. I was among the several hundred people who were invited to join it. While watching *Fire Dragon* for the first time, I was taken back into the unforgettable times that we had together. Puyi seemed to be living with me again. In one scene of the film, I lost control of myself and began to cry. The people around me all tried to sooth me, advising me not to be upset, but to watch the film attentively. I watched the film with red and swollen eyes, filled with tears and wept until the end. Puyi, my dear husband, it has been eighteen years since you left me. Now, your lovely voice and happy manner have reappeared again on the screen. How could I not be excited? How could I not cry?

When the film concluded, the reporters swarmed around me. They asked me whether or not the film was realistic? "Yes, it was," I answered them: "Puyi and I did live that way." I gladly expressed my gratitude to Director Li Hanxiang and all the working staff of the production group of *Fire Dragon*. They produced a wonderful film, which with accurate descriptions, realistically portrayed the second half of Puyi's life, how the "war criminal" Puyi was changed in prison and how the "citizen" Puyi worked and lived. This all demonstrated the greatness of the wise policy of remoulding war prisoners, thought out by the Chinese government. Emperor Puyi always had a large retinue crowding round him, so he couldn't take care of himself at all once he left the Royal Court. Although he had undergone ten years of change, he still appeared very clumsy whenever he tried to do house work. We couldn't have expected him to behave like us in daily life.

Fire Dragon in Chinese

Two days later, on October 17th 1985, was the eighteenth anniversary of Puyi's death. I bought a bunch of flowers and Mr. Li Hanxiang had two of his staff, Mr. Sun and Miss Yang accompanied me to the Eight Treasure Mountain Cemetery. When I gently wiped Puyi's small urn with my handkerchief and looked at his photo again, I felt very sad and my tears gushed out. I whispered to him:

The Last Emperor of China: My Husband Puyi

Puyi, I have come to see you today. You have been away from me for eighteen years. I have been through eighteen long years of sadness and loneliness. Now, I have my pension and free medical care, helping me to live a comfortable lifestyle. I shall never need to worry again about the cost of living and medical expenses. You can rest assured, in knowing that I am very well cared for. A film has been produced about our lives which brings me many happy reflections. I'm sure that you would love it, if you could watch the film.

After I returned to the car, I was told that Miss Yang, as instructed, had video recorded me. While we were having lunch together, the video was shown to us. I was filled with all kinds of feelings, but I did enjoy watching it.

In August 1985, the China Television Play Production Centre started to shoot a 28-part television series *The Last Emperor*. They made a reconstruction of Yangxindian Palace in their workshop, which looked exactly the same as the original one in the Forbidden City.

At the same time, Mr. Bernardo Bertolucci, the internationally acclaimed Italian Film Director, was busy selecting the performers for his film *The Last Emperor*. Mr. Mark Peploe was revising its script, while Mr. Jeremy Thomas, its British film producer, was pleased to announce that the Chinese government had permitted them to film *The Last Emperor* in China. He said, "Our film will be a very magnificent one. We are going to

From left: I, Wang Qingxiang, Li Hanxiang (noted Hong Kong film director), talking about the shooting of *Fire Dragon*

spend five weeks filming it in the Forbidden City, the previous residence of the Chinese emperors. We are grateful to the Chinese government for opening for the first time some of palaces there for us to use."

The colourful wide-screen stereo film, with an investment of $22 million, had commenced being screened at the end of summer 1986. *The Last Emperor* was shown separately on screen and on TV one year later. In the same year, Bertolucci's *The Last Emperor* was chosen as the 1987 "Best Film" in the Oscars, also winning a further eight other Oscars and the American Film Award, thus becoming renowned throughout the world.

I never expected that I, a nurse, would become a celebrity some day in the future. Since 1984, I have often been invited to join various official banquets, receptions, social activities and have also been interviewed by foreign reporters. The press also liked to give a brief account of my activities in the news. While the "Puyi Craze" was increasing, more and more reporters came to knock on my door and their visits disturbed my tranquil lifestyle. During a short period of time, books such as following titles: *Visiting Puyi's Widow*, *Puyi's Citizen Wife* and *The Second Half of the Life of the Last Empress, Li Shuxian* were published one after another. It gave me the feeling of "having nowhere to hide".

A poster for the film *The Last Emperor*. The role of Puyi was played by the American film star, John Lone.

As Puyi's wife, I had been gratified to be both respected and protected by our government and many people. Each year, I received a lot of letters from home and abroad. Although I had no energy to reply to all of the letters, I always tried my best to do what I could to satisfy the senders. But there were a few people who were envious and suspicious of me. They were curious as to why Puyi had married me, a nurse and the daughter of a commoner. I know that there was a lot of gossip about our marriage, but I never worried about what they said. Actually, Puyi didn't have any property when he married me. We needed to survive on our salaries. I married him because he loved me and I loved him. Having no property was not a concern for me. The valuable love he devoted to me will live forever in my heart.

More and more enthusiastic overseas people came to visit me at my home. They

The Last Emperor of China My Husband Puyi

liked to listen to my story about our sweet life together, although I was very sorry that sometimes, when they filled my tiny home, I didn't have enough chairs and stools for them to sit on. In the afternoon of February 27th 1992, the China Comfort Travel Agency invited me to receive an all-female German tourist group which they had organized.

In Russia, Puyi was interrogated.

Most of its members were teachers, engineers, doctors or chemists and they told me that they had decided to visit China, only after they watched the film *The Last Emperor*. When they saw me they were ecstatic and clapped their hands warmly. They told me that one of the purposes for this trip was to see me with their own eyes. I was glad to answer all of their questions and before they left I was included in photos with all of them, as they had requested a photo with "China's Last Empress". They said that they would treasure the photos taken with me as the most precious souvenirs.

What moved me greatly was that at various times some older men, about my age, sympathized with my misfortune. One admired me for being "hale and hearty, quick-minded, kindhearted and virtuous". They all stated that they wished to spend old-age together with me, making offers of marriage to me.

One of them was a retired official. He had joined the Communist Party of China in his early days, but in 1957 had been unjustifiably labelled a "Rightist", who were seen by many as the lowest group in society. The man had suffered a lot and hadn't been rehabilitated politically until the end of the 1970s. In his letters to me he wrote, "From newspapers, I see that you are already sixty-five years old. After experiencing so many frustrations and suffering from five chronic diseases, you look quite weak. I sympathize with you and I'm sure that with my Chinese and western medical knowledge, I would be able to take good care of you and it would be my honour and pleasure if we could marry and enjoy our remaining days together."

I wrote back to him, to express my heartfelt thanks. But at the same time, I had to tell this good-hearted man that nobody in this world could replace Puyi. Although Puyi had been away from me for a long time, I always felt that he was together with me and that I would be with him forever.

Chapter Thirty Five

The Publishing of *The Second Half of Puyi's Life*

Starting from 1979, I worked with Wang Qingxiang to write a series of works about Puyi's life.

The Second Half of Puyi's Life (one of the cooperative achievements of Mr. Wang Qingxiang and I) had been revised frequently since its draft was completed in 1983, but wasn't published formally by the Tianjin People's Publishing House until November 1988. I was ecstatic when its editor came to my home and gladly handed the brand-new sample book over to me. Once again, in my mind I told Puyi I had accomplished another wish of his by publishing *The Second Half of Puyi's Life*.

While reading the sample book, my mind was drawn back to those unforgettable times. I was reminded that it was 22 years ago during the summer of 1966, the storm to "Smash the Four Olds" had finally engulfed our tranquil home at 22, Dongguanyinsi Lane. (The "Four Olds" are old ideas, old culture, old customs and old habits.) That was the day when a group of Red Guards had come to knock at our gate. They fiercely stuck a terrible "General Order" notice on the outside wall of our house. On the top right hand corner it had the words "To Aisin-Gioro Puyi". I remember that the contents of it were to compel Puyi to hand over the photos he had taken alongside State and CPC leaders and himself. Their reason was that he had been condemned by history because of his crimes in aiding Japanese Imperialists, and so he was not then considered to be qualified to stand shoulder to shoulder in photos with those respectable leaders. The order also stated that Puyi must hand over all the luxurious goods in his home. The "General Orders" had been written by the Red Guards from at a nearby middle school.

After the Red Guards had left, Puyi immediately removed from the wall of our lounge and bedroom, the huge pictures in which he had been photographed with Chairman Mao and other State and CPC leaders. He personally sent them to the CPPCC HQ, to be housed there. Puyi was certain that the CPPCC HQ could protect those precious pictures. But we never realized that even the CPPCC HQ had no ability to continuously protect them. The precious pictures were later lost and we never ever received them back.

At that time our only remaining luxury was the telephone in our lounge, installed by the CPPCC HQ. Puyi asked the CPPCC HQ to dismantle it, but the leaders of the CPPCC HQ didn't agree with Puyi. They told him: "Don't worry about it! We shall tell the government to let you keep it." They considered that Puyi was a very special person and that he still needed it.

During that summer, the process of smashing the "Four Olds", had spread across the whole of China. The Red Guards had often burnt books on the streets in frenzy, and many families had to burn their collections of books at home, in order to avoid being accused of keeping the "Four Olds" and therefore getting into trouble. Puyi had also decided to burn books.

After we were married, I borrowed several wooden bookcases from the CPPCC HQ, placing them in our lounge and bedroom. Slowly, they had been filled with the books we had bought, which had been issued by the CPPCC HQ, or sent to us by friends. With a wry smile, Puyi had said to me: "After the Cultural Revolution, we shall never need to read those books." While saying this, he started to move the books down from the wooden bookcases to the floor, and then tore them up, one by one. He asked me to help him to carry the torn books in a bamboo basket to the back courtyard behind our house, where he would burn them. After burning our collection of books, I helped Puyi to take out a large wicker basket from our bedroom filled with the collection of his calligraphy, which was also soon burned in the back courtyard.

Puyi enjoyed writing Chinese calligraphy and always gladly did it for those who had requested him. When he wrote calligraphy, he used to put those that he was unsatisfied with into this large wicker basket. Thus, after a considerable period of time, the wicker basket was filled with rolls of Puyi's calligraphy. But now Puyi personally burnt all of them, turning them to ashes.

Maybe, like many Chinese at that time, Puyi thought that after he had burnt all of his books and writings, he would become a real revolutionary. Or maybe he realized that he couldn't be sure what might happen in the future, so that it would be best to burn all of his books and writings, in case they made trouble for him, if anything else was to happen.

After burning all of his books and calligraphy, Puyi didn't just stop there. He decided to also burn all of his notebooks, diaries and poetic anthologies. First, he tore up his poetic anthologies, page by page, and then handed them over to me to throw them into the fire. I recognized one of the poems that had been written by Puyi in the springtime of 1964, when we visited southern China. Puyi had been moved by the beautiful scenery there, so gladly wrote some poems about it. I was often delighted when he excitedly read one to me. Compared with the melancholy that Puyi was now experiencing, while squatting by the fire, how cheerful he had been on those previous times. What Puyi had recorded in those diaries and notebooks was about the wonderful times we had enjoyed together. Also included were his unforgettable and often pitiful experiences in Fushun Prison, the Beijing Botanical Garden and the CPPCC HQ.

After a short time, I realised that I really couldn't bear watching Puyi burn anymore of the diaries which recorded the glorious times we enjoyed together, so I suddenly had an idea. I said to Puyi: "Puyi, I heard a knock at our gate, would you mind going to have a look while I burn the rest of them?" Puyi who was already nervous, immediately became even more vigilant when he heard what I said and he sneaked cautiously to the gate. After coming back, he told me that at first he had listened carefully inside the gate, but heard nothing. He then opened the gate to find nobody there. Although he was nervous, he then walked along the path in front of our house to the nearby crossing. He had waited and watched for a while, but didn't leave his spot until he was sure that there was nothing dangerous to be concerned about.

But what I had actually wanted was for him to waste his time. It allowed me to quickly stash more than ten of Puyi's diaries and notebooks. Actually, at the time, I didn't realize how crucially important those diaries and notebooks would be in the future. I only wanted to keep them as souvenirs of our wonderful life together. How glad I was when Puyi came back from the gate and I heard his comment: "It's sheer fantasy."

Now, the incident which had involved me hiding the diaries and books has proved that what I did was, in fact a great service for our country and our people.

After Puyi had passed away, I as well as many others had to endure the endless suffering during the remaining years of the ten-year long Cultural Revolution. I had preserved the remainder of Puyi's diaries, notes, meeting records, political study reflections, speech notes, letters and photos until the time when the Cultural Revolution was over and when the Chinese people happily received their "new life".

What I had successfully been able to keep was the Chinese "Last Emperor's" only legacy. The notes and letters reveal how his role as the last representative of the two thousand-year-old feudal system of China was buried in history and how he was changed into a citizen through the process of remoulding, the experience of real life and the caring concern of those people around him.

In the autumn of 1979, Mr. Wang Qingxiang, a young researcher of history from the Jilin Provincial Academy of Social Science, came to see me at my home in Beicaoyuan Lane. He expressed to me his wish to cooperate with me on sifting through and compiling Puyi's original manuscripts (including his diaries, notes, meeting records, political study reflections, speech notes, letters and photos) in order to publish them. Considering that he had graduated in history at the noted Jilin University, he therefore had the ability to do it, and I joyfully consented to his request.

The Second Half of Puyi's Life became popular as soon as it was published. It was listed officially among those for patriotic education, being serialized by many newspapers and given positive book reviews. It can play a role in educating our people.

With sincerity, I would like to convey my gratitude first to Mr. Wang Qingxiang, for he, like some critics commented, showed us "a real Puyi" in the book, and then to the staff of the Tianjin People's Publishing House. For eight years, from 1980, all of the staff cared greatly about the compilation and publication of this book. They quite often gave it their undivided attention. Special thanks go to the editors who were in charge of this book, and who worked very hard towards it's publication. The result of their sustained work is a valuable contribution to our country and people and a tribute to Puyi, "The Last Emperor" and my beloved husband.

Chapter Thirty Six

Apologies from Edward Behr

On August 27th 1990, The Xinmin Evening Paper in Shanghai carried news: "Puyi's Wife is Going to Consult with an American Journalist!"

Recently, Madam Li Shuxian, wife of "Last Emperor", Puyi, was rather disturbed by a biography, concerning Puyi written by an American journalist. She expressed to me that she would consult with this American journalist, who had not researched the history by proper means.

The American journalist was Edward Behr, a noted correspondent and cultural editor of *Newsweek,* International Europe Edition. In 1986, Jeremy Thomas and Bernardo Bertolucci, the producer and director of the film *The Last Emperor* invited Edward Behr to write a book connected with the film. Behr accepted the invitation and expressed that rather than write a book of the film he wanted to try his hand at a serious biography of Puyi and his life and times. The next year, Edward Behr's *The Last Emperor* was published and put on sale by American publishers Bantam Books, Inc.

In September 1988, while visiting me at my home, an Australian scholar, who then taught English at Fudan University in Shanghai, told me that he had already read Edward Behr's book, and that the words in it, some attacking Puyi and I, had aroused his suspicion and concern. He explained that he came to visit me to see whether or not I was the person that Edward Behr depicted. "I don't think that you are a shrewd woman with a fast tongue. Would you mind telling me the truth about it? How about the affection in your relationship with the 'Last Emperor'?" I told him that Puyi had loved me greatly. Because he had previously lacked the warmth of family togetherness since his childhood, he had exceedingly valued our marriage. I also loved him considerably, relying on his love alone. We never had any reason to even think about separating after we were married.

Because I am unable to speak or read English, I wasn't able to read the book, until 1989, when the Chinese version was published. I never would have expected that it had in it so many words which had insulted Puyi and I. Behr said Puyi was a bisexual, a masochist, and even had a pageboy as a lover. As far as I knew, at that time Puyi was cruel and mistreated his retinue whenever he was in bad mood. But what Edward Behr said were simply not true.

As a well-known journalist, Edward Behr lacked the methodical attitude he should have had when he wrote this book. In its postscript, its translator said that in order to write this book he had visited China for as long as six months. During this time he went to visit any survivors that he could find from that calamitous time. Besides that, the postscript says that he read a lot of information about Puyi. Later, he also visited many British, American and German experts of Chinese culture and history, but I really don't understand why he didn't come to visit me, Puyi's wife, who had lived together with him for nearly six years. I was bound to know more than anyone else about his life during that period.

During those years, one of the main activities in my daily life was to receive journalists from home and aboard. Although I was older and not energetic, I always did my best to tell them the facts and to answer all of their questions. At the same time, I hoped that the journalists would report accurately. If Edward Behr had visited me then, I would have received him as willingly as I received other journalists. Of course, journalists have their own right to decide whom they want to visit. But I think that they should at least understand the people whom they want to portray and they must also realise that most people who are hurt by their unrealistic reports, will demand the truth from them.

In the book were depictions about my identity, my age and our courtship and marriage which were far from the truth. Edward Behr described our life like this:

Li Shuxian kept her job, but found that looking after Puyi could be a maddening experience. She had a sharp, nagging tongue.

Puyi was kinder to her than she was to him.

From various accounts, she seems to have been a shrew. But Puyi bore his new misfortune with equanimity.

These venomous slanders made me furious, but at the same time I appreciated the imagination of this famous American journalist whom I had never met. But I couldn't help asking him that by doing this, was it his aim to cause a sensation or for other selfish reasons?

After reading this book, I knew that I had to give people accurate accounts of our life together after we were married, and thus allow the public themselves to judge whether or not our lives together were happy.

One time, Puyi couldn't contain his feelings and told foreign friends: "On May Day,

1962, Li Shuxian and I were married and established our home together. This is the first real 'home' I have ever had." I know that these words were from his heart.

Puyi was born into the Chinese Royal family, but lost the family warmth when he ascended the throne at three years of age. At that time, all people, including his parents, had to consider themselves as servile before him and kowtow to him. But actually he was a person, made of flesh and blood like everyone else with emotions and desires. Like all people, Puyi pursued family happiness.

However, I was an unfortunate orphan. Although our family backgrounds and personal experiences are completely different, we both longed for a happy family life. After we were married, we depended on each other, living a very happy life for five and half years. Our neighbours at 22, Dongguanyinsi Lane often watched us with admiring eyes, when we left home for work together in the mornings.

Since the autumn of 1964, Puyi had been hospitalized many times. As his wife, and as a professional nurse, I knew how to look after him and I had always taken good care of him. But in the book, Behr said:

When Puyi was hospitalized, at first his wife, herself a nurse at another hospital, had come to see him, but her visits became less frequent and eventually ceased altogether. The Cultural Revolution had started a year earlier, and she had a good excuse for not coming, the streets were no longer safe for most adults.

The pain increased steadily too. He wished his wife would come to see him one last time.

Whilst reading the book, my mind was taken back to past times. Actually, in the last two years of his life, because of a serious illness, Puyi had oedema all over his body and had needed my support when he walked. Everyday, I gave him his injection, prepared his medicine and personally cooked his meals. Observing how I looked after him, those who came to visit him at our home often held up their thumbs with admiration for me, praising me and enviously expressing to Puyi: "Puyi, you are lucky to have such a good wife!" Puyi felt proud of me when he heard this comment.

During the summer and autumn of 1966, the streets of Beijing were filled with Red Guards from all over the country. They had been invited to Beijing by Chairman Mao, in order for them to study the "revolutionary concepts". Because of this, I couldn't get on the overcrowded buses and had to walk a very long way to the hospital where Puyi stayed, to give him his meals and Chinese medicinal herbs soups which I had prepared and cooked at home.

Several times, a moved Puyi said to me: "I'm fortunate to have you as my wife! Otherwise who would look after me? I would suffer greatly without you." Hearing this,

I always consoled him and wiped his eyes with my handkerchief.

Edward Behr went so far as to write:

In the final stages, the old man regained a modicum of peace, and the pain abated. But his last wife, whom he had married in 1962, never made it to the hospital in time.

After the old man died, things went from bad to worse. His body was cremated on the hospital premises, like that of a destitute with no family. The ashes were saved, but there was no ceremony of any kind. One of the dead man's relatives braved the rampaging Red Guards, and carried the ashes for safekeeping to Zhou Enlai's home.

This really is an absurd version of events! The fact was that in the last two months before he passed away, I seldom left his ward. As there was only one bed in his tiny ward, in order to doze off for a while during the night, I needed to sit on a stool near the door. After Puyi breathed his last, it was I who put on his shroud for him.

For over three years after Puyi passed away, I had no income, only living on the several thousand yuan he had left for me. I missed Puyi, often weeping and friends kindly soothed me: "You are still young and you must look on the bright side of life."

One night I fell asleep while weeping, and the next morning, I could hardly see anything out of one of my eyes. Immediately, I went to see a doctor. He warned me that it was dangerous to cry in this way. He urged me: "Do you know that your eyes will lose sight, if your eyeballs are always soaked in tears." I tried to restrain myself and didn't cry any more, as I was aware that I would suffer more, if I really cried myself blind in deep sorrow. I comforted myself by recalling the sweet times that I had enjoyed with Puyi.

At that time Puyi took me "as a pearl in his palm", not only devoting his deep love as my husband, but also compensating me with the parent love which I had lost in my childhood. How happy I was then! The only regret from our wonderful life together was that we didn't have a child. I was not yet forty when I married him, and at that time, I never dreamt that I wouldn't bear my own child.

After Puyi passed away, because I was the widow of a feudal emperor, for several years, nobody dared to have contact with me, although many of them actually sympathized with me and wanted to help me. Later, in order to cut down on my daily expenses, three times a day I had to eat noodles served with soy sauce as I couldn't afford any meat and vegetables. I had suffered a lot when I lived with my step-mother in childhood, so I could endure many kinds of difficulties in life. But insomnia at night time had often tortured me, making me feel depressed.

In 1960s China, a widow was an easy target often bullied. All of your actions were under the watchful eyes of some curious and bored people. If you wore beautiful clothes, people would say behind your back: "She must have a lover." By Chinese feudal tradition, a widow should wear black clothes, to show respect and loyalty for her late husband, but if you wore plain clothes, they would gossip about you as though you were pretending to be poor. If the light in your room was on till late, they would say that you had a man in your room, while if there was no light in your room, they would consider that you were not at home, but gone to see your lover.

Although I did my best to see less people, I couldn't refuse my friends and former colleagues coming to my home to see me. Of course, I also heard gossip about this. Finally, I had to believe one of the common Chinese folk adages that "Gossip is a fearful thing".

In the five and half years of our life together and the nearly thirty years after Puyi passed away, I have sacrificed all of my personal interests in taking good care of Puyi and defending his rights and interests. I was most willing to do them, to repay his sincere love to me.

It was about two months after The Xinmin Evening Paper had carried the article about my plan to contact the American journalist for an explanation, asking him to make corrections through the media after setting the facts straight, that I received from Edward Behr, the following letter of apology:

Dear Mrs. Li Shuxian,

I am sorry you have been distressed by the Chinese translation of my book.

In 1987, when I was in China researching the book, I tried to get in touch with you, but in vain. The makers of the film also told me that they had tried to reach you, without success and that you did not want to talk about the past.

I confess that I did rely on the hearsay testimony of a number of people, who knew Aisin-Gioro Puyi after his release. They all, in the main, said the same thing. I am very sorry, if this proved inaccurate and will make a point of altering this part of the text in any new editions of my book.

It would also be very illuminating for me, if, on my next trip to China, I could talk with you and hear something from you about those years.

With very best regards.

Yours Sincerely,
Edward Behr

October 20th, 1990

Chapter Thirty Seven

Drawing a Satisfactory Conclusion to the History

At the beginning of December 1994, Zhou Xiaoqi came to see me at my home. He was the son of Mr. Zhou Zhenqiang, one of the two matchmakers of our marriage and my "fellow townsman" from Zhejiang Province. Mr. Zhou had often taken Xiaoqi with him when he called on our home, after Puyi and I got married. Xiaoqi had always happily called me "Aunt Pu" and I loved him, treating him as my own child. After Puyi and Xiaoqi's father passed away, he still came to see me frequently, until he moved to Hong Kong in the 1980s. Many times he had invited me to visit and tour Hong Kong, but I could never do it, often busy with many matters.

At the Qingming Festival, 1991, I visited the Eight Treasure Mountain Cemetery to show my deep rememberance and love for Puyi.

While chatting with Xiaoqi, I confided in him my anxious concern that as I was already more than seventy years old and in poor health, it was a possibility that I could die at any time but that I still hadn't found an ideal place to bury the ashes of his Uncle

Pu. I told Xiaoqi that I always felt concerned, whenever I thought about the matter.

Xiaoqi replied: "I have heard that a new big cemetery has been built in the grounds of the Western Qing Tombs. Would you be able to go there with me to have a look?" I knew that four Qing Dynasty Emperors had been buried there and that it was located about 130 km southwest of Beijing. I agreed with him, asking him to take me there so that I could have a look when he was free.

A few days later, Xiaoqi drove me there. This was my first time to visit the noted "Western Qing Tombs". I have since heard that it is considered to be 'the most blessed site under the sun'. I found that it was surrounded by green mountains and that the four mausoleums of the Qing Dynasty emperors and 69 other ancillary tombs were nestled comfortably on an adjacent large plain. The entire Western Qing Tomb covered an area of some 800 square km of hilly land with more than 20,000 ancient pine and cypress trees (Chinese believe that pines and cypresses represent longevity), which shaded the winding paths between the mausoleums and the other tombs.

"Aunt Pu, how do you like this place?" Xiaoqi asked.

"It really has excellent surroundings and is close to the Chongling Mausoleum," I replied. (Chongling Mausoleum is the tomb of the previous Emperor Guangxu. Puyi was his adopted son and he reigned in China from 1875-1908.)

"I'm satisfied with this place. I'm sure that your Uncle Puyi would love it too."

Touring Paris in Aprial, 1991

The administrative office of the Western Qing Tombs had appointed a young girl, one of its members of staff, to accompany us on a tour. She didn't know that I was Puyi's wife, but she happened to mention to me that in 1909, when Puyi came to the throne, the building of a mausoleum for him had been commenced according to Chinese custom. However, only about two years later, because the Qing Dynasty was overthrown by the 1911 Revolution, the construction of it had been stopped. It was interesting that finally she said to me: "Our manager said that he would like to find the whereabouts of Puyi's ashes, as he would like to have the ashes buried in the Western Qing Tombs."

For a long time, it had been my anxious wish to find an ideal place to bury Puyi's ashes. It happened to be the high tide of the Cultural Revolution when, in October 1967, Puyi had passed away. Although our esteemed and beloved Premier Zhou Enlai wanted to build a handsome tomb for Puyi, it was actually impossible to do so at that time. After the Cultural Revolution ended, it was fortunate that Puyi's ashes could be sent to be housed at the Revolutionary Cemetery inside the Eight Treasure Mountain Cemetery. The Revolutionary Cemetery was in spacious grounds with tall pines, cypresses and beautiful flowers. I liked it and was glad that Puyi could stay in such an ideal place.

Li Yuqin with me, we became friends in later life.

"Time flies like an arrow," and more than ten years had passed very quickly. When I was nearly seventy years old, I started to worry again because Puyi and I had no children who would take care of Puyi's ashes, after I had gone. I hoped to buy an ideal burial ground to bury the ashes of Puyi and Tan Yuling (Puyi's third wife) and also so that mine could be added to that same location, after I passed away. Since 1991, I had gone to see several cemeteries and all of them expressed that they welcomed Puyi's ashes buried there. Some even offered me burial grounds, but I was unsatisfied with each of them and politely refused the offers.

In the spring of 1994, Mr. Rongqi, Puyi's third brother-in-law, came to tell me that a wealthy Hong Kong man was willing to pay to build a cemetery for the members of Aisin-Gioro Royal Family in the Eastern Qing Tombs area located in Zunhua County in the Hebei Province. Puyi, of course, had been listed as the first likely person to be buried there and he indicated that the Chinese government had cared about the matter. But later, some of the Aisin-Gioro Royal Family members expressed their opposition to it. I knew that all through the ages of the Aisin-Gioro Royal Family, there had been a lot of contradictory opinion, so this didn't surprise me. Therefore, I didn't feel uncomfortable about it.

Several days later, Xiaoqi invited me to have a meal in a Shanghai restaurant. I found that several unfamiliar guests were already waiting for us, when I entered the room. Xiaoqi first introduced one of them to me: "This is Mr. Zhang Shiyi, the General Manager of the Hualong Royal Family Cemetery." This was the first time that I had met Mr. Zhang. While we were eating, a smiling Xiaoqi told me that actually it was Mr. Zhang Shiyi, who had asked him to make the special trip to my home to talk about with me the matter of the possible burial of Puyi's ashes in his Hualong Royal Family Cemetery, located in the grounds of the Western Qing Tombs.

Mr. Zhang was 56 that year and a native of Tai'an, Shandong Province and had graduated from the famous China Scientific and Technological University. He used to be a space engineer and had moved to Hong Kong in 1985. Starting his career there as an basic worker within only five years he had set up his own enterprise. In 1992, he invested in the Hualong Royal Family Cemetery to bury the remains and ashes of distinguished Hong Kong, Macao and Taiwan compatriots, overseas Chinese and also outstanding people from all walks of life in China. The Hualong Royal Family Cemetery covered an area of 20 hectares, located to the north of the Chongling mausoleum. Mr. Zhang had personally directed the workers to build burial grounds, plant pines and cypresses and dredge river courses there.

I had known Xiaoqi from his childhood and I trusted him. I was sure that he wouldn't persuade me to do it, if the matter didn't benefit the country, as well as Puyi and me. Choosing burial grounds for Puyi was an international concern, so I knew that I had to consider it with great care. After taking me to see the Western Qing Tombs, Xiaoqi had immediately informed Mr. Zhang Shiyi in Hong Kong, that I was pleased with its environment. Mr. Zhang was very glad and quickly flew to see me in Beijing. Knowing that I was a native of Hangzhou (Shanghai is next to Hangzhou), he kindly chose a lot of Shanghai dishes, when we ate together.

We had a friendly and frank talk. Mr. Zhang said: "Yongzheng, Jiaqing, Daoguang and Guangxu, four Qing Dynasty emperors are buried in the West-

Li Yuqin with Wang Qingxiang in 1989

ern Qing Tombs. I hope you will agree to bury Mr. Puyi's ashes there, too." He expressed that he would be glad to pay all the expenses for doing that and that he would wait, to hopefully get my permission to do so. He stressed that his Hualong Royal Family Cemetery had also been appreciated and approved by the government. Mr. Cui Naifu, the Minister of Civil Affairs, had inspected it and gladly written the name for it in Chinese calligraphy.

Going to see the Louvre in Paris, May 1991

I asked Mr. Zhang: "You and Puyi are not relatives or friends, why do you want to bury Puyi's ashes in your cemetery, without charge? What do you want to do this for?" Mr. Zhang replied: "Puyi was the Chinese 'Last Emperor', a very special figure with international reputation and I myself sympathized with Puyi's misfortune." Once again, he expressed his willingness to pay all of the expenses for building Puyi's mausoleum there.

Again, I questioned Mr. Zhang: "Besides what you said, are there any benefits for yourself from doing this?" Mr. Zhang answered me: "I established this cemetery as a business. Of course, I hope that my burial grounds will become well-known by many people, even famous people throughout the world. If Mr. Puyi's ashes can be buried in my cemetery, definitely many more people will know about it and some will even hope to be buried there too, so it will bring me economic benefits. Therefore, although I will spend some money for burying Mr. Puyi's ashes there, I'm sure that I can get good return for my donation by selling the burial grounds there quickly and at good prices. I think that it will be worthwhile to build Puyi's mausoleum there, even if I only get back the money that I spend on it." I believed that what Mr. Zhang said was genuine and honest.

As we continued to sit at the dining table, filled with lovely Shanghai dishes, I told Mr. Zhang what my real desires were and that I wouldn't have believed him, if he had said that he did this completely for my benefit and he admitted that he wanted to do this also for the benefit of his own business. Those were reasonable words and I appreciated his honesty and sincerity. I therefore informed Mr. Zhang that I would agree with the burying of Puyi's ashes in his Hualong Royal Family Cemetery, but I'd like to go there to have a look first.

In sincerity and with an earnest desire, I shared with him that I was fortunate to marry Puyi, who had loved me wholeheartedly. After he passed away, I didn't want to marry any other because he was always on my mind. Now after nearly thirty years as his widow, I have nothing valuable that he left to me, but his urn. "It is my spiritual ballast and comfort. I shall have nothing remaining of his, if I give the urn to you," I said.

There was another important reason for me in finally deciding to bury Puyi's ashes in the Hualong Royal Family Cemetery inside the Western Qing Tombs. I have heard two versions about the building of Puyi's mausoleums. One story was that according to the old system of starting to build mausoleums for emperors when they claimed the throne, his burial ground was chosen when Puyi was a child, in the Western Qing Tombs and was named the "Ten-thousand year holy land" by the Qing Dynasty Royal Family. Surrounded by mist, undulating mountains on four sides, Puyi's "holy land" was a basin filled with tall willows, lush green grass and wild flowers which smelled fresh and sweet all year round. It also had a river with winding and clear water, running merrily not far from it. Moreover, the tomb was close to the mausoleum of Emperor Guangxu, Puyi's adopted father (also his uncle). The construction of Puyi's mausoleum had commenced in 1909, but a year later, after the foundations and some basic constructions had just been finished, the 1911 Revolution broke out and the Qing Dynasty was overthrown. Therefore the construction had to be stopped.

Wang Qingxiang and I collaborating on my husband Puyi

Wang Qingxiang and I collaborating on my husband Puyi

Another story I heard was that several years after his abdication, when Puyi was ten years old, the Qing Dynasty Royal Family sent a Fengshui master to find a perfect burial place for him at the Western Qing Tombs. An ideal one for Puyi was chosen there, but later, for some reason, they hadn't proceeded with the building of anything there.

The two versions are different, but both stated that Puyi's original tomb was supposed to be at the Western Qing Tombs. Therefore I felt inclined to bury Puyi's ashes there to actually draw a satisfactory historical conclusion. Besides, Hualong Royal Family Cemetery is located to the north of the Chongling Mausoleum where Emperor Guangxu was buried. I'm sure that if Puyi was buried there that he would be overjoyed to return to be beside his father. While Puyi won't be buried there as an emperor, but as a citizen, this has historical significance.

Later on, Mr. Zhang Shiyi, with his wife and son, came to visit me several times at my home. He asked me for my opinion concerning how to build Puyi's tomb. Considering that my satisfaction would also mean Puyi's satisfaction, Mr. Zhang said to me that since the course of history had given him the opportunity to build a tomb for the Chinese Last Emperor, that he would do his best to do it successfully and he hoped that later generations would praise his work.

I informed Mr. Zhang that in the first half of Puyi's life, his favorite wife was Madam Tan Yuling. When she married Puyi, in 1937, she had been a 17 year-old middle school student in Beijing. With her tender disposition and clever mind, she had soon won Puyi's favour and she had been granted the title "Auspicious Concubine", but she died only five years later. Puyi had been torn with grief, being convinced that she had been murdered by the Japanese. The Japanese authorities didn't even allow Puyi to bury her in the Aisin-Gioro Royal Clan Cemetery, but instead placed her coffin in a

Wang Qingxiang and I accompanying a UNESCO official. We are picking out photos for an exhibition on Puyi's life.

temple in Changchun. It stayed there for three years until after the Japanese Imperialists surrendered. While he was in Russia, Puyi had her body cremated and sent back to Beijing by two of his relatives. After Tan Yuling's death, Puyi always carried with him a lock of her hair and some clippings that he had cut from her finger nails after she died, as well as a photo of her, with his handwriting on the back of it: *My dearest, Yuling.*

After Puyi returned to Beijing in 1959, he took Tan's urn, which had been housed in the home of one of his relatives, back to his apartment in the CPPCC HQ. But after we got married, he had to have it sent back to the home of his relative again, because I was scared of it. On that day, before Tan's urn was taken away, Puyi cut off a lock of his hair and several pieces of his finger nails and placed them in it, "to show his desire to be with her forever". I said to Mr. Zhang: "Since this is Puyi's request, I hope to bury Puyi's and Tan Yuling's ashes together there."

Mr. Zhang Shiyi immediately expressed: "Aunt Li, I promise you that I will do this." I continued: "Someday, I will pass away too. When Puyi was alive, we depended on each other for survival, never separating. After he passed away, I have been missing him everyday. I'm sure he knows this and misses me too. So, I decided not only to bury Puyi's and Tan Yuling's ashes in your Hualong Royal Family Cemetery, but mine too. I'd like to have my ashes buried together with them."

Mr. Zhang said to me again: "Aunt Li, what you have said is reasonable, I promise you that I will do it exactly according to your wishes."

Then Mr. Zhang asked me what kind of tomb I wanted him to build for us. I told him: "I'm sure my desires are easy for you to carry out. As far as I know each of your tombs will cover an area of one and half square meters. How about at least giving Puyi's tomb six square meters, Tan Yuling and mine at least three square meters each, plus some grassland and a tombstone?"

Mr. Zhang answered me without any hesitation: "Aunt Li, be at peace please, I am telling you now that I will do for each of you even better than what you desire."

Then, Mr. Zhang introduced to me his preliminary project for the building of Puyi's tomb. He said: "My Hualong Royal Family Cemetery has three kinds of burial ground. The first kind is for cremated burials, consisting of burial plots of one and half square metres, two square metres, two and half square metres or three metres. The second kind is for standard burials, each occupying an area of five square metres. The third one is a 'VIP section'. All the plots there are at least 20 m^2."

He stated that he planned to build the joint tomb for Puyi, Tan Yuling and myself at the centre of the VIP section and that it would cover an area of 99.9 m^2. This figure was derived from the "9999.5 rooms" in the Forbidden City. He preferred to collect the very best international architectural designs for it. I was overjoyed with the wonderful

The Last Emperor of China **My Husband Puyi**

On January 26, 1995, I held Puyi's urn to bury it in Hualong Royal Family Cemetery. On both sides of me are Mr. Zhang Shiyi and his wife.

scheme.

On January 15th 1995, Mr. Zhang Shiyi and Xiaoqi took me to the Western Qing Tombs to select an ideal burial site for Puyi. As January is the coldest month in Beijing, Mr. Zhang took several warm army overcoats for us. But, surprisingly, that day the breeze was gentle and the sun was warm. Mr. Zhang joked: "Because the heavens know that we are choosing a burial ground for the 'Last Emperor', they have gladly given us a fine day!"

In Hualong Royal Family Cemetery, I selected a piece of land which covered an area of 99.9 m^2, for our joint tomb at the center of its Free Section. It was only about 300 metres from Emperor Guangxu's Chongling Mausoleum, so Puyi would be able to see his father clearly from here. Mr. Zhang asked his staff to mark it brightly with lime. I was very thrilled, for I had finally settled the matter which I had worried about for a long time.

Once again, I was convinced that in this world, most successful matters don't just happen by chance. Suddenly, it crossed my mind that only about a month earlier, I had dreamt a strange dream and it had puzzled me ever since. In the dream, one of my close friends had brought a dragon to my home. It was about a metre long, with its four feet pointing outwards, seeming as thought it was looking for a place to stand. He told me that he would be leaving Beijing to work further away and he trusted me to look after it for him. I held the dragon and was at a loss to where I could keep it. I thought it over and over and then remembered that in our courtyard there was a well. I was pleased with the idea and went to put the dragon in the well. But at the same time, I also worried that it was possible that the dragon might be washed away by the water in the well. I was standing by the well, with the dragon in my arms and feeling anxious about it, all of a sudden, I awakened. I was then sure that the dragon was Puyi and that he was requesting me to find an ideal tomb in which to bury his ashes. It was only a few days after that, Zhou Xiaoqi came to find me. I didn't think that this was just a coincidence. It was clearly arranged by the heavens.

Excitedly, I explained this dream to Mr. Zhang and all the people present. I concluded by saying to them: "I'd like to thank Mr. Zhang and all those present! Puyi has been dead for twenty eight years and I have long been searching for an ideal place to bury his ashes. I would never have dreamt that he would have such a wonderful final resting place. So, I'm ecstatic today. I'm sure that in the nether world, Puyi is overjoyed too."

Soon afterwards, we went to the Longhu (Dragon Lake) Hotel nearby to sign the Certificate of Entrustment. This was the written agreement for the building of the tomb for Puyi. I scrutinized the document, reading every word of it:

The Certificate of Entrustment for the Burial of Mr. Puyi's Ashes

Mr. Puyi, my husband, died of an illness in 1967. Because I'm older now and Mr. Puyi had no children, according to Puyi's request, I am making arrangements with Mr. Zhang Shiyi, the plenipotentiary of the Hualong Royal Family Cemetery, to handle the matter of burying Mr. Puyi's ashes in the Hualong Royal Family Cemetery, inside the Western Qing Tombs, in Yixian County.

Finally, I held a pen to sign solemnly my name on the Certificate of Entrustment. My hand was shaking a little, but I knew that this was because I was greatly excited. I was sure that nobody on earth could imagine how many past events had filled my mind during these few moments. Only I myself could be aware of it. After the signing of the agreement, the "*Fengshui* Master" who had helped me to select the site for Puyi's tomb, asked me to give him the pen that I had just used. A small pen didn't have any value, but it recorded a moment in history that would be forever remembered.

After lunch, we returned to the Hualong Royal Family Cemetery, to dig the first spade of clay from the site of Puyi's tomb. We planned to put it back into the vault until ten days later, when Puyi's urn would be buried.

On the way back from the Western Qing Tombs, I went to the Revolutionary Cemetery inside the Eight Treasure Mountain Cemetery to collect Puyi's urn, so as to leave it temporarily in the care of Xiaoqi.

On the morning of January 26th 1995, in a convoy of six cars, Mr. Zhang Shiyi and his wife, as well as Xiaoqi and some other friends accompanied me in the transferring of Puyi's urn to the Western Qing Tombs. Holding Puyi's urn, I was driven personally by Xiaoqi. Two hours later, we arrived at the mourning hall of the Hualong Royal Family Cemetery.

In the mourning hall, I found that all of the preparations for Puyi's mourning rites had been completed already. A banner with the characters "member of CPPCC, Aisin-Gioro Puyi" hung in front of it. Underneath it was a huge photo of Puyi, when he was in his later years. The four sides of the mourning hall were lined with wreathes, respectfully presented by many departments of the government, democratic parties and other organizations.

First of all, I was asked to place Puyi's carved wooden urn on the altar, which was covered with yellow satin. Next Mr. Zhang announced the commencement of the rites for burying Puyi's ashes. Then in an air of solemnity and respect, Mr. Zhang invited me to make a speech.

I said: "Today, I'm delighted to finally have an ideal resting place for Puyi. I'd like to take this opportunity to convey my gratitude to Mr. Zhang Shiyi and all who accom-

Puyi's tomb in Hualong Royal Family Cemetery

In America, Auguest 1993

panied me today, to place Puyi's ashes here. Now I feel rest assured."

After my speech, all of the people present bowed three times to Puyi's photo.

Then, I was told to put on a pair of black gloves and to hold Puyi's urn. Being supported on both sides by Mr. Zhang and his wife, I was taken to the vault at the center of Puyi's burial ground, about one hundred metres away. Alongside the vault, Mr. Zhang said to me: "This vault was built in the site you personally chose. Its base and four sides are made of rock and reinforced concrete. So, it is dry and safe. Please, would you have a look at it first, and then you may place Mr. Puyi's urn in it, if you are contented to let Mr. Puyi to rest in peace here."

I checked the vault and nodded in agreement. A worker descended into the vault and with great care, took Puyi's urn from my hands and placed it on the bottom of the vault which was covered with yellow satin. He untied the yellow satin which wrapped the urn to position the front of it southwards, so as to face the sun. Then he retied the yellow satin. Finally several workers moved the heavy rock lid to cover the vault and to seal it.

After Puyi's ashes were buried, Mr. Zhang asked me as to where he should place Tan Yuling's ashes, to the right or to the left of Puyi's ashes? I told him that I hadn't decided yet and that I would give the matter further consideration and discuss it later.

That day I was really overjoyed that I had successfully concluded a decisive issue for my dear husband, Puyi and I enjoyed the feeling of having unloaded a heavy burden. Three days later, the traditional Chinese "Spring Festival" came. That day, Mr.

Zhang Shiyi, with his wife and son, came to pay me a New Year call. I thanked him for having helped to relieve my anxiety and that I considered him as one of my relatives.

The news about Puyi's ashes being finally buried at the Hualong Royal Family Cemetery evoked positive responses and intense interest internationally. Many newspapers and magazines reported it, with detailed articles and pictures.

Miss Xiangyan, a niece of Puyi, paid a special trip to Beijing from Hong kong, to convey her thoughts to me. She told me she had already decided to start work to raise funds in Hong kong, so as to build a miniature museum for her Uncle Puyi beside his tomb, to house and portray his photos and the objects that he had used, as well as information, indicating to visitors how Puyi had changed from being an emperor to become a citizen.

On the April 5th, 1995, it was Qingming Festival (the Pure Brightness Festival, the day when Chinese go to pay their respects to their deceased relatives). I returned for the first time to the Western Qing Tomb to pay my respects to Puyi in his new tomb. The following day, the American *International Daily*, under the title of *"Madam Li Shuxian paid her respects to Puyi in his new tomb"*, showed the photo of me in front of Puyi's tomb and a brief news item:

Reuter's News Agency, April 5th, Yixian County, Hebei Province

Today being the Qingming Festival, Madam Li Shuxian, wife of the Chinese Last Emperor Puyi, came here to pay her respects at her husband's tomb. Accompanied by some relatives, friends, monks and local farmers, Madam Li Shuxian (who is now over seventy years old), bowed three times to Puyi's newly-built tomb. Only this January, Puyi's ashes were moved from the Eight Treasure Mountain Cemetery to the Western Qing Tombs. Its small marble tombstone has the words Tomb of **Mr. Aisin-Gioro Puyi**.

The Chongling Mausoleum of Puyi's father, Emperor Guangxu, is not far from Puyi's tomb. Puyi's tomb is apparently quite small in comparison.

I think this is because, although my husband, Puyi used to be an emperor, he had been a citizen for a number of years before he passed away.

THE END

Epilogue

After Puyi's passing away, Madam Li Shuxian lived alone for another thirty years in spite of her poor health. She was highly respected by many people, including the readers of her books. She loved her new life following the implementing of the "pen-Door Policy" by the government. She was often invited to participate in the state affairs activities and parties held by various organizations. Many times, she happily received foreign visitors and friends who enthusiastically enjoyed her company.

Through her co-operation with Mr. Wang Qingxiang, she successfully published a series of books and picture albums on Puyi, some of them being translated into English, Japanese and Korean.

In April 1997, Madam Li Shuxian was diagnosed with lung cancer and was hospitalized. During her final days, there were two matters that always puzzled her. One was that although Puyi's ashes had been buried in the Hualong Royal Family Cemetery, the construction of his tomb had not been completed. The other was that *My Husband, Puyi* had not been translated into English.

She had no children nor close family, so only some of her distant relatives and friends came to see her in the hospital. She did have a maid whom she paid to tend to her.

Early on June 9th, her condition

Mr. Wang Qingxiang at the memorial ceremony for Li Shuxian, June 29th, 1997

suddenly took a turn for the worse and she died just after three o'clock in the afternoon. She only had two friends and the maid with her during the last moments.

On June 29th, a memorial ceremony was held for her at the Eight Treasure Mountain Revolutionary Cemetery. After that, her body was cremated and her ashes were kept there temporarily.

Ten years later, Ms. Ni Na finally translated the book *My Husband Puyi* into English. Here we are extremely grateful to Mr. Stuart Allen. Stuart is from Seaford, England and works in China as an English language/literature expert and private consultant. He is responsible for the final draft of the book and his work on this book was very important. He has lived in China for six years with his wife and child.

Mr. Stuart Allen and Tanslator

Thanks also to Ms. Ruth Bell from New Zealand, who is currently studying Chinese language and culture in China. She has given us her useful suggestions and opinions during the English translation.

We hope the readers in the western world and many other countries, including China, enjoy this book!

Told by: Li Shuxian
Written down by: Wang Qingxiang
Translated by: Ni Na
Managing Editor: Tan Yan (lyty2006@163.com)
Printing Supervisor: Feng Dongqing
Proof read by: Stuart Allen
Art Designer: Wu Tao

All rights reserved: No part of this publication may be reproduced, stored in a retrieval system, or transmitted in any form or by any means, or otherwise, without the prior written permission of the Publishers.

Published by China Travel & Tourism Press
(A9 Jianguomennei Dajie, Beijing 100005,China)
Printed in the People's Republic of China

The Last Emperor of China
My Husband Puyi

责任编辑：谭　燕
责任印制：冯冬青
审　　校：Stuart Allen（英籍）
装帧设计：吴　涛

图书在版编目（CIP）数据

我的丈夫溥仪——中国的末代皇帝：英文／李淑贤忆述；王庆祥撰写；倪娜译．－北京：中国旅游出版社，2008.6
ISBN 978-7-5032-3483-5

Ⅰ．我… Ⅱ．①李…②王…③倪… Ⅲ．爱新觉罗·溥仪（1906～1967）－生平事迹－英文 Ⅳ．K827=7

中国版本图书馆 CIP 数据核字（2008）第 090167 号

书　名	我的丈夫溥仪——中国的末代皇帝
忆　述	李淑贤
撰　写	王庆祥
翻　译	倪　娜
出版发行	中国旅游出版社
	（北京建国门内大街甲 9 号　邮编：100005）
	http://www.cttp.net.cn　E-mail:cttp@cnta.gov.cn
	发行部电话：010-85166507　85166517
经　销	全国各地新华书店
印　刷	河北省三河市灵山红旗印刷厂
版　次	2008 年 6 月第 1 版　2008 年 6 月第 1 次印刷
开　本	720 毫米×970 毫米　1/16
印　张	18.25
印　数	1－5000 册
字　数	280 千
定　价	68.00 元

ISBN 978-7-5032-3483-5

版权所有　翻印必究
如发现质量问题，请直接与发行部联系调换